Cults, New Religions & Religious Creativity

Cults, New Religions & Religious Creativity

Geoffrey K. Nelson

Routledge & Kegan Paul
London

First published in 1987 by
Routledge & Kegan Paul Ltd
11 New Fetter Lane, London EC4P 4EE

Set in Bembo
by Witwell Ltd, Liverpool
and printed in Great Britain
by T.J. Press Ltd, Padstow Cornwall

© *G. K. Nelson, 1987*

British Library Cataloguing in Publication Data
Nelson, Geffrey K.
    Cults, new religions and religious creativity
    1. Cults
    I. Title
306′6   BP603

ISBN 0-7102-0855-3

Contents

Preface

In a work such as this the author is inevitably indebted to a large number of predecessors and contemporary writers and researchers whose work has provided the basic materials, both theoretic and empirical, on which this study is built. In particular I am indebted to the work of that great but unfairly neglected sociologist Victor Branford for the seeds from which many of the ideas on creativity have grown. I am grateful to all those members of religious movements who have provided information and to those research students who worked with me on empirical studies of religion, in particular Janice Campbell, Elwyn Roberts, Mary Blakeman, Derek Walsgrove and Rosemary Clews. My thanks to Mrs J. Gascoigne for her efficient preparation of the typescript.

Finally I am grateful to my wife for the support she has given throughout the years.

1
The problem of new religious movements

The period following the Second World War has seen an unprecedented burst of religious creativity on a world scale. In North America and Western Europe, revivalist, evangelical and reformist movements have not only reshaped the face of Protestantism but have also rocked the stability of the Roman Catholic church. Cults and new religions have sprouted in profusion, old religions such as witchcraft and the occult movements have acquired new life, and missionaries from Asia have successfully introduced varieties of Hinduism, Buddhism and Islam into the West.

Latin America, a traditionally solid Catholic continent, has been deeply penetrated by Protestantism, and Spiritualism in both its Western and Afro-Caribbean versions has flourished.

In Africa numerous nativistic religious and Christian sects have come into existence. While in the wake of her defeats in the Second World War, Japan has been flooded by new religious movements.

The great Asian religions, Hinduism, Buddhism and Islam have reacted to the process of Westernisation, and even in the communist world there have been signs not only of a continuing but of a reviving interest in religion, in spite of the efforts of a somewhat old-fashioned materialist doctrine to eradicate 'superstition'.

In both the communist and the capitalist worlds a scientific interest in the phenomena of religion has led to the growth of the new science of parapsychology.

An outburst of religiosity on this world scale is unique in human history, though it may perhaps be compared with the period in the fifth and fourth centuries BC which included the work of Lao Tse and Confucius in China, Buddha and a number of significant Hindu thinkers in India, the major prophets in Israel and philosophers in Greece.

Within the more limited world of the Roman Empire there was a similar outburst which was centred around the first century AD when Christianity, Mithraism and numerous other cults were struggling for survival.

While some mention will be made of religious creativity in earlier periods, this study concentrates on the modern period starting from the ending of the Second World War. Religious developments in this period have been the subject of numerous articles, papers and monographs, which provide the basis for the analysis developed in this book. It is my intention to develop a theoretical synthesis that is based on an examination of these studies and which will enable us to arrive at an understanding of both the causes and consequences of this unparalleled period of religious creativity.

In the first chapter we examine the evidence for such religious activity and the social and religious preconditions out of which it developed. In the past three decades sociologists have been deeply concerned with discussions of the process of secularisation, particularly in the Western world, largely to the exclusion of discussion of the opposite process of sacralisation or of the processes of religious creativity.

The wave of new religious movements may be seen as one aspect of a rising tide of spirituality that is producing a re-enchantment of the world. It was Max Weber who introduced the term 'Disenchantment of the World' into the language of sociologists. By disenchantment Weber meant that the growing tide of rationality which he acceded and admired in Western culture was sweeping away the elements of magic and spirituality, not only from the mechanisms of thought but also from the everyday lives of ordinary people. A process which both Weber and later Thomas (1971) attributed to the rationalising influence of the Protestant Reformation within the sphere of religion.

One sign of disenchantment was the retreat of the fairies into the remotest and most isolated districts of the British Isles which was too well documented in Evans-Wentz's classical study of the 'Fairy-faith in Celtic counties' (1911).

As Evans-Wentz observed:

The great majority of men in cities are apt to pride themselves on their own exemption from 'superstition', and to smile pityingly at the poor countrymen and countrywomen who believe in fairies. But when they do so they forget that with all their own admirable progress in material invention, with all the far-reaching data of their acquired science, with all the vast extent of their commercial and economic conquests, they themselves have ceased to be *natural*.

He went on to point out that, 'The Celtic peasant – is normally responsive to psychic influences – as much as an Australian Arunta or an American Red Man, who also, like him, are fortunate enough to have escaped being corrupted by what we – call civilisation.' And continues to ask, 'Are city-dwellers right in *not* believing in an invisible world which they cannot conceive, which, if it exists, they – are through environment and temperament alike incapable of knowing.'

As the influence of 'civilisation' has increased, as urbanisation has affected the rural areas in Western countries, the fairies have retreated further, until it is even more difficult than in Evans-Wentz's period to find a 'peasant' who has seen a fairy. Western civilisation has been diffused throughout the world so that today the fairies have disappeared from much of the earth. At least they had, but in recent years there are indications that they are making a 'comeback'. But before pursuing the question of the return of the supernatural we must examine the process of disenchantment and the movements that constantly resisted the attempts to eradicate mystery from the life of man.

While disenchantment may have had its roots in the Reformation, it reached its maturity in the eighteenth-century Englighten-

ment which threw out Christianity together with other superstitions, the baby with the bath water as some might observe. For
the rationalised there was no reason why one should believe the
Bible stories anymore than stories of fairies, witches and pagan
gods, and of course, which is the baby and which the bath water
depends upon whether you are a Christian or a pagan.

To some extent Christianity was able to survive through a
process of rationalising its beliefs, a process which seemed to lead
to a widespread decline in support for the churches in the early
eighteenth century. However, the Enlightenment had scarcely got
into its full stride before a reaction occurred with the rise of the
Romantic movement. In Britain this took two main forms: one
was the religious revival that manifested itself in the evangelical
movement and in Methodism, while the broader movement of
Romanticism influenced the arts and literature, particularly
poetry.

The Romantic movement was a reaction against the emphasis
on reason and the intellect that was characteristic of the
Englightenment; Romantics emphasised feelings and emotion, the
heart rather than the head. Romantics sensed beyond the material
world mysteries that could not be resolved by reason. The
foremost exponents of the philosophy of Romanticism were
Coleridge in Britain and Goethe in Germany, both of whom were
poets. They were surrounded by other poets such as Shelley,
Keats, Blake, Wordsworth, Schiller and Heine who gave
expression to their Romantic ideals.

Romanticism also expressed itself in prose literature
particularly in the Gothic novels of writers such as Horace
Walpole (*The Castle of Otranto* (1764)), Ann Radcliffe and Thomas
Peacock.

Ghosts, witches and black magic which the enlightened had
exorcised made a return not only in the imaginative literature but
in the revival and rise of new secret societies, and in the growth of
movements such as Mesmerism, Swedenborgianism and phren-
ology, all of which contributed to the origins of the Spiritualist
movement which may be seen as one of the most successful of the
nineteenth century's new religious movements (Nelson, 1969b).

Victorian England was a battlefield with rationalism and materialism on one side and spiritual movements on the other. On both sides there were extremists ranging from members of the rationalist societies to those of the revived occult movements such as the Rosicrucians, about whom Lord Lytton wrote in his novel *Zanoni* (Lytton, 1888).

Materialism and mysticism in British and American culture

The dominant culture of both Britain and North America has its source not only, as Weber implies, in the Protestant Reformation but in a peculiarly Anglo-Saxon variety of Protestantism which became known as Puritanism. Puritanism appears to owe much of its form to the influence of Anglo-Saxon beliefs and attitudes. These managed to survive the long centuries of Catholic Christianity and to re-emerge as the base for English Protestantism, which in turn owes more to the work of Wycliffe than to that of Calvin or Luther, the founders of European Protestantism.

First let us consider the fundamental values and beliefs of the Anglo-Saxons.

A major feature of the Anglo-Saxons together with other Norse people was a strong individualism, as Ellis-Davidson (1964) remarks, 'while they were intensely loyal to leaders and kinsmen, they could not be relied on to co-operate in large numbers, and to obey a general's command without question.' 'The myths,' she says, 'are very much stories of individuals, and their reaction to one another; they show lonely gods going their wilful ways, with certain responsibilities to the community and the family to which they belong, but little more to hold them.' The ideal man is the hero, an image that is found in the Norse Sagas and in *Beowulf*. It is a human ideal that has its roots in the legends of the gods. The hero is essentially an individualist.

In the past the credit (or blame) for the cultural contours of British society has been too readily attributed to the Greeks and Romans, while the influence of both Anglo-Saxon and Celtic traditions has been largely ignored. This is probably because

5

emphasis has been given to intellectual influences mediated through the written word. No such records survive of the philosophical traditions of the pre-Christian Anglo-Saxons and Celts, and the influence of their culture has been ignored. But that influence survived in the traditions of the peasants in Britain and can be discerned in the rise not only of peasant movements but also of the later movement of the working class.

Ellis-Davidson goes on to summarise the values of Norse culture:

> They would give up their lives rather than surrender [their] values, but they would fight on as long as they could, since life was well worth while, [but] The danger of their view of the world lay in a tendency towards lack of compassion for the weak, an over-emphasis on material success, and arrogant self-confidence.

The values of individualism and material success are clearly relevant to our understanding of the emergence of modern capitalist society. It may be argued that the role of the hero became 'christianised' into that of the entrepreneur by the Calvinist reformers in England who constituted the sect of puritans in the sixteenth and seventeenth centuries. This set the style for the development of what Tawney (1921) called the 'acquisitive society'.

The English Puritans also showed other characteristics of the Anglo-Saxon tradition. They organised themselves into small 'independent' self-governing churches, a practice that owes more to the Anglo-Saxon concept of self-government than to any Greek ideas of 'democracy'.

Individualism and democratic self-government are complementary concepts; they have continued to form the basis of the values of British and late-American society since the period of the English Civil War, when Anglo-Saxon culture triumphed over the medieval version of the Roman tradition that had been embodied in feudalism and sanctified by the Catholic church. Unfortunately, the 'dangerous' side of this world-view also emerged particularly in the nineteenth century with its emphasis on materialist success, which developed in philosophical and scientific materialism and in the works of the Utilitarians.

Throughout the medieval period, and surviving on through what we may call the period of Anglo-Saxon materialism, there has remained in British society an element which Tiryakian (1974) would describe as 'an esoteric' culture. A spiritual, mystical culture that has survived 'underground' throughout the centuries, in spite of frequent persecution. This culture, I believe, has its roots in the Celtic world which has survived mainly on the fringes of Britain, in Ireland, Wales and Scotland but which has also continued to exist in England, from where it has never been fully eradicated by successive waves of invaders.

Weber's concept of disenchantment has subsequently been vulgarised by sociologists who have focused their attention on the issue of secularisation, this requires some attention as the alleged process through which the social conditions have been set for the rise of new religious movements.

The fountain of youth

Springs and natural fountains are thought to have miraculous and life-giving powers in the mythology of many peoples in all parts of the world. The symbolism of water as the source of youth and eternal life is found also in Christianity. In the Bible we find God described as the fountain of living waters (Jeremiah 2.13), and in the New Testament Jesus promises his followers that they who drink of the water he gives them shall never thirst.

Amongst the American Indians, there was a myth of a fountain of youth which was thought to be situated in the depths of the forests of Florida. Those who found that fountain and drank of its water were said to receive the blessing of eternal youth. The fountain was, however, hidden in a remote valley and the secret of its location was known only to those who had found it through long and arduous searching.

Many years ago I came across a story based on this legend. It tells how a white man, Joe Smith, heard of the story of the fountain and set out to seek it. After searching for many years he entered the most beautiful valley he had ever seen, where he heard the sound of falling water and saw a fountain gushing out of a hill creating a waterfall that splashed in torrents down the hillside. He had found the fountain of youth but what should he do about it? It occurred to him that if he could bottle the water he could make a fortune, so he established a bottling plant at the foot of the hill. In a very short time he was marketing bottles of water to which he clearly gave the trade name 'Youthade'. For many years 'Youthade' was in great demand and the man became extremely wealthy. Of course he had rivals who sought to discover the location of the fountain. For a long time none of them did. But this did not prevent them from marketing rival products for which they made similar claims.

However, as time went on people began to suspect that 'Youthade' did not have the power of conferring eternal youth, and some sceptics claimed that the bottles contained nothing more than tap water. Scientists who analysed 'Youthade' and its rival products agreed that they could find no ingredients that were not present in ordinary water.

Joe Smith retorted that the water contained non-material elements that could not be detected by scientific analysis, and that the drinkers of his product who had not survived to a ripe old age had not been faithful to the product and drunk it as regularly as they should. Then a rival firm discovered the fountain and proceeded to tap it further up the hill. Their product, sold as 'Living Water', became very popular, but again seemed not to produce the expected result.

In the meantime a few individuals had sought for the fountain and a few had not only succeeded in finding it, but had returned home after drinking the water. It became obvious to their neighbours that these people had been transformed by their experience.

Clearly, the water of the fountain conferred all the blessings that had been attributed to it, but the process of bottling removed these qualities. Those who wanted the secret of eternal youth could only acquire this knowledge by finding their way to the original fountain. Some of those who had found the fountain offered their services to guide the seekers on their journeys, and these often developed into organised tours. However such tours appeared to be less successful than the simple pilgrimages conducted on foot, a fact which seemed to imply that the water alone was not adequate but was effective only if its consumption came as the culmination of the considerable effort involved in undertaking the pilgrimage.

The legend of the fountain is found in the mythology of many nations, and is only one form of a wider range of myths which are concerned with a quest: a journey undertaken in a search for a miraculous object that will confer spiritual and/or material blessing upon those who achieve the goal. In the Arthurian legends there is the archetypal quest for the Holy Grail, but long before that Celtic legends tell of the Land of Youth where the nuts of knowledge may be gathered.

In all the great religions there is the concept of the *Way* – the arduous path that must be followed by all who would attain enlightenment or salvation, two terms for what is ultimately the same experience (Schnapper, 1965).

Probably the first use of this concept was by the Chinese philosopher Lao Tse in his book the *Tao Te Ching* which may be translated as the 'Book of the Way', of which there are many translations (Waley, 1958; Lin YuTang, 1949). One of its most recent uses is in the title of a book *The Path of Perfection* written by Bhaktivedanta Prabhapada (1979), the founder of a major new religious movement, the Society for Krishna Consciousness, sometimes known as the Hare Krishna movement.

The quest for knowledge, wisdom, truth, heaven – those who attain the goal say that it is inexpressable – is a universal search, though few people pursue it seriously or persistently. In Christian thought there are said to be two alternative ways open, the narrow path that leads to salvation and the broad road that leads to destruction; all must choose which of these they will take. This view, which in one form or other is implicit in all religions, gives each person the choice of pursuing spiritual advancement or of following a more material life style.

9

The story of the fountain of youth is clearly a mytho-poeic expression of an attempt to comprehend certain human experiences. It is, I think, immediately understandable and probably makes more enjoyable reading than a scientific explanation, but in order to demonstrate the difference between the two modes of thought I propose to state briefly the scientific model that underlies my whole argument.

The fountain, of course, refers to a source of contact with God or Ultimate Reality; contact with Reality is achieved through the pursuit of religious and mystical experiences. The benefits of contact with Reality can only be enjoyed by those who make the effort to arrive at a first hand, face-to-face contact. At least some of those who have experienced such contact which leads to enlightenment will seek to communicate their experience to others, both Buddha and Christ are examples of this. Unfortunately, it is not possible to communicate the fullness of that experience to others, and the Buddha recognised this and only taught his disciples the method by which it could be reached: in a mytho-poeic sense, he gave them a map.

Many religious leaders who attract a following build an organisation through which their experiences can be transmitted to further generations, but the transmitted experience ceases to have any transformatory power for the individuals who receive it. The organisation grows and comes to dominate the lives of whole populations, because of the power which the 'message' gives the leaders (priests) over the lives of their followers. The control that these 'priests' have enables them to prevent the mass of the people from questioning the authenticity of the 'message', and allows them to persecute those who point out that the benefits of contact with God can only be had through personal experience, an assertion which invalidates the claims of the priests to exercise control over contacts between God and human beings.

In every generation some human beings escape the control of the organisation and are able to make personal contact with 'God'. They may be able to acquire followers and set up their own organisations, but they can only do this freely when the power of the 'priests' has been broken. It is only in certain social conditions that this can happen. The power of priests is closely tied up with political power, which is needed to enable the religious organisations to obtain and maintain a monopoly of ideology within society.

For religious creativity to blossom on a large scale, it is therefore necessary for society to become secular and pluralistic. Such conditions tend to exist only in periods of rapid change which may be either the result of internal conflict or of conflict with alien cultures.

Two approaches to knowledge

Building on the ideas of Ernest Cassirer (1925) the archaeologists H. and H. A. Frankfort (1949) developed the idea that there are two basic ways in which men have sought to explain the world, through myth and through science or, to use an even more descriptive term, mytho-poeic and logico-rational thought.

The story of the fountain of youth is a myth since it uses a narrative form in order to explain certain truths about the human search for knowledge, wisdom and eternal life. In the rest of this work we concentrate on the logico-rational method which includes but is not restricted to modern science, which indeed is an extreme form of this method, a form which emphasises the empirical aspect, whereas philosophy emphasises the logical. However, since the topic we are discussing, human spirituality, transcends logic and rationality we find it necessary to integrate the empathetic methods with those of science in order to attempt a comprehensive understanding of the nature of religion as a development of experiential spirituality. Sociology as the science of society must join with anthropology, psychology and history to provide the theoretical and methodological foundation for a study of religion as a human construction based on particular forms of human experience.

These two approaches to knowledge have recently been re-interpreted in terms of the contrasting attitudes of the 'Enlightenment Man' and the Romantic (Shweder and Le Vine,

1984). The enlightenment view

> holds that the mind of man is intendedly rational and scientific, that the dictates of reason are equally binding for all regardless of time, place, culture, race, personal desire or individual endowment, and that in reason can be found a universally applicable standard for judging validity and worth.... From that enlightened view flows a desire to discover universals: the idea of natural law, the concept of deep structures, the notion of progress and development, and the image of the history of ideas as a struggles between reason and unreason, science and superstition (*ibid* pp. 27–8).

On the other hand Shweder and Le Vine (*ibid.*, p. 28) point out that a

> central tenet of the romanticists view holds that ideas and practices have their foundation in neither logic nor empirical science, that ideas and practices fall beyond the scope of deductive and inductive reason, that ideas and practices are neither rational nor irrational but rather *non*-rational. [Hence] The concept of arbitoriness and culture, the subordination of deep structure to surface content, the celebration of local context, the idea of paradigm, cultural frames, and constitutive presuppositions, the view that action is expressive, symbolic or semiotic, and a strong anti-normative, anti-developmental presumption culminating in the view that the primitive and modern are co-equal and that the history of ideas is a history of a sequence of entrenched ideation of fashion (*ibid*).

The Romantic approach seems to have been much more widely developed in anthropology than in sociology, largely because of the obvious weaknesses that result from the application of enlightenment methodologies to the study of alien cultures. The enlightenment method, which consists of the application of alleged universal concepts to the analysis of alien cultures, can only lead to misunderstanding since these alleged universal concepts are the products of a particular culture, that of the Western world.

Concepts that have originated out of the pattern of thought of Western civilisation may prove very useful when analysing the culture in which they arose, but may distort totally the social reality of other cultures, which has to be tortured into shape on the Procrustean bed of Western preconceptions in order to be comprehensible to the Western mind.

The Romantic is concerned with arriving at an understanding of the alien culture in its own terms. Such an empathetic understanding involves the use of hermeneutic methods enabling one to arrive at an appreciation of the way in which people come to understand the universe in which they live, and to give meaning to their lives.

The relevance of this discussion to the study of new religious movements becomes obvious if we consider the idea that such movements are, in fact, alien cultures, alien not only from the point of view of social scientists but also from the point of view of the dominant culture of the Western world. Indeed, from that 'frame of reference' all religion must be considered as deviant.

Anthropologists have, in recent years, developed a new methodology described as 'The New Ethnography' which involves the use of empathetic methods, through which they attempt to understand alien culture from the point of view of 'the natives'. It is clear that such methods are very appropriate to the study of new religious groups since such groups represent cultures that are alien to the paradigms within which the sociologist operates. The symbolic interactionist perspective which has been effectively used in studies of deviant cultures has seldom been applied to religious groups.

With a few honourable exceptions, such as Barker's (1984) study of the Moonies, the majority of studies of new religious movements have simply applied 'positivistic' or scientific concepts to their analysis in a way that is both patronising and dismissive. From the Marxist point of view, they are seen as either new opiates or as 'pre-political movements of protest'. Functionalists are invariably concerned with questions of the extent to which they are socially functional, disfunctional or irrelevant to the development of modern societies; evolutionary theorists tend to see them as retrogressive or 'throw backs' to a more primitive type.

Now, it is true that new religious movements may have their origins in the wider socio-cultural environment and have historical antecedents that must be taken into consideration. It is also true that they have social consequences for the dominant culture, but a full understanding of such movements also involves an in-depth study of the meanings of membership for those involved.

A combination of the approaches of the 'Enlightenment Man' and the Romantic is necessary if we are to arrive at a comprehensive understanding of new religious movements, not only as sub-cultural groups or countercultures within a dominant culture, but as functioning cultures in themselves. The Romantic approach is necessary since no culture can be fully appreciated from outside. But while this method enables us to understand empathetically the content of the culture, it does not enable us to compare cultures. In order to compare it is necessary to use 'universal' concepts which, as we shall see, are extremely difficult to construct. Further, the hermeneutic approach does not enable us to take account of the influences of the environment in which cultures develop.

Are there any universal concepts? A synthesis, perhaps, of the universal aspects of enlightenment, of science and romanticism requiring compromises on both sides. This involves a consideration of the philosophical discussion of the nature of reality, which in the West reached some tentative conclusions in the ideas of Kant and has been pursued by the phenomenologists.

Positivists assume that what human beings perceive through their senses is all that actually exists – that men see things as they are. The opposite view, that of the idealist, particularly in the extreme form of solipcism taught by Berkeley, was that all we know is the content of our own minds. These two epistemologies correspond roughly to the enlightenment and the Romantic world-views respectively.

Between them lies the view that while there is an ultimate

reality, for which Kant used the term Noumena, this cannot be known directly to man through his senses. Man can only know the phenomena – the way in which things appear to him through his senses. According to this view the *Real* may be interpreted in a variety of different ways. While in theory each individual might interpret *Reality* in a different way, there is in fact a great deal of agreement on the way in which people interpret reality at least within a particular culture. This point is made very effectively by the English philosopher Owen Barfield in his discussion of collective representations. 'A representation is something I perceive to be there. . . . As to what is meant by "collective" – any discrepancy between my representation and those of my fellow men raises a presumption of unreality and calls for explanation' (Barfield, n.d.).

The way in which we perceive reality, our representation, is largely determined by the way in which we have learned to perceive the world through the process of socialisation by which the cultural tradition has been communicated to us.

There are, however, those who claim that while *Reality* cannot be directly perceived through our physical senses, it may be directly experienced through the development of latent or perhaps culturally suppressed psychic abilities. Such claims are made by mystics who appear to exist in all cultures, though more frequently and prominently in cultures that include some recognition of their claims to interpret reality.

The mystical view bears some similarity to that of the idealist, since the mystic can only experience *Reality* subjectively. However, there is a significant difference since the idealist can only experience what is in his own individual mind, whereas the mystic claims that his experience of *Reality* is shared with all other mystics, and is thus not a purely individual experience occurring in an isolated mind. Rather, the mystic holds that his experience is of a *Reality* which is objective since it includes all that exists within itself. Each individual is able to experience that *Reality* directly because each is a part of it; in order to experience it each has only to abandon the illusion of their separate individuality and become immersed in the one *Self*.

I make this point particularly because many, if not all, of the founders and some, at least, of the members of new religious movements have this idea of unity with the *Real* as a central aim of their lives.

The interpretation of the nature of the *Real* must always be expressed in socially conditioned terms. Those mystics who have been socialised within a Christian culture are likely to interpret the *Real* as a personal being, God, whereas the Buddhist views it as impersonal and refers to it simply as the *existent*, that which exists.

Mystics have considerable difficulty in communicating their experiences to layfolk for the simple reason that no experience can be adequately communicated to others who have not had a similar experience. How do you explain the taste of an orange to someone who has never tasted one? You can only do this by using an analogy; you might, for instance, say that it's like a sweet lemon, but those who have tasted an orange will know that this by no means conveys the real experience.

Mystics are usually so convinced of the importance of their experience that they attempt to convey it by comparing it with some experience that is familiar to their followers. For example, Jesus expressed his experience of *Reality* as a relationship with God because reality was interpreted in terms of personality in Jewish culture. But since few Jews had a personal experience of a relationship with God, he explained that relationship as comparable to the relationship between a child and its father. He did not use the analogy of the relationship of a child and its mother, which some people in our own culture might consider more appropriate, because of the strong emphasis on the role of the father in the patriarchal structure of Jewish society. The growing influence of the mother in European culture led to the development of the cult of the Virgin Mary in Catholic Christianity, a cult in which Mary is referred to as the 'mother of God'.

While *Reality* remains the same, social change necessitates the production of new interpretations of its essential nature in order that the majority of people may arrive at some understanding of the nature and meaning of life. Traditional religion is often slow to adapt, consequently new religious ideas must arise and be promoted outside the religious institutions.

People interpret their religious experiences in terms of their own understanding of life conditioned by the society in which they live. In times of rapid change these interpretations are often at variance with those offered by the established religious organisations. The deviants form or join new movements.

Mystical experiences are an extreme form of religious experiences and in examining these we can do no better than start from the work of the sociologist Joachim Wach (1958) who drew a clear distinction between religious experience and the form through which it is expressed.

He agreed that the religious (spiritual) experience, which includes the mystical experience we have already mentioned, could not be reduced to a sociological explanation. He pointed out that, 'Those among us who study the sociological implications of religion would be deceived if they imagined that their works are capable of revealing the nature and the essence of religion itself.'

The rise of new religious movements has produced a number of problems for sociologists that we intend to discuss in this study. In the first place there is the obvious question of why these movements have emerged at this particular point in history. Second, what are the common factors that have led to this phenomenon occurring on a world-wide scale? For, as we have already indicated, new religious movements have developed in most countries in the world. Third, we are faced with the problem of the functions that such movements may have within a society or, even more significantly, for the human species as a whole. Fourth, we are concerned with the processes through which such movements originate, grow, decline and die.

A consideration of these problems led to the examination of more profound matters that start from the question of the nature of religion and went on to raise the subject of human nature and of those social relationships that constitute the fabric of society itself. Ultimately, therefore, we find ourselves forced to re-examine the basis of sociological theory and methodology.

2
Religion and sociology

What is religion?

Before we can go beyond a descriptive account of events, it is necessary that we arrive at a definition of the nature of religion. Such a definition has been a subject of debate between theologians, philosophers and social scientists for many years, and numerous definitions have been produced. The social scientists' contribution ranges on the one hand from the purely individualistic proposed by William James (1936) that religion is 'the feelings, acts and experiences of individual men in their solitude, so far as they apprehend themselves to stand in relation to whatever they may consider the divine', to the social definition of Emile Durkheim who proclaimed 'there is no religion without a church'.

On the other hand social scientific definitions may be divided into two categories (Robertson, 1970): (1) inclusive; and (2) exclusive. Inclusive definitions are most typically represented by Durkheim who specified religion as 'a unified system of beliefs and practices relative to sacred things, that is to say, things set apart and forbidden – belief and practices which unite into one single moral community – called a church, all those who adhere to them' (Durkheim, 1915).

Durkheim's definition formed the basis of that used by functionalists: religion is defined not in terms of its content but in terms of its functions. Religion has the function of integrating society. It is assumed that people are brought together, unified and kept together by the beliefs and values they share. The content of these beliefs is irrelevant; they may relate to gods and the supernatural, as in traditional views of religion, but they may equally be atheistic and materialist systems of belief such as Marxism, fascism, nationalism or Rationalism, all of which have been described as secular religions by functionalists.

Indeed, some of these secular movements seem quite prepared to accept the label of religion. Some years ago when a certain English Local Education Authority was setting up a committee to prepare a new agreed syllabus for religious education, I was approached by the secretary of a local Rationalist Society who asked me if they could claim to be a religion in order to obtain a place on the committee and so ensure that Rationalism was included in the Religious Education syllabus.

The difficulty, for this study, of using the inclusive definition is that it is too broad, and would lead us to a consideration of all types of new social movements. We consequently need a definition that will enable us to distinguish between 'religious' and other types of ideological movement, since we believe that the processes involved in the rise of new movements may be related to the content of their beliefs and practices. We also believe that the effects of movements on members and on the general public may vary in terms of the beliefs and values promoted by the movement. Consequently, we seek an exclusive definition.

Exclusive definitions of religion are expressed in terms of the content of the belief system. They invariably include some reference to a belief either in God, gods, spirits, the supernatural or 'other worlds'. We therefore propose that for the purpose of this study religion is defined as a system of beliefs, once rooted in an acceptance of a non-material level of existence which may include a belief in a God or gods, in spirits and the 'supernatural'. Such a definition is broad enough to include 'religions' such as Buddhism where there is no belief in a God in the Western sense of that term, but which will exclude purely secular beliefs such as Marxism.

However, to define religion in terms of beliefs alone would be to ignore other dimensions of religiosity which form essential elements within what is a complex social institution. Not even the solitary practitioner of James's definition would be restricted to the purely intellectual aspect of beliefs, as is clear from James's study in which he emphasised *experiences* as the primary factor. Although religious experiences and beliefs are at the heart of religion, it is, as Durkheim suggested, also a collective activity. Religion involves activities such as ritual and worship, and the need to plan and arrange such collective action gives rise to religious organisations.

Next, religion involves the development of myths, the sacred stories through which both experiences and belief are transmitted, and which develop in literate societies into holy books, dogmas and creeds, until finally theology, the 'science' of God evolves as an intellectual and academic activity.

In defining a movement as a religion, we expect it to have developed, or at least have the potential to develop, most of the characteristics we have listed. For example, the Spiritualist movement has a set of beliefs that have been formulated into what amounts to a creed, 'The Seven Principles of the Spiritualists National Union'. Experience of contact with the spirit world is available to all members through the activities of mediums. Organisations such as local churches have developed to provide venues for both worship and psychic activities, and many of these have united to form national organisations.

While there is no one holy book exclusive to Spiritualism, the Bible is widely used and a number of other works including the Harmonial Philosophy of A. J. Davis and the writings of Dr Stainton Moses are considered to have a key position in Spiritualist thought. Spiritualism like Hinduism has many 'sacred writings', and these constitute the body of the theology or philosophy of the movement.

When we examine the characteristics of Spiritualism we have no difficulty in defining it as a religion. Spiritualism is a 'new religion' which had its origins in the middle of the nineteenth century. It has been one of the most successful of the new religions of that century, together with, amongst others, Mormonism (The Church of Jesus Christ of Latter Day Saints) and Theosophy. We shall frequently use material relating to the history of these movements to illustrate some of the long-term aspects of the development of new religions.

Belief and action – myth and ritual

There has been a lengthy debate in anthropology about the relationship between myth and ritual, between those who argue that rituals are objectifications of myth and those who take the opposite view that myths are created to explain rituals. The relationship is certainly complex and, when we consider the situation in preliterate societies, an unplanned process. Even in modern religious movements it is rare to find evidence that rituals were consciously designed to fit a myth or that myths were invented to explain a ritual. True myth is not consciously created in the way in which a scientific theory is formulated to explain an event. Neither, for that matter, is it deliberately constructed in the way in which a novel is written. We shall return to a discussion of the difference between myth and science later. At this point it is necessary to examine more closely the relationship between myth and ritual, the relationship between belief and practice. In an established religion these are intricately interwoven in the organisational structures of the institution, but we are primarily concerned in this work with the emergence of new movements, and therefore have to ask the difficult question of 'what came first, the chicken or the egg?' When we examine in detail the emergence of a 'new religion', we may be able to trace some part of its source before the tracks become too confused or, to go back to our analogy of a fountain, to find the spring before the waters of the stream become too muddied.

It is appropriate that we should turn now to an examination of the ways in which sociological definitions of religion have been influenced by the positivistic and scientific paradigm in the past, and the effects on future perspectives which recent work in the field of the new science of parapsychology has produced.

Religion and social science

In discussing the visions of the Virgin Mary at La Salette and Lourdes, Michael Carroll (1985) raises a bogey that has haunted the social sciences of religion for many years when he points out that 'to allow even the possibility of divine intervention as the proximate cause of human thought or behaviour could be to move the analysis beyond the bounds of social science.' Whereupon he quickly retreats and attempts to explain the visions as 'similar to hallucinations' (a psychological 'cop-out'). He goes on to offer sociological or social-psychological explanations as to why people experience particular types of hallucinations at particular times and places.

Why should explanations of human thought and behaviour always be restricted to those that fit the current 'social-scientific' paradigm? We may suspect that this is a defence mechanism through which social scientists react to any questioning of the omniscience of their discipline. Such a questioning in turn threatens not only their status within the profession but the very existence of that profession. However, if as scientists we are concerned with deepening understanding, broadening knowledge and arriving at truth, we must not allow ourselves to be frightened by the fear of transcending disciplinary boundaries or even of working ourselves out of a job. If an adequate explanation for events (facts cannot be found within the existing disciplinary paradigms or even within the current cultural world-view), then the scientist must be prepared to abandon the inadequate paradigm and to examine the possibility of using 'culturally tabooed' theories that offer explanations for the phenomena in question.

Before proceeding to an examination of the possibilities of developing new paradigms for the understanding of visionary and religious experience, we may look at some of the points made by Carroll since they are representative of a positivistic approach in social science.

In the first place, the assumption that if we allow the possibility of divine intervention we must automatically exclude a social scientific approach is mistaken. The recognition of the independence of a particular factor such as religious or spiritual experience does not preclude us from considering the way in which that experience is modified or interpreted as the result of social influences.

Secondly, the concept of hallucination is unclear and there is no reason to think that such a concept has any advantages over the concept of divine intervention as an explanatory device. From a sociological point of view, what is important is the meanings that people give to their experiences rather than the 'real' causes of the experiences themselves. An experience such as a vision of a lady may be interpreted in a number of different ways. The different meanings given to the experience may derive from the prior socialisation of the individual, consequently many individuals in a modern secular society might believe that they were having an hallucination. Such an intepretation would not only be meaningful to them but would perhaps have social consequences, in that they would probably consult their medical practitioner or psychiatrist. Alternatively, someone socialised in a religious tradition would possibly consult the priest or, if the social situation were appropriate, set themselves up as a prophet and found a new religion.

3
Parapsychology & the sociology of religion

Religion was a central concern of the founding fathers of the sociological enterprise. Comte, Spencer, Marx, Durkheim and Weber, in different ways, all argued that religion had a key function to play in the structures or processes of society; and as Robertson (1977) noted, there has been a re-emergence of interest in religion amongst those sociologists not confined within the boundaries of the sub-discipline of the sociology of religion. In view of this renewed interest in religion as a central factor in any attempt to understand modern societies, it is important that we re-examine the nature of religion in the light of recent non-sociological investigations, which suggest that previous sociological ones are inadequate.

The sociological study of religion has always presented difficulties that are not present in the study of other social institutions, difficulties that have arisen out of both definitional problems and the substantive differences between the sources of religious action, as defined by religious practitioners, and the sources of social action, as defined by sociologists. This problem has evolved out of the situation of sociology as a discipline which has developed within the general monistic materialist paradigm of the natural sciences. In consequence, sociology, like the natural sciences, has encountered great difficulty in investigating or understanding a religiously inspired form of behaviour or action that is based on either the assumptions of a monistic spiritualist paradigm or on those of a dualistic paradigm.

As a discipline operating within a monistic materialist

24

paradigm, sociology has tended to produce reductionist theories of religion. These have the characteristic of 'explaining away' religion as the product of non-religious or purely 'material' factors, rather than contributing to an understanding of religion as either a source of human action or as expressive behaviour.

Sociological reductionism

In order to appreciate the potential contribution of sociology to an understanding of religion and the equally important contribution that religion may make to our understanding of society, it is essential that we examine the conditions which led to the rise of a sterile reductionism in sociological thought about religion.

While many historical factors have contributed to the rise and dominance of reductionism, these are mainly related to the desperate attempts of sociologists in the nineteenth and early twentieth century to gain scientific respectability for their new discipline.

Sociology has its roots in eighteenth century 'Enlightenment', a mis-named movement based on the assumption that the universe could be understood in the light of reason alone. This was a period in which science was replacing theology and philosophy as the foundation for the dominant world-view of Western society. This rationalist scientific ethos was reflected and given expression in the work of August Comte. Partly because he coined the term 'sociology' for the emerging science of society, Comte is recognised as the founder of modern sociology.

The ethic of the Enlightenment also included a concept of progress (Nisbet, 1980) which Comte included in his 'three stage' model of the development of human thought. A model that introduced into sociology the rationalist concepts of religion which had appeared in the work of such enlightenment scholars as David Hume (1956). This model was extremely important since it clearly influenced the thinking of all the major sociological scholars who have concerned themselves with religion.

Comte claimed that human thought, in its attempt to explain

the universe, passed through three stages. In the first, animistic or theological stage, explanations were couched in terms of the will of 'supernatural' beings. In the second, metaphysical stage, explanations are offered in the form of logical but speculative theories. In the third, positive stage, explanations take the form of scientific laws or of theories that have been substantiated or 'proved' experimentally. It is not our intention to refute the Comtean model which adequately fits the development of scientific thought up to the twentieth century, but simply to suggest that the paradigm shift that is taking place during the current scientific revolution (Kuhn, 1970) demands that we extend the Comtean model to a fourth stage.

But first we must consider the influence of Comtean positivism on sociology. Under this influence religion came to be treated as synonymous with a 'primitive' stage of thought; later metaphysics was expunged from philosophy as mere speculation by the logical positivists who reduced philosophy to the discussion of logic, the use of language and questions of method.

The denigration of religion as an outmoded style of thought had considerable influence on early anthropological as well as sociological studies. For example, Tylor (1958) defined religion in terms of a belief in spirits and attempted to demonstrate the universality of such beliefs, and to examine the ways in which a belief in spirits developed into theistic concepts in 'higher' religions. However, since he did not believe in the objective existence of spirits, he concluded that such a belief must have had its origin in the misinterpretation of some common experiences such as dreams and visions, and in the fact of death. Tylor may be correct in his view that religion has its origins in a belief spirit, but wrong in his reductionist explanations of the sources of that belief. As we shall see, the findings of psychic research and parapsychology indicate that spirits may have an objective base in reality.

Durkheim, in his attempt to establish the objective existence of social facts, argued against any form of reductionism that threatened the autonomy of sociology (1938). Yet, in his own study of religion (Durkheim, 1954) he offered an explanation of origins that reduced religion to an epiphenomenon of society and described its functions as purely social. In a similar way, Marx and Engels (1955) attempted to explain away religion as an epiphenomenon of the economic base of society, and to describe its functions in terms of the maintenance of the stability of class societies.

Weber (1965) did not deal seriously with the ontological reality of religion and even refused to define it, though he did treat it as an independent variable in his analysis of social change. But here, as with the previous theories, Weber emphasises the rational analysis of religion and indeed considers religious change itself as part of a process of increasing rationality.

Parsons and Shils (1937) went some way towards recognising the ontological independence of religion in their claim that religious symbols refer to aspects of reality outside the range of scientific investigation and analysis, but restricted their examination to the social functions of religion.

Although Berger's (1969) social constructionist theory differs widely from the forms of reductionism already discussed, it remains within the province of what may be called sociological imperialism, as a theory which does not admit the inclusion of any variables that are not social. He attempted to defuse the problem of the nature and status of religion by advocating methodological atheism, yet his argument that religion is a human projection, logically neither precludes nor accepts the possibility that the projected meanings have an ultimate status independent of man. Berger suggested that sociologists should engage in a search for 'signals of transcendence' and it is therefore surprising that this did not lead him to seek such signals in the findings of parapsychologists. For these findings indicate that his projected meanings may represent the interpretation by the human mind of levels of reality that have an objective existence independent of the individual, or of any collectivity which, in itself, is assumed to have an existence apart from the individuals of which it is composed.

These findings thus question both the theory that religion is the result of illusions created by the individual mind, as in Freud's theory (1928) and Durkheim's idea that religion is a social creation

27

of a 'collective representation', which presumes the existence of a mythical 'collective consciousness' (Durkheim, 1954).

This critique of reductionism has also been influenced by the work of Robert Bellah (1970) who went on to suggest that an understanding of religious action can only be reached if we adopt an approach which he describes as symbolic realism. This approach treats religion as a 'reality *sui generis*'. As Bellah says, 'to put it bluntly, religion is true ... since religious symbolisation and religious experience are inherent in the structure of human existence all reductionism must be abandoned.'

In addition to the objections to Bellah's proposals arising from the difficulties in operationalising his ideas in empirical research (Robbins, Anthony and Curtis, 1973), there are the problems that arise from Bellah's restriction of his discussion to religious symbols. Although he mentions the importance of 'experience', this is not fully incorporated into his discussion. The problem of restricting his study to symbols is that the beliefs which they embody are frequently treated as objectively real by believers and, consequently, to conceptualise the 'real' as symbolic is to engage in yet another form of reductionism. For instance, to treat angels as symbols is to misunderstand the beliefs of many Christians, just as the treatment of spirits as symbols misrepresents the position not only of modern Spiritualists but also the beliefs of all animists.

Further, the key element in any religion is experience not belief, for beliefs as such have their source in either direct or indirect experience and, therefore, to arrive at an understanding of religion it is necessary to share the experience of believers.

Finally, Bellah suggests that the truth of religious symbols is different from scientific truth since it is not subject to the same type of objective test. In this work, we suggest that at least some of the claims of religion are scientifically or experientially testable, although such testing may involve the researcher in the act of 'suspending his unbelief'.

The question of the extent to which it is legitimate to include propositions about the supernatural in scientific theories of religion has been discussed by Hodges (1974). He argued that if the supernatural exists, it provides a responsive environment that provides feedback to the actor and thus affects his action. Assumptions about the supernatural can thus be feasibly and usefully included in scientific theories of religion if they can be put in the form of postulates.

The concepts of the supernatural that may be derived from the findings of parapsychology conform to Hodges's requirement and we shall later discuss the postulates that may be derived.

However, as Johnson (1977) has pointed out, 'most sociologists of religion still subscribe to the doctrines that science can have nothing to say about the truth of religious ideas'. He goes on to point out that 'this doctrine is based on the methodological principle that science cannot investigate that which is non-empirical.'

It is clear that there are no empirical referents for some of the central concepts of religion: for instance, it may always remain impossible to test the existence of God, as the ultimate existent, by using empirical scientific methods. On the other hand, some proposition about the alleged 'supernatural' may be testable in so far as the propositions in question relate to claims that supernatural agents may influence events in the material world. In particular, it is possible to examine propositions that relate to the nature of man as a spiritual being; these not only refer to truth statements of a religious nature but also to concepts of the nature of man that are central to sociological theorising. It is also possible to investigate the claim that this separable, non-material component, the spirit, can survive the destruction of the material component, the body. Here, also, there is substantial confirmatory evidence.

The proposition that man is a spirit being forms a key part of the belief systems of all religions. It includes the idea that man consists of at least two elements, a material body and a non-material spirit (mind or soul). This idea receives support from many empirical studies of extra-sensory perception, telepathy and psycho-kinesis which show that communication is possible between two human minds without the use of the normal, sensory apparatus and, further, that the human mind can influence material objects without physical contact.

Johnson's article (1977) led to a discussion at the Fortieth

Annual Meeting of the Association for the Sociology of Religion in San Francisco, in which Johnson, Dick Anthony, R. Bellah, William Garrett, Charles Glock and David Stagman were involved (Kelly, 1978). William Garrett (1974) discussed these problems from a different perspective which led him to ponder 'the considerable problems social theorists have encountered in dealing with the troublesome phenomenon of religious transcendence'. He classified the approaches of sociologists to religion into three types: scientific reductionism; symbolic functionalism; and phenomenological nominalism. It is only the last of these which includes a 'non-reductionist category for religious transcendence', and it is this view that has been incorporated into our study.

Non-positivist approaches

The theories we have considered so far have all treated religion as a social or at least a human product, and we may admit that the form religion takes as a social institution, as a structure, and as an organisation, is clearly the result of human action. However, the source of the action which remains the core of institutionalised religion may not be social or even human but may, in the words of Rudolf Otto, be 'the Wholly other' (Otto, 1959).

The core of religion in the rationalist theories considered is belief, but in the phenomenological theories such as those of Otto (*ibid.*) and Eliade (1958), it is experience, and indeed experience of something that is transcendent, non-human or supernatural – that is central to religion. While some psychological studies (James, 1936) and some anthropological works (Humphrey, 1944; Long, 1976) have been founded on this approach, sociologists have tended to avoid research that considers the social effect of non-social variables of this type. Indeed, under the continuing influence of Durkheim sociologists are wary of including any non-social variables in their work. This reaction may also be detected in another field, in the attitude of some sociologists to the theories and research of socio-biologists.

Beyond positivism

As we have seen, the positivist tradition leads to a reductionism from which there appears to be no escape, since the monistic materialist paradigm on which it is based excludes by definition the possibility of the ontological reality of non-material entities. On the other hand, the phenomenological tradition is concerned with the analysis of subjective experiences the existence of which cannot be established objectively.

It is, however, possible to transcend positivist philosophy by the use of empirical methods, and thus to move into a stage of post-positivist thought which we may call animistic positivism. This may be demonstrated by using the methods of positive science to test the existence of non-material entities. It is my contention that empirical methods used within the discipline of parapsychology have already succeeded in establishing the existence of such non-material entities, through the examination of the effects that they may have on the material world.

The findings of parapsychology

It is impossible to provide a comprehensive analysis of the findings of psychic research within the compass of this book, but a brief résumé is essential to our argument.

Parapsychological research is usually referred to as psychic research in Britain. This term is in some way more appropriate since it includes the investigation of phenomena that are assumed to be objective and occur outside the individual mind, and of such events as reincarnation and communication with discarnate spirits – phenomena that have been largely ignored in recent years by the more rigorous parapsychologists. Conversely, Soviet scientists study this type of phenomena under cover of the title of 'paraphysical research'.

The programme of psychic research may thus be divided into the investigation of a number of widely different phenomena that are connected only by the fact that they appear to be generally inexplicable in terms of the accepted scientific theories of the time. For this reason, the discipline is sometimes described, particularly in the USSR, as para-physics or psychotronics. One of the areas currently explored by such researchers is that of clairvoyance, which is usually attributed by scientists either to fraud or delusion.

Clairvoyance is one type of the phenomena of mediumship which constitutes a central problem for the psychic researcher. Clairvoyance is used in a broad sense to refer to the ability to 'see' or perceive objects not perceptible to the 'normal' senses. It is, of course, difficult to test the claims of mediums to clairvoyant experience; indeed, there is only one major way this may be done. In many cases mediums claim to have received messages from the dead; in some instances it has been possible to show that the information disclosed by 'spirit' informants through a medium could not have been obtained by the medium through any material sources.

As in sociology, it is extremely difficult to conduct rigorously controlled experiments on mediumship since the necessary controls may inhibit the phenomena studied, which tend to be of a spontaneous and unrepeatable nature. In consequence, statistical evidence is much more difficult to obtain than in the case of extra-sensory phenomena. There is, however, voluminous evidence based on individual cases, and case studies of individual mediums. Emma Hardinge Britten (1870; 1873) produced two contemporary but uncritical accounts of mediumship in the nineteenth century, but the best critical account remains that of Frank Podmore (1963), while the author (1969a) has provided a more recent review of Spiritualism. Other reviews of the evidence for the survival of personality after the death of the body may be found in Johnson, 1953; Gauld, 1968; Baird, 1944; Crookall, 1961; and Rao, 1966.

Mediumistic evidence is not restricted to the provision 'testable' information (which can be very evidential in individual cases), but also takes a number of other forms: materialisation, psychic photography and automatic writing. In each of these areas there is a solid body of evidence obtained under controlled conditions.

Finally, there is substantial evidence to support the claims of spirit healing. Of course, there are also instances of fraud in all these areas, but that fact does not invalidate all the findings. Indeed, the cumulative evidence is vast and clearly supports the hypothesis that human personality survives the death of the physical body.

Psychic phenomena are by no means restricted to modern industrial society, and evidence of the wide distribution in human experience is well documented (see Paton, 1921; Humphrey, 1944; Eliade, 1964; Beattie and Middleton, 1969; Jackson Knight, 1970; Lewis, 1971; Hitchcock and Jones, 1976). Studies of these types of psychic phenomena may be compared with case studies involving the use of participants and other forms of observation in the social sciences, and the findings may be considered to achieve the same level of validity as those in comparable social science research.

If religion is rooted in experiences of the psychic and the mystical, it may be understood only if one treats such experiences as independent variables and accepts their 'existential validity'.

Reincarnation

A belief in reincarnation forms part of the religious teaching and is widely accredited in many parts of the world, particularly in the East (Stevenson, 1975, 1977, 1980). The theory of reincarnation has been less widely accepted in the West and was progressively rejected by the Christian church. With the rise of 'scientific' theories of personality, it was long ignored by the scientific establishment. In recent years, evidence has begun to accumulate which suggests that at least some individuals may have experienced previous lives. Much of this work has been undertaken by psychologists, psychiatrists and hypnotists such as Guirdham (1970; 1971), Bloxham (Iverson, 1977), Keeton (O'Hara, 1980), Moss and Keeton (1979), Wambach (1979) and Kelsey (Grant and Kelsey, 1969). One of the first cases to be subjected to a thorough examination was that of Bridey Murphy (Bernstein, 1956).

The cumulative evidence is sufficient to suggest that

reincarnation occurs, and consequently supports the hypothesis postulated in relation to evidence from mediumship of a separable entity (spirit) that survives the death of the body.

Extra-sensory phenomena

Much of the work of parapyschologists in the USA and the USSR (Gris and Dick, 1980) has been concerned with the investigation of extra-sensory phenomena (ESP), a general term including telepathy, telekinesis and precognition. The scientific investigation of telepathy had its origin in the work of William McDougal (1915; 1934), the Scottish psychologist who became head of the Department of Psychology at Duke University in the USA in 1927. McDougal established the first parapsychological laboratory at that university and was responsible for the appointment of J. B. and Louise Rhine as assistants. Over a period of thirty years the Rhines conducted a series of tests that firmly established the facts of the direct transfer of information from one human mind to another without the intervention of a normal sensory means of communication. Using the Zennor cards they demonstrated that some subjects were able to produce remarkable results in recording the symbols on cards visible only to the experimenters (Rhine, J., 1936; 1948).

The possibility of precognition was also established in another series of tests which revealed that some subjects were able accurately to predict a card before that card had been seen by the experimenter.

Through a further series of experiments, the Rhines were also able to establish the existence of psycho-kinesis, the ability of the mind to influence material objects. They showed that some subjects could influence the fall of dice and, by concentrating on a particular number, ensure that the die fell on that number much more frequently than would occur by chance (Rhine, J., 1971; Rhine, L., 1972).

These findings, which have been supported by the work of other researchers (Beloff, 1974; Uphoff and Uphoff, 1975), tend to support the hypothesis that mind can operate independently of body. Taken in association with the other evidence we have examined, these results appear to confirm a dualistic theory of human nature.

Other evidence that questions scientific (monistic) materialism includes studies of the psychic abilities of animals (Schul, 1978) and plants (Backster, 1968), and of the effectiveness of various types of 'psychic' healing.

It is noted that parapsychology is not a subjective discipline, but seeks to establish the objective existence of non-material entities by the use of empirical scientific methods. In this way, the methods of positivism are being used to transcend the positivist theories. This represents an advance beyond positivism rather than a retreat from it, which is the method adopted by subjectivists.

There is also some evidence for the concept of mind as an independent entity that interacts with body. The specialist, Sir John Eccles argues that the brain appears to be 'the sort of machine a "ghost" could operate, if by "ghost" we mean in the first place an "agent" whose action has escaped detection even by the most delicate physical instruments' (Eccles, 1970, p. 127). A theoretical explanation for these findings has also been proposed by Eccles and Popper (1977).

This cumulative evidence supports the views of some scientists such as Sir Alister Hardy (1966) that the current materialistic monism which constitutes the paradigm of science is outmoded and must be replaced by a dualistic paradigm. We thus appear to be at the beginning of what Kuhn (1970) called a scientific revolution. Since modern sociology is rooted in the same materialistic monism as the physical sciences a paradigmatic revolution must have equally revolutionary implications for the social sciences including sociology.

The evidence already cited contains indications of the form to be taken by the new dualistic paradigm, but we are concerned here only with the implications of such a new paradigm for the development of sociology and in particular for the sociological study of religion.

The major element of interest to sociologists in the findings of parapyschologists is the implication which these findings have for our concept of the nature of man. In the past, sociologists have tended to operate with an image of man as a *tabula rasa*, as an almost infinitely malleable being. This model appears to have its source in the works of Locke (1706) and is present not only in the positivist schools of sociology but, through the influence of Mead (1934), has provided the base for the concept of self found in the symbolic interactionist and allied schools of thought.

The findings of parapsychology support the notion that the individual is more than the sum of his social experiences and his genetic make-up. Psychologists and biologists suggest that the individual is at least in part the result of his genetic inheritance. But none of these theories accounts for the existence of the self – the common human experience of continuity. The evidence produced by Spiritualists that this self survives the dissolution of the physical body confirms the view that it is not a product of the biological organism. In any case, the body itself is a rapidly changing organism, in which cells are constantly dying and being replaced. In view of this, it is clear that self cannot have its foundation in biological factors. Neither is there any evidence that man's experience of self-continuity is derived from his social experiences. Hence we may conclude that the consciousness of self is the result of the experience of an 'existent'; that the individual experiences a self because the self as an entity pre-exists the birth of the biological organism, survives its death, and is independent of that organism. This self may influence the behaviour of that organism and in turn be influenced by the physical organism and by the organism's social contacts with other organisms.

The existence of a 'self' cannot be demonstrated by an objective 'Scientific' test. The only evidence is experiential and consequently subjective. Testimentory evidence of experiences of self are to be found in the writings of mystics. As Staal (1975) says 'If mysticism is to be studied seriously, it should not merely be studied indirectly and from without but also directly and from within.' The techniques that may be used to obtain knowledge of the Self have been given by many mystics including Patanjali (1978),

Shankara (1964), Conze (1956), the author of *The Secret of the Golden Flower* (Wilhelm, 1972), Baker (1977), Wood (1961) and Steiner (1969).

The existence of such a 'self' provides the only adequate base for the assumptions of action theory, for the universal experience that men have of 'free choice' and for a sociology that rejects deterministic explanations of a behavioural type and introduces explanations in terms of the individual's ability to make choices.

Implications for the sociology of religion

The new dualistic paradigm has important implications for the sociological study of religion in general and for our study of new religious movements in particular. In the first place, religion can no longer be treated as a purely social product and thus 'explained away'.

It is clear from our previous discussion that religion has its roots in certain relatively common experiences which, under the influence of positivist thought, have been treated as illusory, but which have been established as having a base in objective reality by psychic research. Recent research into religious experience (Hay and Morisey, 1977) has shown that such experiences are relatively common and that most individuals have at least one such experience during their life. The experiences in question include the impression of being in the presence of gods or supernatural beings, of spirit or faith healing, of seeing ghosts or other supernatural beings such as fairies or perhaps, in more recent times, of encounters with UFOs.

If, as we have argued, such experiences are not purely subjective but have some referent in objective reality, then we are justified in proposing that they form the basis of all religions. Indeed, this may explain the common features of all human religion since the practitioners of all religions engage in psychic and mystical practices which include attempts to contact 'gods' and 'spirits'.

Religion, however, embraces dimensions other than the

'experiential'. A number of attempts have been made to classify these dimensions. But while many of these are illuminating within previous paradigms, we must now root our dimensional definition on the *experiential*.

Given that experiences are the basis of action, we may then postulate that beliefs arise out of man's efforts to interpret and understand his experiences. There is a reciprocal relationship between experiences and beliefs in that beliefs, once institution-alised, react upon and influence experiences. Beliefs related to categories of experience in question have a tendency to acquire a sacred quality, when the term sacred is used in a Durkheimian sense (Durkheim, 1938). The reason for this lies in the elusive quality of such experiences. In view of the sacred character of such beliefs it is important to believers that their beliefs should be transmitted in a pure form to their children and succeeding generations, in consequence *ritual* and *myth* develop and these may, in certain circumstances, evolve into liturgy and formal theology which constitute a doctrinal dimension of religion. In the case of religions that arise in more complex societies, it becomes necessary to develop an organisational structure with the formal aim of promoting the beliefs of the religion.

This study of new religious movements is based upon the assumption that psychic, mystical and religious experiences are real and not illusory, and that such experiences provide the base upon which new religious movements grow. We shall therefore proceed to examine the influence of religious experience in the origination of new movements in the following chapter.

4
Human nature

The work outlined in the previous chapter raises certain fundamental questions about human nature which underlie any study of religion from a sociological angle. We start with an examination of the proposition that sociological theories have their foundation in assumptions about human nature, but this is not all, for the ideas of religion are also rooted in conceptions of the nature of human beings.

One of the problems that arise in a sociological discussion of religion is that sociology and religion start from different assumptions about human nature. While there are obviously some differences between religions, there is one major characteristic on which almost all religious philosophies would agree – the assumption that man is a spiritual being. Further, that each individual consists of an essence or distinct self which may be described as a soul or spirit and this spirit is a non-material being which pre-exists the body and survives the death of the physical organism.

Such an ontology is related to a cosmology which assumes that the material world is not the only order or level of reality. Indeed, some religions believe the material world to be unreal, a creation of human minds and not independently existent. All religions accept the reality of a non-material universe though some do not distinguish clearly between the material and the non-material worlds.

When we turn to the scientific philosophies of the Western world we find human thought dominated by very different ontologies and cosmologies, as a result of the processes of 'disenchantment' discussed by Weber (Gerth and Wright Mills, 1947), and the secularisation that has been a major topic of debate in more recent times. Western conceptions of human nature rest on very different ideas about the nature of the universe. Since the period of the Enlightenment, scientific thought has tended to see the universe as purely material. Only that which can be perceived by the human physical senses and can be measured is considered to be real, because only this reality can be subjected to scientific methods of study.

In consequence, scientific materialists have held that conceptions of spiritual or non-material worlds were based on illusion. Human beings were purely biological organisms having no spiritual essence or soul. Their behaviour was thus to be explained in terms of genetic and other biological or physical factors. If 'spirit' was an illusion, mind was almost equally illusory since it merely represented the epiphenomena of brain activities. Conceptions of human nature used by biologists and psychologists are still largely of this type, and the biological view of human nature still deeply colours the ideas of many lay people.

The third major conception of human nature, that of a *tabula rasa*, is distinctively sociological in form. While it seems to have been expressed first in the works of the philosopher John Locke, it reached full fruition in the positivist sociology of Comte, particularly as developed by Emile Durkheim. The concept of the *tabula rasa* is quite simply that human beings are born into the world as a 'blank sheet' on which society writes: they are almost infinitely malleable and are shaped by society.

The attraction of such a concept to sociologists is quite clear, for it provides an ontological foundation for their imperialistic aims in its denial of the existence of either a spiritual or a material essence to human nature. It opens up the way to the assertion that humans are entirely a product of society and consequently legitimates the claim of such sociologists to be the sole interpreters of the nature of 'man' and society. As Andreski (1974) pointed out, sociologists have thus tended to assume the role of sorcerers or priests.

Let us turn to an examination of the concepts of human nature as expressed in the works of some of the most influential sociologists.

In the theories of Durkheim the positivist concepts of human nature are united, as De Coppens (1976) says:

> The central assumption of Durkheim's theory of human nature is that Society fashions and organises man's psychosocial nature and to know man, it is necessary first to know and understand the Society which made man what he is at the human level.... All that transcends and surpasses animality and biological life is of social origin.

The consequence, is that in his research Durkheim in fact ignores the biological and concentrates exclusively on man as a social product.

De Coppens goes on to compare Durkheim to what he calls the classical traditions in which humanity is seen as a *homo duplex*, 'a being reduced to a physical body, a biological organism; and to a soul, a microcosmic and psychic reflection of society, which is purely psychosocial and which has nothing spiritual or trans-cendental in it.' It is this concept of 'soul' as a social product that is the subject of Durkheim's work. Quite clearly, it is a very different definition of soul from that used in theology but is the one that underlies Durkheim's conception of a 'Conscience sociale'. As a product of nineteenth-century materialist thought, Durkheim totally rejected the idea of the individual as incorporating a self-existent soul. It is clear that he uses a modified *tabula rasa* concept in which the blank sheet may vary in colour and size, but where the message written on it is dictated by society.

The other major founding father whose ideas have extensively influenced sociological thought on human nature is Karl Marx, another to see the human individual as a social product. It is true that in his early writings (Bottomore, 1963), where the influence of Hegel is more obvious, he would seem to imply that 'man' is free to make choices. However, his statements are unclear and perhaps ambiguous, as where he states that man as a species/being 'treats himself as the present living species, as a universal and consequently free being' (Bottomore, 1963, p. 187), and later when he points out that 'as society itself produces man as man, so it is produced by him' (*ibid.*, p. 157).

In his later works Marx moved further from Hegel and the overall impression that we get of his views has been well expressed by Seve (1978, p. 394) who claimed that 'Marx absolutely destroys the belief in an illusory abstract human essence inherent in the isolated individual.' In other words, the effect of Marx's work was to set up a view of human nature as largely, if not completely, a product of social, and indeed economic forces. Of man as a being without essence, whose nature differs from one society to another, from one historical period to another. Such beings would almost amount to a different species, able to communicate with each other only with great difficulty.

Marx and Durkheim thus both contributed to the development of a sociological relativism that presents great difficulties for the study of man as a species. Is it true that human beings differ greatly from society to society? It is of course impossible to test that theory historically, though the fact that we are able to understand the ideas of Plato or Confucius and of Buddha suggests that we have much in common with them in spite of the differences between their societies and ours.

Anthropologists are very centrally concerned with attempts to understand contemporary societies of which they are not members; while they may not always be successful, their undertaking does not appear to be inherently impossible. Indeed, it may be no more difficult to understand a human being from a geographically or temporally remote society than it is to· understand a contemporary neighbour. The problems which arise are the result of inherent difficulties of communication that affect all relationships between individuals. The central methodological problem in sociology is that of understanding the actions of others; the very existence of sociology depends upon the possibility of achieving such an understanding. Understanding can only be reached if there is some common ground upon which individual minds can meet, and this is to be found in a constant and shared element in human nature which is not a produce of social or environmental conditions. There is of course an additional factor necessary if understanding is to be reached, and this is a common means of communication – they must be able to use a common language.

Both the Marxist and Durkheimian varieties of sociology offer us a deterministic version of human nature. The mystical philosopher Gurdjieff (1950) suggested that the human race faced the choice of becoming human ants or human bees, and that indeed is the choice offered by political extremists, on the left and on the right, a choice between two varieties of collectivism. Even in the Western democracies there is a growing tendency to see human beings as products of their genetic make-up or of the social environment. These two alternatives are combined in models such as those of the socio-biologists who see human behaviour as a product of a complex mixture of biological (genetic) and social factors. This view has the consequence of dehumanising man, of legitimating the development of bureaucratic and other forms of state control, of encouraging the development of new technologies that facilitate the control of individuals by elites, and may eventually eliminate the need for human beings altogether since the functions of most people may be more efficiently carried out by machines.

It is paradoxical that sociology, traditionally seen as a liberating discipline, should have become the major philosophical and 'scientific' basis for a thoroughly deterministic view of human nature, one that justifies the denial of the significance or indeed the essence of the individual human being.

This view of human nature negates the possibility of the very phenomena that sociology should be concerned with – the phenomena of sociability and of social relations – for only autonomous beings can have meaningful social relationships with each other. Society as a network of social relationships is consequently only possible if individuals can be identified as units that have an 'essence' which is not simply the product of their interaction with other units.

This takes us back to Gurdjieff's analogy of the ants and bees. Marais (1937) in his study of the white termites suggested that termite behaviour can best be understood if we treat the unit of analysis, not as the individual termite, but as the colony and see this as a biological organism of which the individual termites are but cells. Spencer's concept of society as an organism displays many similarities with Marais's model of the termite colony, a model that underlies much structural, functional and systems theory, and treats the individual as being as insignificant as the ant whose behaviour is determined by the 'ant hill', or a bee who is controlled by the 'hive'. In my view it is impossible to develop a sociology of the hive or ant hill. This may be the reason why sociology was banned in the Stalinist Soviet Union and in Nazi Germany. There can be no sociology of collectivist human hives and any attempt to practice sociology in such societies is thus seen as a subversive activity, because it draws attention to the fundamental defects of a system that denies the individual 'essence' of man.

In the West determinism is still frequently disguised by appeals to traditions of free will which insist that human beings are still able to make choices, and it is true that opportunities for free action still exist on the margins of such societies, and become available because of the institutional complexity that creates conflicts particularly during the socialisation process. In consequence it is possible for alternative concepts of the nature of man to persist and to express themselves not only in alternative sociologies but also in the rise of new religious movements, which are the main concern of this study.

However a major thrust to changing attitudes towards the conception of the nature of man has been produced by development in cosmology within the natural sciences.

Until recently, the natural sciences have tended to take a deterministic view of the nature of the universe and consequently of human nature, though cracks began to appear in the structure of nineteenth-century determinism early in the twentieth century when Einstein published his theory of relativity (Einstein, 1920). Further developments including Hiesenbergs Quantum theory led Eddington (1928) to declare that 'physics is no longer pledged to a scheme of deterministic law', and point out that the abandonment of the concept of causality in physics led directly to the necessity to abandon determinism in accounting for human behaviour. However, in a desperate effort to be 'scientific' social scientists have continued to strive for a positivist stance more appropriate to nineteenth-century than to late twentieth-century science.

It is unfortunate that sociology has continued to be unduly influenced by antiquated concepts of science imbedded in the philosophical grounding of its founding fathers, and that its practitioners have largely ignored philosophical idealism and vitalism as represented in the works of such thinkers as Bergson (1911), Berdyaev (1952), Eucken (1912) and Schopenhauer (1891). Their writings provide the foundations for an alternative sociology more appropriate to the discussion of contemporary problems, including that of new religious movements, for they are particularly concerned with questions of creativity, spirituality and free will.

It is equally unfortunate that orthodox sociology is so rooted in a philosophical ethnocentrism that has excluded the potential contribution of Eastern thought, for the philosophical traditions of both China and India have much to offer to the sociologist who seeks to develop a concept of human nature that will enable him to understand the religious life of the human species. In particular, the concept of human beings as essentially spirit beings was developed in greater depth in Eastern philosophy than in the theological thought of the Christian world out of which Western civilisation has grown.

It is interesting to note that the findings of parapsychology tend to confirm the insights of Eastern religion, and that these are also in line with the more recent developments in the natural sciences. We shall take up these points later since they relate to the way in which some new religious movements appear to attempt to bring together philosophy, religion and science. Spiritualism, which I have cited as one of the first of the 'new religions' of the Western world, has from the nineteenth century been overtly claimed by its followers to be, 'a philosophy, a science and a religion' (Nelson, 1969a).

The mystic Gurdjieff produced a system of philosophy that

synthesised the mysticism of the East and the science of the West (Bennett, 1963). During his life he gathered around him a fluctuating group of disciples but founded no surviving organisation.

Gurdjieff's concept of human nature is curious, for he views the universe as material, though the way he uses this concept simply indicates that he considers the universe to be of one substance, and therefore he makes no distinction between spiritual and material. His view of human nature has been well expressed by Wilson (1978), 'Man's being is like a vast mansion, yet he seems to prefer to live in a single room in the basement.' As Wilson (1980) has also pointed out, Gurdjieff's aim was to wake up the individual to the immense potentialities of human nature, an aim that differs little from that of most religious and occult movements though it is presented in a different form.

The concept of human nature that emanates from the philosophical systems of both East and West which we have mentioned, and which is currently supported by the findings of parapsychology and recent developments in the natural sciences, is one that provides the basis for a new world-view on which future sociological paradigms will rest. It is a perspective that underpins many of the new religious movements which may thus be seen as collectively paving the way for fundamental changes in the outlook, attitudes and values not merely of the Western world but of the human race. It is clear that some such core of belief must come into existence as the basis for a unification of the species – a stage in human development that must be reached soon if mankind is to solve the problems with which it is faced and move forward into the future with confidence.

The image of human nature that is emerging is that of the individual as a spirit being incarnated in a physical body, a being which is itself a facet of a universe that exists as a unified whole, and is conscious and purposeful.

Human beings inevitably associate with other humans and experience mutual influences. Sociology is primarily concerned with the relationships between individuals, with the ways in which individuals form groups and societies and the relationships between such human groups, with such problems as power and authority, control and deviance, but it must treat these within the broader context of the concept of human beings as integral parts of the whole universe.

5
Church - sect and cult

Typologising religious organisations

In simple, small-scale societies religion is integrated into the whole fabric of life to such an extent that in many languages there is no word to express the ideas covered by the concept of religion in English. If we disentangle the aspects of life that might be included in that concept, we find that most of them are part of the everyday activities of the individual. In such societies the only social organisations are those connected with kinship and territory. In so far as there are cults these are family cults connected with the family's continuing relationship with its ancestors, and the ritual activities of such cults tend to be led by the head of the family. But even in such societies, specific roles related to 'religious' activities begin to emerge. The first such role is that of the Shaman who specialises in contact with spirits and in healing, both of which functions require skills and abilities that are not universally, or even widely, distributed in society.

As society becomes more complex so religious roles become more clearly differentiated and religious institutions and organisations are created. In the West the Christian church became the first large scale organisation apart from the state. Before the rise of Christianity, the rulers of the Roman Empire had realised the integrative functions of religion, and in order to unite an Empire in which there were innumerable gods and cults they instituted the worship of the Emperor.

When the cult of the Emperor was replaced by Christianity as the state religion, a large number of independent Christian churches were welded together to form a vast organisation with the headquarters in Rome, the capital of the Empire. Not only did the churches lose their organisational independence but they also lost their doctrinal freedom. The state, anxious to use the church as an ideological instrument in integrating the Empire, could not tolerate disunity within the church. It must be centrally organised so that the local churches could be effectively controlled and it must present a consistent and coherent ideology.

Within the Empire the Roman church was given a monopoly and state support in suppressing heretics and pagans; it held a position similar to that of the Communist Party in the Soviet Union at the present time. But outside the Empire some independent churches survived including the Syriac and Ethiopian churches.

The Roman church was so effectively organised that it was the only major social institution to survive the destruction of the Western Empire. The continuing Eastern Roman Empire, which later became known as the Byzantine Empire, reorganised its own ideological wing, the Orthodox church, with its headquarters in the imperial capital, Constantinople.

With the collapse of the Empire a number of independent churches appeared particularly around the margins, in those countries which were largely cut off from Rome by pagan invasions. A good example was the British Celtic church which survived in Wales, Ireland and Scotland. As Rome reasserted control over the European churches they began to send missions to recover the lost areas; the Augustinian mission sent to Britain ostensibly to convert the pagan Anglo-Saxons ended up by suppressing the independence of the Celtic church.

The organisational structure of religious movements became of interest to sociologists largely as a result of the work of Max Weber and Ernst Troeltsch. They pointed out that an examination of the history of Christianity disclosed two major types of religious organisations, the church and the sect, and that these very different types of reaction had their roots in a fundamental ambiguity in Christian teachings regarding attitudes to the state and society. This ambiguity is to be found in the earliest Christian literature and has continued to influence the actions of Christians up to the present period.

The first attitude is that the Christian should, in the words of Jesus, 'render therefore unto Caesar the things which be Caesar's (Luke, 20:25); as Peter expressed it 'submit yourself to every ordinance of man' (1 Peter, 2:13). Peter also instructed his followers to 'Honour the King' (1 Peter, 2:17).

This attitude may be summed up as the view that Christians should obey rules because as all rulers are only able to assert authority in as much as their power is willed by God. On the other hand, we find suggestions in other texts that earthly authority is evil because the world is ruled by the Devil (Satan). Those who take this view believe that Christians should, as far as possible, withdraw from the world.

Consequently, since the period of the Apostles there has been a division within Christianity between those who believe that Christians should involve themselves fully in the social, economic and political life of their society, and those who believe that they should either actively resist the evils of society or shut themselves away from these evils.

Troeltsch (1931) argued that these conflicting attitudes led to the development of two types of religious institutions, the church and the sect. The church is an institution held to be endowed with divine grace, which it mediates to the world through the priesthood. It claims universal authority and consequently seeks to include everyone. In order to provide for a universal membership, the church tends to relay its moral requirements, and to adapt to the culture of the social environment in which it operates. While it seeks to include members of all classes, it is dependent on the upper class and therefore lends its support to the ruling group and to legitimate social order. Once established the church is naturally not very concerned with proselytizing, but generally relies on recruiting the children of members. Typically, one is 'born into' rather than converted to membership of a church. Churches emphasise doctrine and sacrament. They are relatively strict on matters of faith but are less inclined to enforce moral rules.

On the other hand, sects are voluntary organisations which actively proselytize though of course they also attempt to retain the children of members. However, one is not born into a sect and typically the children of members are expected to go through the same conversion experiences as outsiders who join the organisation. Sects reject compromise with secular values and constitute small groups which separate themselves from the world and stress the virtues of 'perfection' and an ascetic life style. They tend to recruit mainly from the lower class, the oppressed and the underprivileged and consequently are either hostile or indifferent to both the existing social order and the existing religious establishments. They tend to look forward to the Second Coming of Jesus when all the existing authorities, which they consider to have been instituted by Satan, will be destroyed and the 'true believers' (usually restricted to those who are members of the sect in question) given authority to rule the world under the direct instructions of Jesus.

The dynamics of sect development

Troeltsch's ideal typology came under criticism as providing only a static framework of analysis. It became apparent that many religious movements that engaged the attention of sociologists did not fit into either of the dichotomous ideal types that Troeltsch had proposed. Certain of these had some characteristics of a church combined with other features that were characteristic of a sect. This led to the proposal that the church and sect typology needed to be seen as a continuum rather than as two opposing ideal types.

The model of a continuum also introduced the idea of dynamic change into what had been a static dichotomy, and H. Richard Niebuhr (1954) in particular introduced the idea of a unidirectional process of development through which all religious organisations passed on their way from being sects to becoming churches.

Niebuhr suggested that all religious movements started life as sects, that is as movements among the poor, oppressed and under-privileged, who were opposed to the social order and to the dominant values of society. Such movements recruited their members through active proselytization and the use of conversion techniques. He went on to argue that in the strict sense, no religious organisation survived as a sect for more than one generation. The reason for this is that all sects encourage their members to ensure that their children join the sect, so that a large proportion of the second generation have not been converted from disbelief but have been raised and socialised from birth to become members of the group.

This was not the only reason why sects developed into denominations, according to Niebuhr. He pointed to the change in attitude which has become known as the Wesley effect since it seems to have been first noted by John Wesley as a process taking place within the Methodist societies he formed.

Wesley noted that over time the membership of his societies seemed to change. In the early days the membership consisted of poor working-class people, but as time went on he observed that it seemed to become more middle class. The process appeared to be related to the effect which Max Weber later ascribed to the Protestant ethic. That is to say that workers who joined the Methodist movement tended to work harder, to stop spending money on drink and other leisure activities. They saved their money and invested it in small business enterprises, so that by the second generation their families had experienced upward mobility. These children would have been brought up as good Methodists and would continue to remain members of that society. However, their enthusiasm for the strict Biblical teachings would have waned, and it was this effect that Wesley regretted.

Many studies of Methodism show that a process of denomination took place within that movement which was offset by the rise of new Methodist sects that sought to restore Methodism to its original teachings and also to return it to the working class for whom it had originally been intended. A major breakaway movement was that of the Primitive Methodists, but there were others such as the Bible Christians, a subject to which we shall return later.

Cults

The concept of cult had its origin in the elaboration of Troeltsch's church-sect typology by Howard Becker (1932) whose four-fold classification stretched from Ecclesia through Denomination and sect to cult. He argued that those 'tendencies toward religion of a strictly private personal character fairly well-marked in the sect ... came to full fruition in the cult as here defined.' He summed up his model of the cult in the following words:

> The goal of the adherent of this very amorphous, loose-textured, uncondensed type of social structure ... is that of purely personal ecstatic experience, salvation, comfort and mental or physical healing. Instead of joining a cult, an act which implies the consent of others, one simply chooses to believe particular theories or follow certain practices, and the consent of other members of the cult is not necessary. It therefore verges on the abstract crowd, although its well-marked ideology probably entitles it to a place among the abstract collectivities.... The cult is the most ephemeral of all types of religious structure (*ibid.*).

As I pointed out (Nelson, 1969a), the Spiritualist movement is a classical example of a cult, as defined by Becker. It is true that there are many formally organised Spiritualist churches and societies, but it is not necessary to belong to any of these in order to be a Spiritualist. A Spiritualist is simply defined in terms of the type of beliefs he holds and the only contact he may have with other Spiritualists, except for any psychic contacts, may be in reading Spiritualist literature. He is under no obligation to attend services or meetings or to join any organisation. However, as I also pointed out, the loose nature of the organisation does not, as Becker suggested, necessarily mean that such cults are ephemeral.

The modern Spiritualist movement has survived for over 130 years in spite of the fact that individual societies and churches, specific magazines and papers have ceased to exist. Becker was correct in suggesting that cults in general are short lived and Spiritualism is one of those exceptions that are said to prove the rule.

J. Milton Yinger (1957) developed and extended Becker's typology into a six-fold interpretation by subdividing Becker's Ecclesia and sect types. In my study of Spiritualism I summarised Yinger's definition of his six types in the following way:

1 The Universal Church which Yinger suggests is the most successful in supporting the integration of society and satisfies most of the personality needs of individuals in all strata of society. The best example of a Universal Church would be the Catholic Church in Mediaeval Europe.

2 The Ecclesia is less successful in incorporating sect tendencies, and while it is adjusted to the needs of the dominant strata in society, it tends to frustrate the needs of the lower strata. A good example would be the Church of England.

3 Denomination or Class Church is in Yinger's typology limited either in class or racial membership or in regional distribution. It is in substantial harmony with the existing social order. It is conventional and respectable in its outlook and has often developed from a middle-class sect. The Congregational and to some extent the Methodist Churches fit into this category.

4 The Established Sect is a sect which has resisted development towards a denomination and is usually one which had originally been concerned mainly with the evils of society. An example of the Established Sect is the Quakers.

5 Sects were divided by Yinger into three types according to their responses to and means of dealing with the undesired situation which had given them birth.

A Acceptance. Sects arising from this response are basically middle-class organisations. The middle classes tend to accept the social pattern. Their difficulties arise from lack of faith, selfishness, isolation and other personality problems, not from the evils of society. An example of this type of sect would be Moral Rearmament or Christian Science.

The underprivileged may react to the evils of their situation by aggression or avoidance, and consequently two types of sect may result.

B Aggression. In this type of sect arising from aggressive feelings the teachings of Jesus are interpreted in radical-ethical terms and the efforts of the members are directed towards obtaining social reform.

C Avoidance. In sects arising from avoidance the hopes for a better life are projected into the supernatural world or into Chiliastic hopes for the early establishment of the kingdom of God.

6 The Cult. Yinger suggested that this is normally a small short-lived group, often local, which develops round the personality of a charismatic leader. Its beliefs differ widely from those generally accepted in the society concerned and it is basically concerned with the problems of individuals. Yinger pointed out that the best examples of this type are Spiritualist groups (Nelson, 1969a).

However, since Yinger's definition of cult is similar to that of Becker, my study of Spiritualism pointed out the inadequacy of both their definitions.

Type of cults

In the course of my study of Spiritualism (Nelson, 1969a), I found that there were many difficulties in applying the church-sect model even in its modified form (Wilson, 1966) to that movement. In the first place, such typologies as systems of classification offer no basis for a theoretical explanation of the origins of a new movement, for the particular organisational form it takes or for the way in which it develops.

As we have already seen, I sought to offer an explanation of origins by suggesting a 'needs' theory as a logical development of deprivation theory. However I was at that point more interested in the organisational form and development processes through which such movements grew.

The second problem I then encountered was that church-sect 'theory' is very difficult to apply to religious movements that are not products of the Judaic-Christian-Islamic tradition. This of course was not surprising since Troeltsch devised that typology as a tool for his analysis of the history of Christianity, and subsequent modification had been made by scholars also interested in the study of Christian churches.

Benton Johnson (1971) had argued that the difficulty arose from the differences in the charismatic source of Western as compared with Eastern religions. He pointed out that Western religions have their origins in emissary prophecy, while Eastern religions have their base in exemplary prophecy, a distinction which was also used by Martin (1962b). The concepts of emissary and exemplary prophecy are based on Max Weber's concepts of the ethical and exemplary prophets (Weber, 1965).

Johnson argued that it was the fact that Western religion was rooted in ethical prophecy that gave rise to those social reactions exemplified in the church-sect typology. In my view exemplary prophecy gives rise to religious reactions that do not fit into that typology, but which require the development of new concepts. I argued that the concept of cult should be used as the basis for the initial classification of such new movements.

It was clear that wide differences in structure could be observed between cults, and it became obvious that a basis for classifying them into two main types existed in Troetlsch's concept of mysticism which he had defined as 'simply the insistence upon a direct inward and present religious experience'. According to him mysticism is a form of 'radical individualism' best described as 'a parallelism of spontaneous religious personalities', which gives rise to the 'conception of a purely spiritual fellowship'. Mystics get together and form organisations because of the need they feel for 'the give and take of intimate fellowship with other souls'.

Troetlsch suggested that two types of organisation might develop within mysticism. One which he labelled Philadelphianism was the result of 'the formation of groups round spiritual directors and deeply experienced leaders'. The second type for which Troeltsch had no label but which might be called Religious Communities, were organisations 'formed on the family pattern ... by people who lived the community life'.

Both these types are clearly useful in classifying new religious movements and in the examination of processes of organisational growth. However, it is clear that within each of these types there are sub-types which depend upon the structures of power and authority. For in both cases power may either be concentrated or diffused, giving four ideal types (see Fig. 5.1).

CULT

Authority	*(Philadelphianism)*	*Community*
Concentrated	Charismatic	Autocratic
Diffused	Spontaneous	Democratic

Figure 5.1   *Organisational types within mysticism*

In my study of Spiritualism I was concentrating on a case study of a spontaneous cult. Such cults are rare. They come into existence not out of activities of one charismatic leader but from what Martin (1962a), following Troeltsch, described as a 'parallelism of spontaneities'. In other words, individuals who have common or similar interests, ideas or experiences come together, often informally to give mutual support and encouragement, or because their interests and activities require the co-operation of others.

My study of the Spiritualist movement showed that in the early days in America and Britain small groups of individuals interested in psychic phenomena gathered together informally. Many of these cult groups had very short existences but those that survived tended to develop democratic structures and to make contact with other such groups. This led in the first place to loose federations of groups, and in Britain to the formation of a democratically structured Spiritualists National Union.

But within the broad Spiritualist movement there were from the first some charismatic cults, composed of groups of disciples and followers that gathered round charismatic mediums. These often ceased to exist or transformed themselves into democratically organised groups on the death of the charismatic founder, though some evolved a structure through which charisma became institutionalised and an autocratic power structure was maintained.

The major example of this last process may be seen in the case of the Greater World Christian Spiritualist League. This organisation developed out of a Spiritualist Circle that formed around the charismatic medium Winifred Moyes. After her death the organisation continued to exist with control centralised in a small self-perpetuating group. Another example is that of the White Eagle Lodges which developed from the mediumship of Mrs Grace Cook.

The charismatic cult

Psychologists such as Stoner and Parke (1977) have concluded that the leaders of many modern cults are engaged solely in promoting their own interests and are prepared deliberately to manipulate their followers in order to obtain wealth and/or power. Such persons are quite prepared to use fraud and deception in the promotion of their organisations. They may claim to have received divine revelations, to have the gift of healing or to be God, and then proceed to maintain their charisma by whatever means they feel to be necessary. The sociologists Bainbridge and Stark (1979) in their review of three models of cult formation have also discussed what they call 'the entrepreneur model'. This model sees cults as businesses and cult leaders as businessmen engaged in producing and selling a product. As they point out, a number of cult founders have in fact made a considerable fortune out of their organisations. They quote the case of Arthur L. Bell whose cult Mankind United had an income of some four million dollars between 1934 and 1944 (Dohrman, 1958, p. 41) and L. Ron

Hubbard who became very wealthy as a result of the establishment of his Church of Scientology (Cooper, 1971, p. 109). Another
case is that of Sun Moon the founder of the Unification Church
(Moonies). Other cult leaders have exploited their followers
sexually.

Bainbridge and Stark go on to point out that there have been
many cases of entrepreneur cults that have been based on fraud,
and quote the somewhat dubious case of Uri Geller, the Israeli
spoon bender (Randi, 1975). Fraud in this case, however, has not
been proved and subsequent investigations have shown that similar
results can be produced under experimental conditions using
subjects other than Geller. A clearer case is that of the Phillipine
and Brazilian psychic surgeons who were definitely detected in
fraud (Flammonde, 1975). However, one of the best examples of
chicanery quoted by Bainbridge and Stark was Arthur L. Bell's
claim that his movement was a branch of a universal spiritual
hierarchy similar to that claimed by the Rosicrucians. Bainbridge
and Stark go too far in asserting dogmatically that no such
hierarchy exists, though they appear to be justified in their claim
that Bell was not legitimately connected with any such hierarchy.

The question of fraud in religion raises many difficult problems.
It has been suggested by sceptics that all religion is fraudulent, in
that (a) God (or gods) do not exist! (b) only material facts that can
be tested by scientific methods exist, and that all claims that
cannot be tested in that way are untrue; consequently the claims of
religion which cannot be tested objectively are untrue.

Such a rubric would clearly lead to the conclusion that Christianity was untrue, and largely fraudulent, indeed it has been
claimed that (a) Jesus never existed, or (b) that if he did he was
only a man who made fraudulent claims to divinity.

The status of claims made for or by religious leaders, whether
Jesus or Sun Moon, depends upon their acceptance, as a matter of
faith, by their followers, and there is no way in which we may
ascertain objectively if Jesus or Moon are who they profess to be.
It has been suggested that the claims of a religious leader can be
tested by the effect that they have on the lives of the 'true
believer'. But the life of the believer in the teachings of Marx or

Adolf Hitler may be equally influenced, albeit in different ways, to that of the lives of the Christians or the Moonies. Perhaps this is because the teachings of Marx and Hitler also constitute religions, and indeed communism and fascism are often labelled secular-religions by functionalists.

Perhaps we need here to revert to our earlier distinction between religion and spirituality, but while this enables us to concentrate on the spiritual based cults we are still faced with the problem of distinguishing between false and true spirituality.

The mystical experience which is the essence of spirituality is ineffable and can only be understood by another mystic. It might be concluded that only a genuine mystic can detect fraudulent claims to mystical experience, but while the mystic can often enter into the experiences of fellow mystics and understand empathetically their descriptions of those experiences, there are some difficulties in that view. Although the core of the experience is the same, it is clothed by the conscious mind in symbols that are socially derived and consequently differ not only from one society to another but also over time in the same society. The symbolic presentation of the experience of medieval Christian mystics presents difficulties not only to mystics from the Hindu and Buddhist faith but also to modern Western mystics.

In most societies those who seek to establish new religious movements will be expected to have had religious experiences, and those who have not had a genuine experience will probably make a claim to such an experience. Because of the inherent difficulty in transmitting the essence of such an experience to those who have not had one, it is relatively easy for a fraudulent cult leader to create the impression amongst his followers that he has been blessed by a divine revelation. This deception is facilitated by the fact that most religious seekers will not themselves have had any very profound experiences, but have become followers either in search of access to such an experience or because they need the reassurance that can be given by an inspired leader. If they are seeking 'mystical experience' them-selves, they will soon detect that the leader is unable to provide them with the knowledge and techniques necessary for achieving spiritual enlightenment, and will probably leave the movement. It is clear from many studies that within the cultic *milieu* there is a heavy turnover of membership. Lofland (1965 and 1978) distinguished a category of 'seekers' who drift from one cult to another in a search for 'knowledge'.

This way of searching for knowledge is more likely to be characteristic of those who join or form occult or Eastern-type cults. Cults in the Western Christian traditions tend to offer 'salvation' rather than spiritual knowledge. Their leaders claim divine revelation rather than mystical experiences. The claim to divine revelation made of such a prophet is usually one to a unique status – the prophet has a 'hot line to God' which is not available to his followers. The follower can only contact God through the mediation of the leader, whereas the mystic experience is usually considered to be available to all who follow the necessary course of training. The followers of a mystic may achieve the same experiences as their master; the followers of a prophet cannot hope to do so, at least in this life. Some such leaders promote themselves from the rank of prophet to that of God, usually in the form of claiming to be an incarnation of God, or a reincarnation of a previous incarnation as in the case of those who claim to be Jesus returned. In some cases the relatively more modest leaders wait for their followers to proclaim them God, and they seldom refuse the honour. Mr Moon appears to be an example of one who waited for his followers to make the claim. For an example of a leader who rejected divinity we probably have to return to Gautama Buddha, though in the present century Krishnamurti denied the role planned for him by his masters. The claims of the prophet are very different from those of the mystic but no less difficult to prove or test.

The third type of cult leader is the psychic who claims to be able to contact the spirit world and to heal. Psychics usually do not claim to have received a revelation directly from God but rather to be in communication with less elevated spirit beings through whose aid they may mediate messages to the living and heal the sick. Their assertions are open to testing at least at the level of their claims to communicate with the dead and to heal.

All three types of cult founder depend for their authority to some extent on charisma, though in certain cases an element of tradition is also involved.

The concept of charisma as a basis for authority was first proposed by Max Weber, who argued that three types of authority could be distinguished: traditional, legal-rational and charismatic. In the field of religious leadership the authority of a Catholic priest is largely traditional, that of a Protestant minister legal-rational, while founders of sects and cults tend to be charismatic. The role of charisma in religious leadership has been discussed by many authors including Barnes (1978), Richardson (1977) and Wilson (1970).

The concept of charisma has been widely extended and almost indiscriminately applied in recent years and has, therefore, been subjected to considerable criticism on the grounds that it is both 'theoretically ambiguous and methodologically inprecise', as asserted by Burke and Brinkerhoff (1981) in their report of an attempt to construct a method for measuring the concept.

It must be remembered that Weber saw charisma not as a personality trait characteristic of a leader but as the product of the social relationship between the leader and his followers. The leader makes demands upon the followers but he can only be described as charismatic if the followers respond. Indeed, initially the potential leader has no followers, he proclaims his message to a relatively uncommitted public. If the message evokes a response from his audience he begins to acquire followers. It is clear that a number of factors are involved including: (1) the nature of the message; (2) the appropriateness of the message to the situation of the audience; (3) the general social environment, the place and time at which his message is communicated; (4) the effectiveness with which he presents his message; and (5) the form and style of presentation.

In all of this the personality of the leader is involved particularly in the construction and presentation of the message, but also in his ability to choose the appropriate time and style of presentation.

This takes us back to a second model of cult formation discussed by Bainbridge and Stark (1979), the psychopathology model which attributes cult innovation to individual psychopathology.

They outline the main features of this model in the following way:

'1   Cults are novel responses to personal and societal crises.

2   New cults are invented by individuals suffering from certain forms of mental illness.

3   These individuals typically achieve their novel visions during psychotic episodes.

4   During such an episode, the individual invents a new package of compensators to meet his own needs.

5   The individual's illness commits him to his new vision, either because his hallucinations appear to demonstrate its truth, or because his compelling needs demand immediate satisfaction.

6   After the episode, the individual will be most likely to succeed in forming a cult around his vision if society contains many other persons suffering from problems similar to those originally faced by the cult founder, to whose solution, therefore, they are likely to respond.

7   Therefore, such cults most often succeed during times of societal crisis, when large numbers of persons suffer from similar unresolved problems.

8   If the cult does succeed in attracting many followers, the individual founder may achieve at least a partial cure of his illness, because his self-generated compensators are legitimised by other persons, and because he now receives the true rewards from his followers.' (*ibid.*)

Given the positivist assumptions of those who have used this model, the model itself provides a logical explanation for cult formation, but, of course, it totally ignores a whole series of problems that beset all theories that rest on such assumptions. In the first place it ignores the problem of defining 'mental illness', 'psychic episodes' and 'hallucinations'. In each case the definition is always relative and culture bound; and labelling of certain types of behaviour as 'insane' or a symptom of mental illness is a consequence of cultural definition. Indeed, the perceptional experiences and consequent actions of some people are defined as symptoms of insanity, simply because they differ from the experiences and actions of the majority. The kind of experiences that may commonly underlie the actions of cult founders are of the precise type that, because of their unusual and infrequent nature, tend to be labelled deviant or insane. These religious experiences include such occurrences as seeing visions, hearing voices and trances. In modern Western societies these are generally perceived not only by the psychiatric profession, but also by the general public who have adopted the perspective of scientific materialism, as indications of mental illness. In societies that are not dominated by that perspective, perceptional abnormalities of this type might be considered either as an indication of the favour of God (or the gods) or of the curse of demonic possession.

Many people who have such experiences in the Western world suspect their own sanity and consult a psychiatrist because they have learned to define such experience as symptomatic of insanity. However, some people brought up within a religious sub-culture such as that which Tiryakian suggests has survived as an underground movement in our culture, may recognise their experiences as being those of contact with another world. The nature of their recognition, the way in which they interpret their experiences, will depend on their previous religious socialisation. For example, someone who has been educated within a Catholic culture may well describe the experience as a vision of Our Lady, whereas a Hindu might interpret a similar experience as a vision of the God Krishna. Those brought up in a generally scientific culture may see visitors from outer space in 'flying saucers', where those steeped in ancient pagan beliefs see 'fairies'. It is clear that such visions are subjective, though they may be shared, and they therefore tend to be labelled as hallucinations. Now the best definition of an hallucination is that it is something you can see but I cannot. On the other hand, you might claim that since I do not see what you see I must have defective sight.

People who see visions are sometimes described as imaginative, which may simply mean that since visions are subjective phenomena some people are able to objectivise their subjective experience more effectively than others. On the other hand, there is a great amount of evidence that so-called visions have some base in the objective world.

We here encounter a further difficulty for materialists, that of distinguishing between the subjective and the objective. Indeed, it raises the whole question of the extent to which we can know the objective world, in view of the fact that all knowledge must ultimately be subjective in that it takes place within the mind.

While we can only touch briefly on the subject of epistemology, these questions are clearly of central importance to any social scientific inquiry into the field of religion, for the social manifestation of religion has its base in religious experience.

As in the case of entrepreneur cults, certain of which may be fraudulent, it is also clear that some cults may have been created by persons who were mentally ill. All we wish to point out is that religious experiences are not by themselves a sufficient condition for labelling an invididual insane. Religious experiences are a perfectly valid form of human experience, and it has been claimed that as such they may constitute the peak achievement of human life.

Mysticism and cult

David Moberg (1961) in a critical discussion of church-sect typology, pointed out that developments of the typology although largely derived from Troeltsch's ideas, had completely ignored his concept of mysticism. Moberg's comment led me to a reconsideration of this concept where I argued that its omission from discussion of types of religious action

> Would appear to be a serious defect – since the inclusion of Mysticism would convert a bi-polar continuum and two-dimensional analysis into a tri-polar continuum and necessitate three dimensional analysis.... [Further] It would appear that these three concepts treated as 'ideal types' should be placed at

the points of a triangle and not represented as lying along a unilinear continuum (Nelson, 1969a).

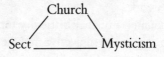

Figure 5.2   *Mysticism – tripolar analysis*

In presenting the typology in this way, it is intended to emphasise that there is no necessary unilinear connection between these types.

It is important to consider Troeltsch's definition of mysticism since mysticism is a form of religious experience which, it can be argued, is a key feature in the rise of new religious movements.

Troeltsch said that mysticism, as a type of a formation, is based on 'purely personal and inward experience . . . [which] leads to the formation *of groups on a purely personal basis*, permanent form, which also tends to weaken the significance of forms of worship, doctrine and the historical elements' (Troeltsch, 1931, p. 993). He claims that, 'Mysticism has an affinity with the autonomy of science, and it forms a refuge for the religious life of the cultured classes; in sections of the population which are untouched by science it leads to extravagent and emotional forms of piety.'

In applying this concept to the Spiritualist movement, I found close parallels between mysticism and Spiritualism, and in the subsequent studies of the wider range of 'new religious movements' which form the basis of the present book the Troeltschian concept of mysticism has proved extremely enlightening. It is consequently unfortunate that this concept has continued to be ignored by sociologists to the extent that Swatos (1981a) has recently repeated Moberg's and my pleas to 'bring mysticism back in'.

6
Cults & social movements

Cultic milieu

Colin Campbell (1972) suggested that cults arise from a general cultural ethos which he described as the *cultic milieu* that constitutes a sort of reservoir from which they draw their members. He argued that the cultic milieu includes all deviant belief systems and their associated practices: 'Unorthodox science, alien and heretical religion, deviant medicine, all comprise elements of such an underground. In addition it includes the collectivities, institutions, individuals and media of communication with these beliefs' (*ibid.*).

It is doubtful whether all these elements compose a single milieu in any meaningful sense, since cults differ widely from each other. Many cults are not only opposed but strongly antagonistic to all other cults, and indeed also to other manifestations of the cultic milieu. Like many other cults the Moonies claim to have exclusive access to the truth, they are right and everybody else is wrong. They are good and all others are evil. The same is true of the Krishna Consciousness movement on one hand and Jehovah's Witnesses on the other. The only characteristic that such movements share is an intolerance of all other movements whether these are within the cultic milieu or more widely situated in the broader culture of society. It is true that all the types of movement included in Campbell's concept of cultic milieu share an attitude of opposition to established cultural traditions of the society in which they exist.

The concept has certain similarities with that of counter culture

(Roszak, 1968), and suffers from the same defects. The opponents of the dominant culture do not agree on their criticisms of that culture and consequently they do not agree on the form that a replacement for the dominant cultural tradition should take. Indeed, different cults offer radically different solutions to the problems of the human situation; and offer constructions of reality that are opposed not only to the dominant tradition but also to each other.

Let us first consider the nature of the dominant tradition of the Western world against which new religious movements are protesting.

It would appear to us that the dominant culture of modern Western capitalist societies may be described as a combination of scientific and economic materialism. The ethic of the communist world is not very different, consisting as it does of a form of historical and dialectical materialism which includes important elements of scientific and economic materialism. Since Marxism is only a variant of the Western patterns of thought, in practice both systems contain residual elements of a Christian tradition which have become secularised.

We have already mentioned the Weberian views on the origins of capitalism, and we may conclude that the ethic of economic materialism has its origins in the revision of the Protestant ethic. The latter manifested itself largely in the Anglo-Saxon world as a consequence of the revival of the tradition of 'this worldly' individualism which in turn is a result of the Reformation and the re-emergence of the 'English' culture after centuries of suppression by the Norman-French aristocracy.

While the Protestant ethic, with its emphasis on 'hard work' and 'frugal living', may indeed have provided the stimulus for the emergence of the commercial capitalism usually described as mercantilism, it is clear that an ethic of frugal living could not have produced the incentive for a modern industrial capitalist system.

While the ethic of 'hard work' continued to provide an important base for exploitation of the working class, it has been clear, at least since the work of Lord Keynes, that no capitalist system can prosper without a wide and expanding market. Profits can only be made if there are customers to buy the ever increasing quantity of goods being produced by the new mechanised industries.

In consequence, the ethic of 'frugal living' was abandoned in favour of the ethic of 'consumption'. The general population was encouraged to expect an ever improving standard of living, which became a major measure of the 'progress' that was conceived to be normal in Victorian society. Advertising became an essential adjunct to industry and the masses were encouraged to 'want' more and more of the material goods being produced by capitalist industry.

Economic materialism may therefore be defined as a system in which the consumption of material goods is seen as the major aim of life. It rests on two assumptions (1) that wants (as distinct from needs) are unlimited, 'the more you have the more you want'; and (2) that there are unlimited resources to satisfy these wants.

These features of economic materialism are as characteristic of Marxian communism as they are of capitalism, since these two systems only differ in terms of means not ends.

As we shall see most 'new social and religious' movements reject the 'ends' aimed at by economic materialists.

We must next give some consideration to 'scientific materialism'.

Followers of Weber such as Merton (1938) have argued that modern science has its roots in the same processes of change that gave rise to modern capitalism. Marxist historians such as Hill (1958) and other socialists such as Tawney (1926) have pointed to the connection between the rise of the bourgeoisie and the origin of science. There is at the very least an historical coincidence between the rise of the middle class, of capitalism and of science which occurred in the same places and times, Britain and Holland in the seventeenth century. No one would suggest that these are unconnected events, but the exact causal relationship between them remain as yet, unresolved.

There is evidence (Hagen, 1966) that many of the English scientists of the seventeenth century, including Newton, were Puritan Protestants. However, Bacon, who is usually considered to be the philosophical founding father of modern science, was far from being an orthodox Protestant and seems to have been a member of the Rosicrucian movement (Yates, 1972), an occult order which was considered heretical but which has survived and, indeed, been revived in recent times (McIntosh, 1980).

By the eighteenth century, a split between science and religion was becoming evident in the works of the 'Englightenment' writers who attacked the teachings of Christianity. These attacks were delivered not only at the intellectual level but also through popular works such as those of Tom Paine (1794).

To some extent the effects of the 'Enlightenment' attack on religion were offset by the Romantic movement of the late eighteenth and early nineteenth centuries, which was not unconnected with the Wesleyan revival in the British Protestant churches and pietism in Germany. The influence of science was firmly re-established by the controversy over evolutionary theory largely promoted by Darwin's follower Thomas Huxley (Huxley, 1967) and Herbert Spencer in Britain, and Ernst Haekal (1910) in Germany.

Scientific materialism which differs little from the positivism of August Comte (1875), may be summed up in the following way:

1   The universe is purely material;
2   it can be understood, explained and controlled by the application of scientific methods;
3   in consequence religion is false, since its proposition cannot be tested by scientific method.

Scientific materialism in this sense became very widely accepted in the West during the first half of the twentieth century.

Again, we find that the basic assumptions of scientific materialism and economic materialism are challenged by the rise of new religious movements.

Set off against this dominant culture, Edgar Tiryakian (1974) sees esoteric cultures constituting a sort of underground movement constantly present as an underground counter-culture which emerges at times, and 'has been a catalyst in the modernisation process (spanning many centuries), both in its "break-downs" and in its "build-up"'.

In his work Tiryakian was, at least at that time, more concerned with the occult revival than with the wider question of new religious movements; but he pointed out that this esoteric underground may be a significant source of innovation and thus be much more important for sociologists to study than might at first seem likely. In earlier works on social change, Tiryakian (1967) had proposed that important ideational components of change (i.e. change in the social consciousness of reality) may often originate in non-institutionalised groups or sectors of society. The paradigms of reality of such groups may, in certain historical moments, become those which replace institutionalised paradigms and become in turn new social blueprints: 'I would propose that esoteric culture, and groups of actors mediating esoteric to exoteric culture, are major inspirational sources of cultural and social innovation' (Tiryakian, 1974, p. 273). He went on to suggest that one task for sociologists would be to follow up Weber's study of 'the affinity of ascetic Prostestantism and the ethical basis of modern Capitalism' with a similar study of the affinity of 'esoteric' culture to social innovations in exoteric culture'. Unfortunately, this challenge has not been taken up, though in this work I propose to outline what appears to be the relationship between the 'ethic' of certain types of new religious movements and changes that are taking place in modern societies, and more particularly those that we may foresee as taking place in the near future.

We may conceive a counter-culture, whether it be an esoteric culture or a cultic milieu, as being composed of the disaffected members of society irrespective of either the cause of their dissaffection or of the type of solution they may propose. However, it would be more realistic to suggest that we may arrive at an understanding of the forms of cults and new religions, if we consider the causes of disaffection and the proposed solutions, and use these as a means of classifying the resultant cults into a number of differing 'cultic milieu'.

There are three main elements in the dominant culture of

modern Western societies: Christianity, scientific materialism and economic materialism and, while these are interrelated, the connections are not indissoluble. Thus, a situation is created in which individuals may become disaffected with one of the elements without rejecting the others; some people may reject two of the elements, and others all three.

One of the factors leading to the rise of new religious movements in the present century has arisen out of the tensions and strains that exist within Western culture as a result of the inherent conflicts within that culture consequent on the incorporation into it of the three main elements we have distinguished. Of course, it will be clear that other minor elements also exist within Western culture, notably those which Tiryakian designates as 'esoteric'. However, as I have already pointed out, there is a 'folk' culture, a culture of the lower classes in Britain, and also regional cultures particularly those of the Celtic nations on the one hand and the ethnic minority groupings within Britain on the other, all of which have contributed to the general cultural mixture; in effect the dominant culture of Britain has the consistency of a stew rather than a soup. If we examine the United States, the stew contains at least as diverse a variety of components, and when we refer to Western culture as a whole the analysis of the mixture becomes even more difficult to undertake.

No individual can possibly accept all the diverse elements within the Western cultural mix, but most people may be said to accept the major elements and to tolerate the minor differences without too much strain. Extreme commitment to a specific element, however, may result in the rejection of other major elements and even in intolerance of those elements that appear to be inconsistent with one's own major commitment. The events in Northern Ireland and the activities of the Klu Klux Klan in the USA, seem to be instances of the breakdown of a culture which can only survive in an atmosphere of toleration of internal differences.

Let us return to our attempt to construct a classification system of new movements, based on our sub-division of Western culture into three elements. It would seem that we may treat each of these elements as a continuum from emphatic acceptance to complete rejection with a central zone of toleration.

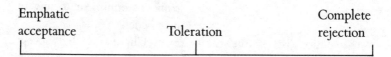

| Emphatic acceptance | Toleration | Complete rejection |

Figure 6.1 *Dimensions of commitment*

If these are cross classified with the three major elements we can find nine possible types (see Table 6.1).

Table 6.1 *Cultural orientations*

	Christianity	Scientific materialism	Economic materialism
Emphatic acceptance			
Toleration			
Complete rejection			

Because of the fact that emphatic acceptance of one element may lead to complete rejection of others, there is a connection between these two types of reaction.

Let us consider in some detail the major types that may be distinguished.

| 1 | Enthusiastic conformists: | claim to accept all the major elements, though an emphatic acceptance of all three elements would seem to be possible only to the schizophrenic. |
| 2 | Conformists: | are best defined as those who register as 'tolerant' on all three |

scales. This is the position held by the majority who 'go along with things' without expressing strong commitment to any of these beliefs.

3	Rationalists or atheists:	reject Christianity but accept both scientific and economic materialism.
4	Marxist rationalists:	as above.
5	Socialist rationalists:	reject Christianity and economic materialism.
6	Evangelical Christians:	(New religious right) reject science, accept Christianity, tolerate economic materialism.
7	Mystical Christians:	reject science and economic materialism.
8	Rejectionists:	reject all three main elements, but may replace these with a variety of different substitutes.

a   Reject Christianity and replace with an alternative existing religious belief system, for instance Buddhism or Hinduism. Such a process of conversion tends to involve a replacement not simply of Christianity but of the other elements in the Western culture system, and in this case the convert will probably join an Ashram or other type of monastic religious organisation and completely abandon the Westerners life style.

b   However, in some cases only a partial rejection/replacement takes place and a religious convert may continue to occupy a normal work and social role within Western society. For example, one of the major Western advocates of Buddhism continued to pursue his career in the legal profession and indeed became a judge.

c   Other rejectionists may join a new religious movement.

d   Some rejectionists may join new movements of a secular or political type, socialist or anarchist movements, new life or new age movements that demand levels of commitment that vary from total immersion in the life of a commune to nominal membership.

e Finally some rejectionists, unable to find an existing movement that fills their needs, will formulate their own 'privatised' religious or secular belief systems, which may attract followers and lead to the establishment of a 'new religion'.

While this system of classification is complex, it does enable us to understand the great variety of new movements that have come into existence and to appreciate that no one theory can explain the reasons for the rise of all new religious movements, other than the vague and useless concept that they all stem from economic, and social change and strain, concepts which themselves do not enable us to understand the origins and functions of specific cults.

We shall return to this point later, but first we must explore the relationship between the typology proposed and the more traditional forms of church-sect typology commonly used to classify such phenomena.

Churches

The term church is used to embrace what we have described as conformism which also covers those organisations usually defined as denominations or, in America, 'mainline churches'. In Britain this would include the liberal denominations such as the Church of England, the Methodists and the United Reformed Churches, all of which accept the 'dominant' culture. The typical conformist is a Christian scientific materialist who claims to belong to a church, but is only an occasional participant in worship. He verbally assents to Christian morality, but in practice largely ignores it in his work and social life. He accepts the world and the social order and considers material satisfaction to be paramount in his decision-making. He is acquisitive and not radically opposed to a capitalist or mixed economy. He accepts relatively uncritically the 'findings' of modern science and welcomes technological innovation. He is individualistic and only adopts collective action, such as that involved in membership of a trade union, when it is necessary to promote his own self-interest.

If we take this model as an 'ideal type' construct of Western industrial man, we may perceive that such an 'ideal man' is not an integrated personality. He contains within himself the seeds of conflict, the contradictions that exist between the materialist attitudes, acquisitiveness and individualistic self-interest on the one hand, and the Christian traditional virtues of love and charity on the other. There is also a potential for conflict between that other Christian value, faith, and the values implicit in scientific materialism, which include the value of 'doubting' every idea unconfirmed by scientific investigation, and the materialistic assumption of science which questions the spiritual foundations of Christianity.

The problem for the conformist in a Western society is therefore that the dominant culture is internally inconsistent and he is consequently caught up in the necessarily impossible task of maintaining an equilibrium. The conflict is also not one that can be resolved in the dialectical process of thesis-antithesis-synthesis, but involves a much more complete process of internal negotiation which seldom results in a fully integrated personality. It is not surprising that only relatively superficial people are able to survive as conformists, for those who think seriously about the contents of the culture package they are supposed to accept must inevitably find themselves rejecting some components of that package.

At the social-cultural level the process is equally complex, for the main elements within the dominant culture are so at variance with each other that they give rise to potentialities for social conflict within society as well as personality conflict within the individual.

It is thus clear that new social movements may arise from conflict within the dominant culture as well as from a total rejection of that culture.

Let us look at some of the conflicts that may arise at the social and cultural levels as a result of the complexities of the value system in modern Britain. At the level of economic values the value of maximising self-interest obviously leads to discord since all must naturally conflict or at least compete for the possession or use of scarce resources. A major example of this is the conflict between employers and trade unions. At a different level, there is conflict between those who wish to exploit natural resources and conservationists, an issue which has led to many new movements devoted to the conservation of the environment varying from the National Trust to nature conservation trusts, the Friends of the Earth, and has even given rise to new political parties, the Greens. In this case extreme environmental-conservationists may develop a stance that represents a total rejection of the contemporary Western cultural tri-system and replace it with a system that develops a new religion as well as economic philosophy, for example, the GAIA movement, which is only one of a range of New Age movements advocating radical social-cultural change. (The GAIA group is a branch of the Green or Environmentalist movement which believes that the Earth is a living being.)

Sects

Sects are reform movements that emphasise certain elements within the Christian tradition while rejecting other elements within either the religious traditions or the factors of science or economic materialism.

The term sect, as used here, includes not only such organisations as Jehovah's Witnesses and the Pentecostal churches, but fundamentalist, evangelical and charismatic movements within the mainline denominations. It may be useful to illustrate this through the examination of some sects.

Jehovah's Witnesses concentrate on particular aspects of Christian teaching notably those referring to 'the second coming and the end of the world'. The evil condition of the world is the result of man's disobedience to the will of God. There is no way in which human beings can improve conditions on earth, this can only happen when God personally takes over the government of the world. However, only those who have been 'saved' by a faith which includes strict adherence to the Watch Tower teachings will survive to live in the 'New Earth'. These will be joined by the faithful who have died before the 'Last day' who will be physically resurrected.

Jehovah's Witnesses do not reject the use of technology but only those scientific theories that question Biblical teaching, as in the case of evolutionary theory in biology. They do not reject the economic ethic of capitalism and in fact encourage the practice of the 'puritan ethic'. They do, however, reject all earthly authorities, condemning equally all governments of whatever political persuasion. The Watch Tower organisation has for the past thirty years been one of the most rapidly growing religious movements in the world, having branches not only in the Western countries but also throughout the Third World. They also have members in the communist countries, but there they encounter repression by the authorities.

In view of the obvious failure of the human race to solve its major problems, it is perhaps not surprising to find that large numbers of people are turning to organisations, such as Jehovah's Witnesses, which teach that humanity will be saved from its folly by the intervention of God or non-human beings.

Another movement that is concerned with the solution of world wide problems through the intervention of God is the Unification Church, founded by Sun Myang Moon, a Korean prophet, and whose members are consequently known as 'The Moonies'.

Pentecostal, fundamentalist and evangelical churches

These three types of churches (sects) are all primarily concerned with the salvation of the individual. They all treat the Bible as the literal word of God, but emphasise different aspects of Biblical teaching. For example, the Pentecostal churches emphasise the practice of the 'gifts of the spirit' which were originally manifested at the meeting of the disciples at the first Pentecost recorded in the Bible. These gifts which include 'speaking with tongues' (glossolalia) had been neglected by the Christian churches for many centuries until their revival in the early years of the present century. In England the movement had its origin within the Anglican church but, like Methodism a century earlier, it met so much opposition within the establishment that Pentecostals were forced to organise their own churches outside the established churches. In this way two main Pentecostal denominations came into existence, the Elim Four Square Gospel Mission (later the Elim Church) and the Assemblies of God. These churches include healing among the gifts of the spirit which they practice. In addition there are some independent Pentecostal churches.

In more recent years the practice of the gifts of the spirit has become more widely accepted and groups have been formed within most of the more traditional denominations including the Church of England and the Roman Catholic Church. In order to avoid confusion with the Pentecostal churches these groups usually refer to themselves as charismatics. The charismatic movement within the established churches tended to engage in the same practices as the Pentecostal churches.

The retention of the new charismatics within the established churches is an interesting development from the sociological point of view, since it indicates a growing spirit of toleration within the major organisations, not only on the side of the establishment but also on the part of the reformers, a willingness of both parties to co-exist within the same organisation. This trend is also to be observed in the Ecumenical movement which has brought together many previously antagonistic organisations into a single movement.

However, it has been suggested that toleration and ecumenism are indications of the growing weakness of Christianity in that 'the churches now have to huddle together for warmth in a cold world.' There has, on the other hand, been a considerable reaction by 'religious extremists' who range from fundamentalist-evangelicals on the extreme edge of Protestantism, to Roman Catholic groups who resist the liberalising movements within that church. Such groups within the Christian tradition may be thought of as new religious movements for they display a creative vigour that is missing from the 'established' churches.

Most of such movements reject certain aspects of the scientific ethos and some question the economic ethics of the Western world. In this area there are organisations such as the Christian Socialist Movement, Christian CND, and a range of Christian Pacifist movements, some of which are interdenominational while others operate within a specific denomination.

It is debatable whether such movements can be sociologically defined as sects, but I have treated them briefly under this general heading because sociologists have so far not produced a classificatory system that includes them. This failure to classify has also led to such organisations being largely ignored by sociologists. They do however constitute an essential part of Christianity within the Western world in the present century and it is not possible to arrive at a true understanding of the role of religion in modern societies without giving serious attention to the activities of those specialist pressure groups that exist within Christendom. I use this phrase rather than 'the churches' because such 'movements' often cut across denominational boundaries and must therefore be treated as organisations that are separate from and sometimes independent of the organised churches. For these reasons they come within the definition of 'new religious movements' that form the subject of this study.

These movements vary widely in their aims and organisation and the only logical term that may be used to describe them is 'religious social reform movements'. This avoids the ambiguity and value judgments that have crept into the use of the term 'moral crusades', though movements that have been defined in that way must obviously be included, movements such as Mrs Whitehouse's organisation and the Festival of Light.

Finally, we cannot ignore secular movements for social reform that are reacting against Christian ethics, some of which have already been mentioned.

Secular social movements are often difficult to separate from religious movements partly because of the ambiguities we have noted in the definition of religion, but also because there are often unrecognised connections between religion and secular activities. The classical example of this was the subject of Weber's (1930) study of the influence of the Protestant Reformation on the rise of a new economic system, capitalism, a development also recognised by Tawney (1926) who further suggested that religion had an influence on the rise of socialism. The influence of religion on a wide range of social movements has been widely documented. For example, the influence of the Evangelical movement in Britain on child care, prison conditions and a wide range of social welfare movements was thoroughly examined by Kathleen Heasman (1962).

Cults

While sects are reform movements within the major religious tradition of the society studied, cults reject that tradition. Within the Western world we have used the concept of sect to describe movements that are concerned with reform within the general Christian tradition, and shall use the term cult for those that reject either the Christian religion and/or science and/or economic materialism, the three major elements which we see as constituting the Western culture.

There are a number of ways in which cults may be classified, but we shall utilise and develop our previously outlined scheme as the base for suggesting that cults may be classified into the following major types which constitute possible cultic milieux or counter cultures.

1 The mystical/occult culture

This consists of groups that reject the Christian tradition, but replace it with mystical or occult ideas derived from other religious traditions. Such movements tend to reject scientific materialism replacing it with occult philosophy, and also to reject economic materialism, which is replaced by a collectivist and world-rejecting life style.

These groups vary, mainly as a result of the sources from which they draw their inspiration, and a number of sub-types may be distinguished:

a   *Buddhist based groups*. These vary from Buddhist Ashrams and monasteries which are mainly led by immigrants from Tibet or some other Buddhist country, through organisations such as the Western Buddhist Order to Western Zen movements, all of which adapt Buddhist practices for the Western world. As offshoots of the Buddhist influence in the West, we must also include the organisations that promote the practice of Asian martial arts most of which have their origins and legitimation in Buddhist philosophy.

b   *Taoism*, a Chinese mystical religion, is much less organised in the West, small groups do however exist and it has had a wider influence on Western mystical movements through the publication of the major Taoist scripture. It is also related to the practice of the Chinese martial arts.

c   *Hinduism* has had a wide influence partly through the large number of Indian immigrants who have settled in Britain, but also because of the residual effect of the British Raj which created a situation, dating from the mid-nineteenth century, of interest in Indian ideas. Hinduism in its native form has not attracted large numbers of converts, but the influence of Hindu thought has been apparent in such movements as Theosophy since the late nineteenth century. Since the 1960s, the West has been visited by a succession of Hindu gurus, many of whom have established permanent organisations in the West. Amongst these are the Maharishi Mahesh Yogi, who for a time attracted the attention of the Beatles, and whose movement Transcendental Meditation continues to grow. Another, the Mahara-Ji was only 13 when he arrived in the West in 1971, but rapidly attracted a wide following to his Divine Light Mission. Other important Hindu gurus who have had considerable influence are Swami Prabhupada whose Krishna Consciousness movement attracted much attention in the 1970s, Sai Barba, Sri Chinmoy, Shree Rajnesh and Maher Baba, all of whom have attracted a following in Britain and America.

d *Witchcraft movements.* Modern witchcraft appears to date from the 1930s when it was revived by Gerald Gardiner. Gardiner claimed that he had discovered the existence of a cult which had survived in secrecy for a thousand years. His critics have claimed that he invented the Witchcraft Cult and that his ideas were largely derived from the work of Margaret Murray (1921) whose writings have also been subjected to severe criticism. It is clear that a 'secret' movement, particularly one composed, for much of that period, of illiterate peasants would be unlikely to leave many written records. But there is a persistent tradition in the literature of the enemies of witchcraft, of the existence of such practices throughout the period in question, and even in the nineteenth century one finds newspaper reports of the persecution of witches in remote country districts. It seems that not only did most people believe in witches, but some people claimed to be witches. None of the arguments about the existence of witches should be confused with the question of whether 'witches' are able to exercise the powers they claim to possess. Many people who claim that witches do not exist do so because they believe that the powers attributed to witches are impossible in terms of scientific theory. Even though modern science has moved away from the materialist determinism of the nineteenth century, people may still *believe* that the 'miraculous' is impossible.

e *Paganism.* The revival of witchcraft is one aspect of a revival of interest in the pre-Christian religions of the West. The first indication of this occurred in the nineteenth century with the reawakening of interest in Norse mythology that found a major expression in the works of Wagner, and in a general curiosity about our Celtic myths that showed itself on the one hand in Tennyson's rewriting of the Arthurian legends, and on the other in the writings of A.E. (G.W. Russell) and Yeats on Ireland, and Fiona Macleod on Scotland, all of whom were representatives of a movement known as the Celtic Twilight. In Wales the Druid Orders were revived or perhaps recreated, while in England, King Arthur's Order of the Round Table was re-established with its meetings held at Tintagel. Glastonbury, said to be the site of the first Christian church in Britain and before that of ancient pagan worship, has become a centre for pilgrimages and festivals.

f   *Occult movements.* Paganism may be seen as one aspect of the occult movement which is worldwide though differing slightly in its manifestations from one country to another. Occultism is characterised by the concept of secret knowledge that is not available to the general public, knowledge that will be revealed to members, usually in stages, as the initiates progress through a series of ranks, from neophyte to Grand Master or some equivalent terms.

Most occult movements have, or claim a long history and also profess to preserve and transmit knowledge discovered by their founder who in some cases may be a god or mythical figure. A typical example of such a movement is Rosicrucianism, a movement which claims to have been founded by the Egyptian Pharoah, Akhnaton, but which in its modern form seems to date from the fifteenth century. In 1614, a tract entitled 'Fama Fraternitalis' was published in Germany. This claimed to give the history of the Rosicrucian Order, which it said had been founded by Christian Rosenkreuz. The teachings of the order are said to have been derived from occult sources in the Middle East and some claim that the order was founded by the Egyptian King Akhnaton. The order claims to possess secret knowledge derived from Spiritual Masters.

The order has been a secret society from the early days since its teachings are thought to threaten not only the church but also the secular authorities. In the late nineteenth and early twentieth centuries the movement has revived and its existence has ceased to be 'secret' though it still protects its 'secret knowledge' – while proclaiming that it possesses such knowledge openly in the media. The best known branch of this movement is the Ancient and Mystical Order of the Rosey Cross (AMORC) which has its headquarters in California.

While what may be called the occult establishment claims a long ancestry of well established traditional beliefs and practices, there have also been in recent years, sectarian tendencies within the occult church. This is not a completely new development since there have always been new reform movements within occultism and indeed, there have in all religions, but the twentieth century has been a period of growth in occultism as it has in other religions.

Micro-deterministic theories

Deprivation theory

The most widely used concept is deprivation theory which relates the growth of new religious movements to the individuals' feelings of being deprived.

The role of deprivation in the origin and development of religious groups and movements was, apparently, first suggested by H. Richard Niebuhr (1954). Niebuhr argued that new religious organisations arise as movements of a sect-type among the economically deprived and develop into denominations and later into church-type organisations as a result of a change in the economic conditions of their members.

Sects encourage the virtues of hard work and frugality among their adherents and the inculcation of this value system helps their members to lift themselves out of the economically depressed class into the middle class. This transition occurs over a period of some generations. The group at the same time gradually abandons its sect-like character and accepts the predominant value system of society thus transforming itself into a church.

Niebuhr's theory has been criticised on several grounds, the first being that some groups retain their sect-like characteristics over long periods, or even indefinitely.

The American Amish and certain other Menonite groups are cases in point. The second major objection to Niebuhr's theory was that some religious movements have not arisen among the economically deprived, although they display many of the characteristics of sect-type organisations, for example the Quaker's (Society of Friends) (Isichei, 1967), and Christian Science (Gottschalk, 1978).

A third objection is based on the argument that certain religious groups have never been sect-like, but from their inception have had the characteristics of a denomination or a church. A case in point are the Independent or Congregational churches who have been typologically a denomination from the earliest period (Martin, 1962a). Both these last two types of religious organisations have not arisen among the economically deprived but among members of the middle class.

In 1965 Charles Y. Glock set out to justify the claims for the role of deprivation not only as a source of the origin of religious groups but also as the explanation for the origins of other social movements. In order to achieve his aims, he extended the concept to include not only economic deprivation but also other forms of deprivation, and moreover he insisted that objective deprivation was less important than 'felt' (subjective) deprivation. The concept of relative deprivation was also used by Runciman in the context of political rather than religious action.

Glock argued that deprivation may be not only economic, but social, organismic, ethical or psychic, and that persons who are comparatively well off economically may suffer from one or more of these other types of deprivation. Religious groups may arise largely to compensate for one or more of these forms of deprivation.

Glock said that the concept of deprivation, 'refers to any and all of the ways that an individual or group may be, or feel disadvantaged in comparison either to other individuals or groups or to an internalised set of standards' (Glock and Stark, 1965).

He pointed out that *economic deprivation*, which had 'its source in the differential distribution of income in societies and in the limited access of some individuals to the necessities and luxuries of life', may be judged on objective or subjective criteria, and he considered the subjective to be more important when one is considering the effect on human action notably in the creation of new social movements.

Social deprivation he said, 'is based on society's propensity to value some attributes of individuals and groups more highly than others'. The person who possesses few of these desired attributes has lower status and feels deprived relative to others. Social and economic deprivation tend to be associated in industrial societies but it is possible to distinguish between them at least in some cases.

Organismic deprivation arises when individuals are disadvantaged, relative to others through physical or mental deformities, ill health, or other such stigmatising or disabling traits.

While these three types of deprivation are reasonably clearly defined his other two types are much vaguer concepts. *Ethical deprivation* Glock said, 'refers to value conflicts between the ideals of society and those of individuals or groups', though why this should give rise to feelings of deprivation is not made clear.

Psychic deprivation is said to occur, 'when persons find themselves without a meaningful system of values', but this appears *not* to be an independent variable, for he says, later, 'such a condition is primarily the result of severe and unresolved *social* deprivations, which, by denying access to rewards, cause men to lose any stake in, and commitment to, existing values' (*ibid.*)

The term psychic as used by Glock is a misnomer since the form of deprivation to which he attaches this term seems to correspond somewhat to the concept of anomie. If employed at all, the term psychic deprivation should be used to refer to deprivation of the psychic needs of human beings, by which we mean the specifically religious need that people have for contact with transcendental or ultimate reality.

The concept of deprivation as used by Glock seems at one level to be too wide and, at another, to be too narrow to be useful. It is this thought that led me to publish a paper (Nelson, 1971) in which

I proposed that the concept of deprivation should be replaced by one of need, an unpopular suggestion with sociologists and one which has so far been ignored. In the article I pursued the argument by pointing out that at the level of the use of deprivation theory as an explanation of the rise of social and religious movements, it appears too wide, since any action that leads towards the formation of a new movement can in retrospect be attributed to a pre-condition of felt deprivation, but that it is extremely difficult to discover the existence of felt-deprivation before the action takes place that it is supposed to explain. It is also difficult to establish, after the formation of a movement, the mental condition of the members before they formed or joined that movement. On the other hand, deprivation may not be consciously felt but may exist at the unconscious level and may also contribute to religious action.

Attempts to test the deprivation theory have inevitably encountered difficulties.

Deprivation theory may also be said to be too narrow, particularly if we consider the problem of religious action in general and not only the problem of the formation of *new* movements. The concept of deprivation necessarily implies a recognition of the concept of needs, since one cannot be deprived of that which one does not need.

Needs may stem from the physiological or psychological nature of a person, or they may arise out of the nature of society and make themselves felt as pressures upon the individual. Needs may thus be biogenic, sociogenic, or they may be psychogenic. Durkheim's theory is based on the proposition that religion arises out of the nature of society (Durkheim, 1956), and functional theories tend to be based on the same assumptions though some of the early founders of functionalism realised that religion had a role to play in satisfying the needs of individuals as well as fulfilling certain social functions. This idea is found particularly in the work of anthropologists such as Malinowski whose definition of needs is particularly useful:

By need . . . I understand the system of conditions in the human organism, in the cultural setting, and in the relation of both to the natural environment which are sufficient and necessary for the survival of the group and organism. A need therefore, is the limiting set of facts. Habits and their motivations, the learned responses and the foundation of organisations, must be so arranged as to allow the basic needs to be satisfied (Piddlington, 1962).

It is unfortunate that sociologists have tended to ignore the concept of need, though Parsons in the development of his social action theory did evolve a concept of need-dispositions (Parsons and Shils, 1965) which themselves become organised into need-patterns. To some extent, it appears that Glock's organisation of a typology of deprivation may have its basis in Parsons's 'need-patterns'.

However the discussion of needs was largely left to anthropologists (Aberle, 1962) and psychologists. Numerous lists of needs have been drawn up, but the most useful is probably that produced by Abraham Maslow (1964) which includes a 'need for self actualisation' which has often been interpreted as a recognition of the 'spiritual element' in humanity. Maslow's studies of what he calls 'peak-experience' also clearly relate to ideas of religious and spiritual experience which are discussed elsewhere in this study.

Maslow is one of the founders of a new school of psychological thought, humanistic psychology. While mainly concerned with therapeutic methods, it has moved psychology away from the positivist attitudes implicit in both behaviour therapy and psychoanalysis. Humanistic thought of this kind has had some influence on the development of sociology, particularly in the study of religious movements where it is increasingly being recognised that the positivist approach to the study of religions lacks a dimension, in fact the very dimension that makes religion a distinctive form of human action.

However, Maslow is mainly remembered for his formulation of a theory and typology of needs. As a psychiatrist, he came to the conclusion that neurosis and other psychopathological disorders were deficiency disorders that resulted largely from the frustration or deprivation of basic needs. This led him to attempt to specify these basic needs. He argued that neuroses, as well as other psychic illnesses, were due primarily to absence of certain gratifications (of objectively and subjectively procurable demands or wishes). These he called basic needs and termed them instinctual because if they were not gratified, illness (or diminution of humanness) would result'. He went on to hypothesise that 'health is impossible unless these needs are gratified' (Maslow, 1964).

He argued that the most basic requirements are physiological and include the need for food, water and sleep. The next most basic is the need for safety. Above these are needs for a sense of belonging and love, then that for esteem, and finally the need for self actualisation.

These needs are arranged in a hierarchy of dominance in which the most basic must be satisfied first. Once they are satisfied, higher needs dominate the motivation of individual action.

Rodney Stark, who was associated with Glock in the production of his deprivation theory, has more recently been associated with Bainbridge in the production of a theory of new religious movements. They argue that human beings pursue *rewards* and claim that

> 'in pursuit of research, humans seek *explanations*,' statements about how and why rewards may be obtained and costs are incurred.... 'rewards are anything humans desire – some rewards are very scarce, including some that cannot be definitely shown to exist at all. In the absence of a desired reward explanations will often be accepted which posit attainment of the reward in the distant future or in some other non-verifiable context (Stark and Bainbridge, 1979).

They then introduce the concept of *compensators* which they define as 'postulations of reward according to explanations that are readily too susceptible to unambiguous evaluation'. 'Compensators merely refer to postulations of reward based in hope and faith rather than in knowledge.' They go on to say a 'Compensator is an intangible promise which substitutes for the desired reward.' They see religion as a major source of compensators, and indeed go so far as to define religion as 'a system of general compensators based on supernatural assumptions.'

While Bainbridge and Stark (1979) made a number of useful suggestions in their comparison of models of cult formation, their attempts to construct a theory have been seriously weakened by adherence to a concept which reduced religion to an activity compensating for rewards which are, by their very nature, unattainable.

In order to understand religion, it is necessary to treat it as a reality in itself, to go beyond the symbolic realism that Bellah (1970) advocated and treat it as having an objective as well as a subjective reality (Nelson, 1982).

If we treat religion as real, then a religious innovator is engaged in the production, not of new compensators, or even of new 'rewards', but of new methods of obtaining 'rewards', or of drawing attention to the existence of desirable ends of which people may not have been previously aware.

The rewards of religion may be no less real or attainable than the more material rewards for which Bainbridge and Stark see them as compensators. Indeed, from a religious perspective the rewards of spirituality may be infinitely more desirable than material rewards.

7
Religious creativity

Creativity

Religion has its origins in certain types of human experience. Those which have to be categorised as religious include both mystical and psychic experiences, as well as those more heavily charged with emotional impressions. They range from inner experiences of at-oneness with God or the Absolute, through feelings of the presence of supernatural beings, to trance experiences and visions of the so-called supernatural.

The evidence for the objectivity of psychic experiences has been examined in chapter 2 where we consider their implications for the sociological study of religion. In this chapter we shall consider the broader implications not only of psychic experiences but also of mystical and other types of religious experience.

Religious experience

In our examination of religious experience we shall follow the way indicated by Joachim Wach who drew a clear distinction between religious experience and the forms through which it is expressed.

The religious (or spiritual) experience, he argued, could not be reduced to a sociological explanation: 'Those among us who study the sociological implication of religion would be deceived if they imagined that their works are capable of revealing the nature and the essence of religion itself' (Wach, 1944).

In this respect the religious experience can be compared with the aesthetic experience (Dufrenne, 1953) which must be taken as datum on which psychological and sociology analysis can be based. To carry the analysis any further than that is a self-defeating exercise of crude positivism through which the data themselves are destroyed. Attempts to explain such experience scientifically end up by reducing it to a cause or series of causes, either in the psychology and biology of the individual or in the social environment, that are held to determine not only the external (objective) behaviour but the internal (subjective) experience of the individual. Such theories explain away the events that should (at least for the purpose of this study) form the basis for the explanation of the subsequent social behaviour with which we are concerned.

To attribute religious experience to the social institution of religion is comparable with explaining eating as a product of the establishment of restaurants. We eat because we have need for food; restaurants are established to facilitate the satisfaction of that need. No sociologist would consider that he must produce a sociological explanation for eating, why therefore should he assume that religious experience needs to be interpreted sociologically? The main explanation for this is that most sociologists have started from the positivistic assumption that religion was 'untrue'. As rationalists they have been either biased or atheists. As we have seen, one has only to examine the assumptions on which the theories of writers such as Marx, Durkheim and Weber were based to appreciate the reasons for the neglect of the study of religious experience by sociologists.

Of course, few would deny that religious experiences take place within a social context which both shapes the experience itself by creating expectations, and also determines the way in which the experience is interpreted. For example, a Catholic who has a 'religious' experience of a certain type may interpret this as a vision of Our Lady, a) because s/he is a devotee of Mary, and b) because Mary the mother of Jesus has frequently been the subject of such experience by others in the past.

In similar circumstances the Hindu might interpret his experience as one of contact with Krishna, or some other God to whom he pays devotion, whereas a Chinese Buddhist might well perceive himself in communion with Kuan Yin the Chinese goddess of mercy. The essence of the experience may be identical but the form in which it is perceived may be socially conditioned.

Visionary experiences are, of course, only one form of religious experience. The more profound type of experience involving trance-like conditions and usually following on meditational practice, seems to present a similar pattern everywhere. In earlier stages visions may appear. At the more advanced levels, there is the unitary experience described by Bucke (1972) as cosmic consciousness, which in the Christian tradition may be interpreted as union with God, while in Buddhism it is described as Nirvana, and in Taoism as at-oneness with the Tao (way). Such experiences are ineffable and in consequence all mystics would agree that they suffer in the attempt to describe them.

In view of the common core of religious experience that is found in all human societies, we feel justified in treating experience as an independent variable in any analysis of religion. Indeed, we may justifiably claim that experience is the only independent variable and that all other forms of religious behaviour and belief may be seen as the products of experience modified by social factors. As we have already noted, the expression of religious experience is itself always conditioned by social factors, so that the existence of a central common core can only be confirmed by personal experience, a fact which has important methodological implications for those who would undertake the study of religion. Any study which is not based on an existential understanding of religions is bound to be superficial, distorted or mistaken.

The scientific study of religious experience seems to have had its origins in the work of Leuba (1896), Starbuck (1899) and James (1902), from then on it received little attention until Glock and Stark (1965) published their taxonomy.

They divided experiences into those that were divine and those that were diabolical. They arranged the experiences within each of these categories into types in hierarchical order and in terms of the closeness of the interaction between the human and the supernatural actor.

Divine experiences

1   The confirming experience. This confirms the prior belief of the human actor who 'simply notes (feels, senses etc.) the existence or presence of the divine actor'.
2   The responsive experience. Here 'the divine actor is perceived as noting the presence of the human'.
3   The ecstatic experience in which, 'The awareness of mutual presence is replaced by an affective relationship akin to love or friendship.'
4   The revelational experience is one in which 'the human actor perceives himself as a confidante or a fellow participant in action with the divine actor.'

In the same way, they point out, individuals may have experience of the diabolic.

Diabolic experiences

1   The confirming experience, in which the individual has a sense of the presence of evil.
2   The responsive experience, in which the individual perceives the evil being to respond to him.
3   The terrorising experience, in which the human actor feels 'intimate and loathsome contact with the diabolic'.
4   The possessional, in which the human actor feels that he is taken over by the Satanic.

While these categories may be useful in the classification of the experiences of actors socialised within a Christian culture and probably also within Judaic and Islamic cultures, they do not prove useful for the analysis of religious experiences within other traditions including new religions.

In view of the difficulties of applying Glock and Stark's taxonomy even within the Christian context (which I discovered in the course of conducting an empirical study of religious experience (Nelson, 1972)), I proposed a typology based on the location or source of the stimuli that gave rise to the experience.

There are two possible locations for the source of these stimuli, either in the environment or in the individual. The internal stimuli may be sub-divided into those located in the physical body and those having their source in the psyche.

The individual becomes aware of objective stimuli in the world outside himself through his sense organs. He perceives the objects in his environment as they impinge upon his senses and in so far as his attention is directed towards them. Because of the immense flood of impressions which arrive at his sense organs, it is impossible for him consciously to perceive all these impressions simultaneously. He therefore learns to select those to which he will give his attention, and which register themselves upon his consciousness. Through the process of socialisation the individual learns to select from this flood of impressions those which are used in the situation in which he finds himself, and those to which his society gives approval. Further, he interprets these perceptual experiences in terms of the conceptual framework which he has introjected from his social environment. Not only the selection but also the interpretation of sense data is thus influenced by social factors. The way in which the individual perceives, interprets and understands the world outside his own mind is thus influenced not only by the efficiency of his sense organs but also by the process of social conditioning.

The second location is in the mind of the individual. Mental stimuli are directly perceived without the intervention of external sense organs, though it might be possible to argue that they are the result of changes in the physical condition of the organism itself. Thinking, remembering, imagining and the emotional experiences of love, hate, fear and pleasure are subjective experiences located in the mind as are those experiences usually described as mystical.

Objective religious experiences

This type of experience arises as a result of the interpretation of the perception of something external to the individual. For example, he may experience a feeling of awe and wonder in the presence of an impressive work of nature such as a waterfall or a beautiful sunset. Such feelings are often the source of great works of art or literature through which the experience may be transmitted to others, and thus human works of art may also provide the stimulus for religious experiences. Indeed, it is probable that mystic experiences of the more profound type can only be communicated through art or poetry.

Religious experiences may also be the result of human action and certain types of action are specifically designed to create conditions in which participants may have such experiences. These situations may vary from those in which the action is designed to induce a change in the attitude of the participant through conversion techniques, to situations intended mainly to reinforce the existing attitudes of participants through religious ritual or prayer.

Further consideration will be given to the process of conversion later, but there is no doubt from accounts given by converts that this involves a genuine religious experience.

Within specific religious cultures certain material objects may call forth a religious experience because of the religious ideas which they symbolise. The cross in Christianity or the image of the 'god' in many other religions are symbols that may evoke religious experiences. A particular architectural style may become traditionally associated with religion and thus become a symbol evoking experiences, and there are many accounts by Christians of the religious feelings that they have experienced when entering a church.

Most religious ritual is intended to create an environment in which the individual may experience a relationship with the divine which is presented to him through the symbolic act in which he participates. For instance, in the Sacrament of the Holy Communion the believer is symbolically united with his God through the act of drinking wine and eating bread in a ceremony that re-enacts an historical event central to his faith.

Subjective religious experience

In this type of experience, which is frequently described as mystical or ecstatic, the individual has a sense of standing outside socially defined reality. This may involve a feeling of loss of personal identity and culminate in an experience of unity with God or Ultimate Reality.

Such experiences may occur spontaneously, that is to say without a deliberate effort on the part of the individual or others, or they may be induced by techniques of meditation or taking drugs.

These experiences vary in depth and profundity, from feelings that the truth has been revealed and one's eyes have been opened, through feelings of the presence of the divine and that one has received divine aid, to feelings of being at one with nature or with the God-head itself.

It is appropriate to sub-divide this category into mystical experiences, which include the rather rare types of unitary experiences, and extend the term ecstatic to other types of experience included in this general category.

Psychic experiences

This category includes a wide variety of experiences, such as encounters with ghosts, communication with supernatural beings and the phenomena of Spiritualism. It is questionable whether this type of experience is objective or subjective because it is not always clear whether such experiences are triggered by external or internal stimuli.

There is a close connection between psychic experiences of all kinds and religion. Such experiences involve contact, or an event that is interpreted as contact, with a supernatural or spirit world, or with forces that are not explainable in terms of known scientific laws. Such experiences may be direct or indirect. In the case of direct experiences, the subject has a personal visionary experience, he perceives spirit beings through what appears to be the agency of his senses; he sees, hears, feels or 'senses' their presence. In the indirect experience the subject is dependent on observing the experiences of others. For example the Spiritualist who has no psychic experiences of his own but depends on a medium who transmits what are claimed to be messages from the spirit world or who is the agent for the production of materialised spirit phenomena. One aspect of the material effect of psychic phenomena seems to be of sufficient importance to constitute the separate class of psychic healing.

The two major types of religious experience form the poles of a continuum (see Figure 7.1). Most actual experiences are mixed in type. In principle this typology may be used to classify experiences encountered within any religion or indeed any cultural system and would be applicable to 'non-religious' ecstatic experiences.

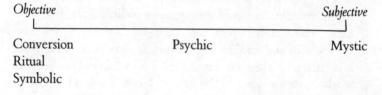

Objective   *Subjective*

Conversion   Psychic   Mystic
Ritual
Symbolic

Figure 7.1   *Base of experience*

For a religion to come into existence, the fountain of religious experience must be tapped, the experience must be expressed in terms familiar to the understanding of the mass of the people. The act of expressing the basic experience is one of 'religious creativity', an act which brings a distinctively new religion into existence. A religion which brings into everyday life the unique expression of a universal experience. A new channel through which the waters of eternal life may flow, clear and fresh for a new generation of people living within a particular cultural environment.

Religion growing out of the initial spiritual experience of a religious innovator is thus concerned with the transmission of that experience in such a way that it will promote the spiritual advancement of those who come in contact with it; unfortunately, it frequently becomes directed to the pursuit of less spiritual ends.

But let us turn briefly to consider the nature of creativity.

Creativity

George Bernard Shaw once observed that genius is 10 per cent inspiration and 90 per cent perspiration, and Abraham Maslow implies a similar relationship between the flash of inspiration and the hard work involved in acts of creativity (Maslow, 1973). However it is doubtful if hard work alone can produce any genuinely creative work. As Ghiselin (1952) pointed out,

> Production by a process of purely conscious calculation seems never to occur.... Not only Shelley, Blake, Ernst, Henry James and many other artists of great note or of little have described some considerable part of their invention as entirely spontaneous and involuntary – that is, as automatic. Automatic invention in this sense is claimed also by a variety of intellectual workers, such as Spencer, Nietzsche, Sir W. Rowan Hamilton, C. F. Gauss.

As Brockington (1934) pointed out, there is always a mystical element in the creation of poetry. The Irish poet George William Russell, writing under his pen name A.E. (1932), provides us with the most detailed account of the creative inspiration for his art yet offered by a poet.

A.E. did not found a religion but he has so clearly described the process of inspiration and creativity that underlies such an activity that it is worth considering his views more deeply. A.E. was a nature mystic similar to Richard Jefferies (1883); nature mystics seldom establish religions because their inspiration is found in solitary communion with nature, and for the same reason they

100

seldom become members of existing monastic orders.

A.E.'s description of his return to the country indicates the source of his inspiration.

> I had travelled all day and was tired, but I could not rest by the hearth in the cottage on the hill. My heart was beating with too great an excitement. After my year in the city I felt like a child who wickedly stays from home through a long day, and who returns frightened and penitent at nightfall, wondering whether it will be received with forgiveness by its mother. Would the Mother of us all receive me again as one of her children?

But even in his office in the city he gets hints of the spirit forces which he perceived behind the natural world, 'a shaft of glory from the far fire in the heavens spearing the gloom of the office, the blue twilight deepening through the panes until it was rich with starry dust' (A.E., 1918). He described certain poems as oracles out of the psyche which, he said, 'Imply they were conceived and fashioned by some high part of our dramatically sundered being and were breathed into the waking consciousness', and gave an example which he says 'came to me almost as swift as thought'.

> Its edges foamed with amethyst and rose,
> Withers once more the old blue flower of day
> There where the aether like a diamond glows
> Its petals fade away.
>
> A Shadowy tumult stirs the dusky air;
> Sparkle the delicate dews, the distant snows;
> The great deep thrills, for through it everywhere
> The breath of Beauty blows.
>
> I saw how all the trembling ages past
> Moulded to her by deep and deeper breath
> Near to the hour when Beauty breathes her last

And knows herself in death.

(A.E., 1932)

A poem which goes as far as language can reach toward an expression of the experience of mystical unity with the cosmos.

As a poet whose work is clearly mystical in origin, A.E. leads us into a consideration of the mystic experience as a source of religious creativity. His contemporary W. B. Yeats, who has achieved a wider fame than A.E., also shows clear indication of mystical inspiration in his poetry. Indeed, he became involved in the occult revival in the early years of the present century as an active member of the Order of the Golden Dawn.

The poet and philosopher Dave Rudhyar (1977) sees creativity as the process through which the individual human being 'acts as a guide to a creative process occurring at a certain place and at a particular time, because Space itself (the whole cosmos) there and then is pregnant of as yet unrevealed but needed forms.' The human creator is thus merely a channel through which knowledge that exists in the universal mind is expressed at the human level.

According to this theory, the universe is a process through which the noumena (real) presents itself as phenomena (appearances) to human beings, who are the means by which the universe becomes self-conscious. Individual human minds are thus instruments through which the universe obtains views of itself from specific points in space and time. These instruments operate in two directions, they not only enable the universe to see itself but to act in such a way as to effect change.

This theory is not necessarily deterministic since individuals may choose between the infinite number of creative influences that exist in the universal mind. It is interesting to note that this selection process is often unconscious and, as we have seen in the example given by A.E., ideas may slip through into consciousness from what Jung would have called the collective unconscious (Jung, 1916). In the case of many religious leaders there has been a deliberate effort to eliminate ordinary consciousness in order to allow the human mind to register ideas in the universal mind, and indeed to experience unity with the all-existent. In the condition of trance or deep meditation the individual mind contacts the universal and such conditions are sought by mystics. This type of mystical experience is commonly the precondition for the origination of new religions. Some individuals are so open to the influence of the universal mind, and at the same time responsive to the needs of their society, that they become uniquely creative influences in shaping the direction in which culture develops. In many cases these have been religious leaders in the narrow sense, such as Christ or the Buddha, but philosophers such as Plato and Confucious and political thinkers such as Marx may also be included. Since the universal mind contains all that exists, we must also consider those such as Adolf Hitler who had considerable influence on history to be instruments of the processes of change.

Looked at in this way we see that the leaders of new religions and ideological movements are instruments through which the forces of history are working to effect social change.

However, the forces of change are constantly counterbalanced by the inertia not only of the social establishment but also by systems of thought which become entrenched. As we shall see, new ideas once established also tend to become resistant to change. There is thus a continuing need for creativity which we see symbolically presented in the legend of the fountain of youth.

In the case of religion, creativity clearly includes the discovery of new ways of expressing eternal truths. This involves the innovator in the exploration of the use of language and symbol systems to express in culturally acceptable terms the underlying experiences of spiritual reality. Creativity does not mean producing something out of nothing, but implies the innovatory use of existing forms to express a knowledge that has become stale and neglected because the current form of expression no longer fits the new forms of societal and cultural images of reality.

A classical example of a recognition of the need for new expression of religious knowledge is to be found in Bishop Robinson's book *Honest to God* (1963). Unfortunately, Robinson's attempt to reformulate the fundamental Christian experience was only in tune with the cultural experience of a small intellectual minority; consequently it failed to revitalise Christianity as an expression of the religious needs of the mass of the people in Western societies.

Let us turn now to an examination of the way in which some religions have come into existence.

Religious innovators

In the first place all historic religions whose foundations can be traced, start from the decision of an individual to follow the Path, to set out on the Way in search of the fountain of youth; or, in more prosaic terms, to make the decision to develop his own spiritual life.

All historical examples will have been born and socialised within a particular society which has its own religion and approved methods of seeking spiritual advancement. We shall therefore briefly examine what is known of the early lives of some of the great spiritual innovators and religious founders, to discover what common features they may have in their spiritual lives. In many cases what is known about them is shrouded in mystery because contemporary records referring to their early lives were not kept, but it is useful to examine the common features of the way in which this factor has been treated by their followers and by others who subsequently wrote about them.

Gautama Buddha

One of the major examples of the founder of an historic 'new' religion was Siddartha Gautama.

Siddartha was born around the year 560 BC, the son of the chief or king of the Sakya tribe who lived in the foothills of the Himalayas in what is now Nepal. He seems to have shown no unusual interest in religion until he reached the age of thirty when, as the result of observing the facts of poverty, sickness and death in the society in which he lived, his mind turned towards consideration of the meaning and purpose of human life. He abandoned his wife and child and set out as a poor pilgrim to seek an answer to the question that troubled his mind.

For some years he travelled around India visiting and studying with the major religious teachers and gurus of the time. However, none of the teachings or methods of the Hindu religion seemed to provide the answer he was seeking. Eventually he abandoned his search and, we are told, he sat down under a Bo tree determined not to leave the spot until he achieved enlightenment. While sitting under the tree he had a revelation which gave him the experience of nirvana. Buddha was tempted to keep the experience to himself but decided instead to devote his life to teaching the secret of the way in which enlightenment is obtained to all those who were interested. An examination of his teaching shows that he developed and systematised ideas already existing in Hindu thought and methods of meditation. He spent the following thirty years of his life teaching his 'Middle way' throughout India, in the course of which he gathered round him a group of disciples who travelled with him. He also established a 'monastic order' the Sangha which organised groups of converts who were situated in many of the places he had visited.

Jesus

In the case of Jesus we have less information on the circumstances that led him to commence his 'ministry' when he also was thirty years of age. The New Testament provides no information on the period of his life between the ages of 12 and 30, but there are legends that indicate that he also spent this period in a search, during which he is said to have visited India and also spent time with the Jewish Essene sect.

According to the Biblical account, Jesus spent some time in solitary meditation in the desert which culminated in his temptation by the 'evil one', an episode which closely parallels the experience of Buddha who, after solitary meditation under the Bo tree was also subjected to temptation by the 'evil one'. In both cases the holy men resisted temptation and returned to 'the world' to engage in an active ministry. Like Buddha, Jesus also chose a small group of disciples who followed him throughout his ministry. Jesus, however, did not establish a formal organisation – this only emerged after his death. The social circumstances in which Jesus worked (Thiessin, 1978) led to the rise of active opposition culminating in his execution by the political authorities who saw his movement as a threat to their authority. His followers continued his mission which they extended from a mission to the Jews to a potentially world-wide movement, establishing churches (groups of followers) in the major cities of the Roman Empire.

During its first three hundred years the movement grew steadily in spite of periodic outbursts of persecution and the competition of other cults. It is not our purpose here to explain the success of Christianity, but it is clear that by the third century the movement had become widespread throughout the Empire. At that point (313AD) the Emperor Constantine, probably for political reasons, legalised the position of the church and himself became a convert shortly before his death. In 381AD Christianity became the established religion of the Roman state, and the elaborate structure of the Catholic church began to be formulated.

Religious innovation

We shall now turn to an examination of the process of innovation particularly in relation to religiosity.

Individuals are constantly faced with the problem of making choices, coming to a decision about what action they should take. Many choices are trivial, what should I eat for breakfast? what clothes should I wear today? and many actions become routinised or habitual. I eat the same cereal this morning as I have eaten every other morning and I get quite upset if it is not available. In this way much of human life becomes automatic, no conscious decisions are made. I may decide to go for a walk, but I do not consciously have to decide to move one leg in front of the other in order to walk.

However, many choices are made at the conscious level, and one of the most important of these is the decision to adopt a particular style of life, in the context of this study the choice of taking a path of action that will lead to spiritual growth.

Decision-making is, of course, strongly influenced by the culture of the society in which we live. There are societies such as those of the modern Western world in which the dominant cultural patterns or ideologies tend not simply to play down but to deny the existence of a spiritual element in life. In such circumstances the young person who has psychic or spiritual experiences learns to suppress them, so that even he becomes 'unaware' of their existence. He forgets such experiences because to remember them, or even worse to continue to have such experiences, would set him apart from his contemporaries, would lead to ridicule or to his being labelled as insane.

The awareness of the repressive effect of immersion in the socialisation processes of modern societies is evident in the work of Wordsworth who described it thus:

> Our birth is but a sleep and a forgetting:
> The soul that rises with us, our life's Star
>   Hath had elsewhere its setting,
>   And cometh from afar.
>   Not in entire forgetfulness,
>   And not in utter nakedness,
> But trailing clouds of glory do we come
>   From God who is our home:
> Heaven lies about us in our infancy!
> Shades of the prison-house begin to close
>   Upon the growing Boy,
> But he beholds the light, and whence it flows
>   He sees it in his joy:
> The Youth who daily farther from the east
> must travel, still is Nature's Priest
>   And by the vision splendid
>   Is on his way attended;
> At length the Man perceives it die away

And fade into the light of common day.

For some people these experiences are so impressive that they cannot be entirely forgotten or denied and, if they continue into later life, and encounter a more favourable environment, may lead to the individual becoming a spiritual or religious practitioner or innovator.

In the course of my study of mediumship I asked a sample of mediums to tell me about their early experiences. A few said that they came from homes in which their parents did not believe in spirits. Some of these claimed that as young children they had seen spirits of relations who had died, and had been punished by their parents for telling lies when they claimed to have seen an uncle, aunt or grandparent who had died. In these circumstances some children stopped 'seeing' spirits while others simply stopped telling other people that they had seen such things (Nelson, 1972).

One person who demonstrated an ability to sense people's feelings, particularly of pain, and who could describe the location of the pain they felt, told me that as a young person he was shocked when he discovered that most persons did not have his ability. That case demonstrates the more general problem that we all have (including sociologists) of understanding other people's experiences. We all assume that other people perceive the world in the same way that we do, but we have no way of confirming that assumption.

Until recently we have tended to assume that spiritual (or religious) experiences are rare (if they actually occur at all), and consequently have labelled those who have such experiences as deviant. A major reason for such a reaction has been that such experiences have been culturally defined as impossible in the context of the dominant paradigm of scientific materialism.

In recent years, however, evidence has emerged that shows that some 36 per cent of the adult population of Britain admit to having had a religious experience (Hay and Morisey, 1977). Hay and Morisey have also pointed out that there is similar evidence from America.

Because of the adverse cultural influences, the choice of

following a spiritual life style has been limited in most Western societies. In Britain, for instance, there has been a decline not only in the number of those having a religious vocation that would take them into a monastic career, but also in those choosing to become a priest or minister.

In many non-Western societies the option has remained more open since scientific materialism has not completely irradicated the native cultural traditions in which the existence of a spiritual order of existence is 'taken for granted'.

Looked at cross-culturally it would appear that in all cultures, even those most secularised, some individuals feel a need for spiritual growth. In every society, even the secularised, there are institutions that 'claim' to exist in order to fulfil spiritual needs. In the West such institutions are Christian churches, and it is clear that these still provide a means by which some people can satisfy at least some of their religious needs.

The strength of a desire to satisfy a need differs from one individual to another, as much in the field of the spiritual as in that of the sexual or indeed of any other drive. Some people with a strong spiritual yearning may find it impossible to satisfy this within the existing structure of religious organisations, and may therefore seek satisfaction outside institutional religion. We shall return to this later in more detail, here we are setting the broad framework for the emergence of religious innovation, by constructing a model that conforms to what is currently known of the form taken by religious innovation in previous cases. This may be formulated in the following way:

1   Religious innovation occurs when an individual who has strong spiritual needs
2   is unable to satisfy these within the context of the existing religious institutions.
3   Consequently he either withdraws from or is expelled from existing institutions
4   and retreats to develop his own methods of spiritual growth and expression
5   leading to the establishment of new religious movements.

As we have seen, after spending some years seeking for enlightenment within the existing institutional arrangements of the Hindu religion, Buddha withdrew for a period into isolation. At the end of this period he achieved enlightenment. Jesus withdrew to the desert for a period of solitude before starting his ministry. Mohammed also withdrew to the mountains before beginning to teach. There is a point at which religious innovators realise that they are unable to achieve their aims within the structure of the existing religion. A period of thought and meditation is necessary in which they develop their own spiritual life.

Not all seekers for spiritual life find it necessary to reject existing religious organisations. Indeed, most religions recognise that they must provide an outlet for such 'seekers' within the organisation. For instance, from the earliest period the Catholic church has attempted to institutionalise spirituality by the establishment of monastic orders. Such orders were formed in the first place by religious innovators who were unable to gain satisfaction within the existing structure of the church and whose organisations were accepted into the structures of the church. Some like Francis of Assisi had difficulty in gaining the approval of the church for their innovatory movements, others were condemned as heretics and their movements suppressed; but some such as Bernard of Clairveaux were readily received into the religious establishment.

Such acceptance has always imposed limitations upon the interpretation of spiritual experience. In order to be accepted the mystic must express his spirituality in a way that conforms to the expectations of the religious establishment. St Francis had difficulties with the authorities of the Catholic church but his group of followers were eventually accepted as an order of friars within the church.

Many of the most significant mystics of the medieval period managed to function effectively within the church as members of religious orders or as secular priests, though some of the more extreme thinkers incurred ecclesiastic displeasure. One of these was the Meister Eckhart (1260–1328?) who in modern times has been considered the greatest of all the German mystics. He joined the Dominican order rising to the rank of Provincial Minister of the Order for Saxony. He became a very popular preacher but the views he expressed led to his being charged with heresy and summoned to appear for trial by the Archbishop of Cologne in 1326. He appealed to the Pope and appeared before a papal court at Avignon in 1327. At this court he recanted his heretical views. He died the following year, but after his death a Papal Bull was issued condemning a number of ideas expressed in his published works (Clark, 1957).

On the other hand, Jan van Ruysbroeck (1293–1381), a priest in Brussels, encountered no such difficulties. This was in part because his religious experiences were expressed in a more orthodox form, but also because he was actively concerned in contesting the heresy of Bloemardine and the Brethren of the Free Spirit, with which we shall deal later (Wautier D'Agalliers, 1925).

At all times there have been Christian mystics who have neither formed nor joined a religious order, and such persons frequently became hermits. There were many such hermits in England in the Middle Ages, but two stand out (mainly because their writings have survived), Richard Rolle and Dame Julian of Norwich (Bullett, 1950).

Richard Rolle who was born around 1290 seems to have come from a wealthy family. He became a student at Oxford but, returning home at the age of 19, he adopted the dress of a hermit and his family thought that he had become mad. He fled from his home but found refuge with Sir John Dalton whose sons he had known at Oxford. The Daltons provided him with a hermit's cell where he lived for some time.

Less is known about the social circumstances of Dame Julian. She seems to have been born around 1342. Her writings show that she sought mystical experience for some years and that at the age of 30, following a serious illness, she had visionary experiences that she interpreted as revelations from God. She is said to have left home and become a hermit living in a cell built on to the wall of the church of St Julian at Norwich. The name by which she is known is said to come from her association with that church (Julian of Norwich 1901: Molinari 1959).

The Protestant churches, influenced as they were by the 'this wordly' theology of Luther and Calvin (Weber, 1930), made no institutional provision for mystics. Calvin, in particular, detested mysticism and the Calvinist churches were particularly severe in their attitudes towards 'religious experiences'. The Church of England was far from being a Calvinist church, although the monasteries were closed by Henry VIII, and mystics were able to co-exist within the church either as priests, academics or laymen. John Donne the poet was Dean of St Paul's, London; George Herbert, an academic; Henry Vaughan and Thomas Traherne were both parish priests; while William Law became a schoolmaster.

One of the most outstanding English mystics was William Blake (1757–1827), the son of a non-conformist. Blake made a living as an engraver. His religious experiences led him to make a violent attack on the conventional Christianity of his day, but he did not found a religious movement, though his work has had considerable influence on mystical thought.

The earlier mystic George Fox (1624–91) had attracted a following which became organised into the Society of Friends, popularly known as the Quakers, an organisation that did much to provide for the needs of the mystically inclined in a period in which they were unwelcome in most of the other churches and denominations in Britain.

In Europe the greatest of the early Protestant mystics was the German shoe-maker Jacob Boehme (1575–1624). Boehme's first book was privately circulated amongst his friends. It offended the authorities of the church and Boehme was forbidden to publish. He continued to write but few of his works were published during his life.

The significance of spontaneous religious experiences began to be recognised more widely by Protestants as a result of the activities of the Wesleys and their followers in Britain and the pietists in Germany. Though these experiences frequently manifested in a crude evangelical enthusiasm, beneath that many of the more sensitive souls such as the Wesleys themselves, had deeper inner experiences. The attempts of the later leaders to control and suppress the popular enthusiasm that gave early Methodists a bad name amongst the middle class led to splits in the movement. The fountain kept bursting forth in unexpected places and a stream of new sects was formed. The foundation of Primitive Methodism provides us with a case study of this process.

The evangelical revival was largely the work of John Wesley the son of an Anglican clergyman. While at Oxford in 1738 he had a religious experience of contact with God that led to a transformation in his life. At that time he had already been ordained as a clergyman of the Church of England and his conversion to a more evangelical form of religion followed on his attendance at a meeting of the Moravian mission.

Seeing the condition into which the Church of England had fallen at that time and the decline of religion generally that seems to have resulted from the rationalism of the enlightenment, Wesley set out to spread his message as widely as possible throughout the country. At first he carried out his work entirely within the established church, preaching only when given permission within the parishes. He set up societies of followers called Methodists because of the methodical way in which they were to conduct their lives; these societies were not in competition with the Anglican church but simply complemented it.

But in many places he found that he was not welcomed by the local clergy and consequently he took to holding open air meetings. So many people wished to attend his meetings that they could not be accommodated in the local church. The success of his ministry was resented by many of the clergy and in some places they were so violently opposed to his work that they incited mobs to break up his meetings.

The first Methodist chapel was opened in 1739 and by 1744 annual conferences of preachers were being held. In order to make provision for the spiritual needs of those Methodists that were refused admission to Anglican sacraments, Wesley ordained Ministers and a complex system of church officers grew up, including lay preachers, stewards and class leaders. The success of Wesley's activities was largely the result of the way in which he organised his followers and particularly the organisation of members into classes, each with its own leader, that met regularly throughout the week for prayers and Bible study. Wesley, however, was no democrat and the control of the movement was kept firmly in his hands and in those of his ministers, the so called 'Legal Hundred'. Wesley never broke completely with the Church of England but after his death in 1790 Methodism increasingly took on the role of a free church. The attempts of the clergy to retain control within the new Methodist church led to the first secession, when some 5000 members led by William Thorn and Alexander Hilham withdrew and established a new denomination called the Methodist New Connexion in which greater powers were given to the local churches and lay members.

A few years later a second secession took place. This arose from attempts by the Methodist leadership to control methods of evangelism. The denomination had become increasingly 'respectable' and sought to restrict preaching activities largely to conventional methods, Hugh Bourne, an active evangelist, sought to return to the methods of John Wesley and organised outdoor meetings, known as Camp Meetings. Bourne was ordered by Conference to discontinue these meetings which were held at Mow Top in Staffordshire. He ignored the order and was expelled from the church. However, Bourne and his followers formed a new organisation, the Primitive Methodist church, in 1807.

A few years later in 1815 very similar events led to a further split in Methodism in Devon and Cornwall when the denomination of Bible Christians was established.

The history of Methodism in nineteenth-century Britain illustrates our thesis, that as religious organisation becomes restricted by the growth of oligarchy and bureaucracy, religious creativity will inevitably break through the restrictions that men seek to place on human freedom. New prophets will arise who will develop new organisations that in their turn will become more rigid, and thus men must always be ready to resist the attempt of others to restrain their freedom.

8
Charisma & organisation

Charisma

While creativity is a necessary precondition, it is not a sufficient cause for the rise of a new religious movement. There are a number of other conditions that must exist before a movement will arise, and yet more are necessary if the movement is to survive and succeed in achieving its aims.

The first of these additional conditions is perhaps best summed up in the Weberian concept of charisma. The existence of a creative thinker or innovator will have little effect on religion or society unless s/he attracts a sizeable number of followers. No studies have yet been conducted into the critical size the following must reach if it is to have a social transformatory effect. There is, of course, no limit to the period of time over which such a movement may grow before it reaches the level at which it may produce transformative effects on society as a whole. For instance, it was about three centuries before Christianity became the dominant religion of the Roman Empire, whereas Hitler's Nazi movement took only 13 years to obtain power in Germany.

The concept of charisma, which had its origins in theology, was appropriated by Max Weber (1965) and applied to the idea of power located in the person of a leader whose source of authority rested solely in his own personality and did not have its legitimation in either tradition or a legal-rational system. As he put it (Gerth and Mills, 1947, p. 295) 'Charisma shall be understood to refer to an *extraordinary* quality of a person, regardless of whether this quality is actual, alleged or presumed.' In another passage he points out that 'the "natural leaders" – in times of psychic, physical, economic, ethical, religious distress – have been neither office holders nor incumbents of an "occupation" in the present sense of the word, that is men who have acquired expert knowledge, and who serve for remuneration' (*ibid.*, p. 245). The natural leaders in distress have been holders of specific gifts of the body and spirit: and these gifts have been believed to be supernatural, not accessible to everybody.

We may agree with Gerth and Mills that

> Charisma – is used by Weber to characterise self-appointed leaders who are followed by those who are in distress and who need to follow the leader because they believe him to be extraordinarily qualified.... Although Weber is aware of the fact that social dynamics result from many social factors, he nevertheless places great emphasis upon the rise of charismatic leaders. Their movements are enthusiastic, and in such extraordinary enthusiasms class and status barriers sometimes give way to fraternisation and exuberant community sentiment. Charismatic heroes are thus viewed as truly revolutionary forces in history (*ibid.*).

In spite of subsequent criticism of Weber's concept (Burke and Brinkerhoff, 1981; Swatos, 1981b; Bensman and Givant, 1975; Gerth and Mills, 1947) there is no doubt that Weber saw charisma as 'the specifically creative revolutionary force in history', and that Gerth and Mills were substantially correct in their claims that

> Weber's conception of the charismatic leader is a continuation of a 'philosophy of history' which after Carlyle's *Heroes and Hero Worship*, (1899–1923) influenced a great deal of nineteenth-century history writing. In such an emphasis, the monumentalised individual becomes the sovereign of history (*ibid.*, p. 53).

This assumption underlies Weber's interpretative methodology. It is therefore not surprising to find that the concept of charisma has been denigrated by sociologists in the Durkheimian and Marxian traditions who see man as a social product.

A comprehensive return to the concept of sociology as an attempt to understand human beings in terms of an interpretation of their social actions is basic to our task. We see human beings as engaged in an effort to understand the world, both physical and spiritual, in which they find themselves, and as involved in a process of personal growth which results from a constant struggle with their environment. Sociology is one manifestation of that struggle and its place in the individual's effort to understand the social world will be discussed later.

It is implicit in this analysis that social change is ultimately the result of human action, and that the potentialities for change that exist within the social situation only become manifest when they are triggered by the activities of charismatic leaders.

The charismatic leader focuses the forces for change and brings them to bear upon cracks in the edifice of the existing traditional establishment. In this way, over time, the new movement inspired by the charismatic leader may come to overthrow the existing power structure, whether this be political or religious in form.

But in order to complete his task the leader must not only attract followers he has also to develop an organisation, and it is out of this requirement that many difficulties arise.

We must consequently examine next the processes that lead to the growth of a viable movement around the personality of an innovator.

Charisma is a potentially fragile basis for the establishment of a movement, because in its primitive (or ideal-typical) form it depends on the ability of the leader to succeed in achieving the aims he has set and to satisfy the needs of his followers. The movement survives as long as it is successful, but when the leader fails to keep his promises the movement may break up. I say 'may' because there is evidence that movements may not only survive the failure of their leader, including his death, but may actually grow more rapidly after the death of the founder.

The first major study of the survival of a movement after the failure of the predictions of its leader was that carried out by

Festinger and Riecken (1956). There are numerous other examples in history; Christianity was on the verge of collapse with the death of its founder but survived to become probably the most successful religious movement in history.

We shall return to consider sociological studies of contemporary charismatic cults in a later chapter. At this point we need to examine the ways in which movements may deal with two sorts of problems: firstly, how to avoid the failure of charisma during the lifetime of the founder; and secondly, how to maintain charismatic authority after the death of the founder.

Weber did not consider the first of these problems though he dealt effectively with the second, so that to understand the first we must turn to other considerations.

The causes of the failure of charisma in a living leader may be attributed to a failure to keep his promises, this may take two forms: (1) the failure of the policies he pursues to achieve the ends envisaged; and (2) the failure of prophecy, by which we mean the failure of events beyond the control of the leader to happen at the time, place or in the manner predicted by the leader. The most common form this takes in religious movements is the unsuccessful prediction of the 'end of the world'. The Festinger study was of a case of this type of failure of prophecy.

Leaders usually deal with the first type, a failure of policy, by scapegoating – by blaming the failure on the work of enemies. The wise leader may avoid the whole issue by making vague promises so that, whatever the outcome of a policy, he may proclaim a success. However, many charismatic leaders are so convinced of their own divine calling by the adulation of their followers, that they make rash promises which they have no realistic hope of achieving.

In the case of prophecy it is clear that wise leaders will avoid making such predictions. Here again, however, their claims to leadership often rest on the assumption of divine revelation, that they have a special relationship with God which can only be effectively proved through the performance of miraculous acts, including the prediction of future events. In such cases the failure of prophecy would seem directly, to rebut the claims of the leader;

and in such circumstances one would expect that the movement would disappear along with its discredited leader.

In addition to the case investigated by Festinger there are a number of instances in which the movement survived the leader's downfall. A classic case is that of the Southcottian movement. This movement was founded by Joanna Southcott who had been born in Devon in 1750. In her forties, she began to hear a voice that convinced her that she was the Bride of Christ. She attracted little attention until 1801 when she published a short pamphlet. She travelled widely through England and obtained a considerable following. In 1814 at the age of 65, she declared that she was pregnant and would give birth to a son who would rule the world. Doctors who examined her declared that she was indeed pregnant and the birth was expected in July 1815. It did not occur and by November she became seriously ill and told her friends 'It all appears delusion' (Balleine, 1956), and a few weeks later she died.

The prophecy failed, the prophetess died admitting that she had been deluded, surely one would expect the movement she had founded to disappear. But it did not. The followers divided into a number of sects focused round her major disciples. They managed to retain their faith by a reinterpretation of many of her published prophecies. For instance, one group claimed that the child had been born but had then been 'snatched up to heaven'. Another group claimed that the birth had never been intended to be understood as a physical birth but rather as a spiritual one.

The movement seems to have grown during the nineteenth century but continued to split into new sects. At least one branch of the movement still survives. It is known as the Panacea Society.

An even more successful movement, the Seventh Day Adventists, which claims to have over a million members world-wide, had its origins in the failure of prophecy. In the 1830s one William Miller, a farmer living in New York State, proclaimed that the Second Coming of Christ would take place in March 1843. He obtained a large following within New York and neighbouring states who were disappointed when the date passed without any sign of the prophesied event. Miller returned to the Bible and recalculated the date for October; when that too failed to materialise, he set the date in the following year. After this third failure Miller gave up attempting to predict the exact date. In spite of this, his movement continued to grow even after his death in 1849 and was finally organised into the Seventh Day Adventist church in 1860. Jehovah's Witnesses is another movement that has successfully survived failures to predict the end of the world.

The problem of ensuring the survival of an organisation after the death of its charismatic founder was discussed by Weber. He introduced the concept of the 'institutionalisation of charisma', that is of devising methods whereby the charisma of the founder may be transmitted to his successor as leader of the organisation. This involves us in considerable modification of the concept of charisma. If charisma is a unique attribute of an individual then it would be impossible to transmit it or to ensure that the successor had charisma of his own. Indeed, it is very rare for a charismatic leader to be succeeded by another leader with personal charisma; this usually happens only when the first leader has lost his charisma and been deposed by a rebel.

Because of the dangers of a charismatic rebellion, charismatic leaders usually take care that their lieutenants are lacking in personal magnetism. One way for the founder to ensure the continuation of his teachings is for him to select and train a successor, a practice common among ageing charismatics. Failure to establish a line of succession or to define the principles upon which selection rests may lead to conflicts between the most influential disciples after the death of the founder.

The term institutionalisation of charisma covers all organisational forms and processes, through which succession of leadership may be ensured and through which the charisma of the founder may appear to be perpetuated and the legitimacy of the leadership confirmed.

In the case of Christianity it appears that Jesus designated Peter as his successor and that the leadership has subsequently passed in a relatively ordered manner to those selected to hold the office that Peter acquired as Bishop of Rome. This is certainly the claim of the Roman Catholic church, though there have been schisms within that church over the claims of succession to that office. Indeed, a number of churches have broken away from the Catholic church on this very point of the legitimacy of the claims of the Bishop of Rome to be the Vicar of Christ and thus successor of the founder.

In long surviving organisations such as the Christian churches, the institutionalisation of charisma became transformed gradually into the establishment of a bureaucracy. Priestly bureaucrats come to fear charisma, as Weber points out; the charismatic prophet presents a threat to the priest, because the prophet claims his authority directly from God whereas the priest's authority comes indirectly through a hierarchy.

It is this formalisation of authority within rigid organisational structures that gives rise to resentment and eventually rebellion by religious innovators who see the dead hand of bureaucracy between them and God.

The charismatic reformers such as Luther and Wesley break down the structural barriers to form their 'sect', but within a generation the structures are being rebuilt within the new movement. The Wesleyans, for example, gradually developed an organisation not unlike that of the Church of England from which they originally emerged.

The process of piping, tapping and bottling the water of the fountain of youth appears to repeat itself cyclically in Christian history. In each generation there are some who go to the fountain itself but they usually end up bottling the water for distribution to others. So to some extent this analogy may be applied to other religions, though Eastern religions usually point out to consumers that if they want the full benefits they must stop drinking the bottled water and go to the fountain to obtain the water for themselves.

In all religions there are some leaders and some organisations that claim to have a monopoly of the truth, but there are equally always those who doubt their claims, and it is these people who become religious seekers, who form and join new religious movements.

As John Curran remarked, 'Eternal vigilance is the price of

liberty' (Hoyt, 1907), and this applies to spiritual freedom as well as political. There is a clear tendency for all religious organisations to fall into the hands of elites whose main aim is to maintain their power and authority over the members of the organisation.

The process through which leaders, even in democratically organised movements, endeavour to retain power was the subject of a study by Robert Michels (1908) who propounded his 'iron law of oligarchy'. Michels was studying democratic political parties in Imperial Germany in the period before the First World War. His model has been successfully applied to other voluntary associations, including trade unions, but only one study has thrown any light on the methods that may be used to circumvent the iron law (Lipset *et al.*, 1956).

Michels's theory has seldom been applied to organisational developments in religions, though there are implications in Harrison's (1959) study of an American Baptist denomination, in Isichei's (1967) work on the Society of Friends (Quakers), in my (1969a) study of the growth of organisation in the British Spiritualist movement or the later study of organisational change in British Congregationalism (Nelson and Campbell, 1977).

Before proceeding to an examination of the ways in which the Quakers, Spiritualists and Congregationalists have avoided many of the dangers of the iron law of oligarchy, we need to consider other processes through which elite groups tend to gain and maintain control of organisations. The first and possibly most important is the growth of bureaucracy; Max Weber claimed that bureaucracy was the most efficient form of organisation. Efficient it may be for the achievement of the aims of rulers and administrators whose main claim is that they know what is good for the people better than the people themselves. In modern societies one of the main complaints voiced by the majority of the people tends to stem from their perceptions of the way in which the bureaucracy, with its 'red tape' procedures, restricts the freedom of the people, and even hinders their attainment of goods which are specifically recognised as rights within society.

A bureaucracy is essentially defined in terms of a hierarchy of status positions, in which the role of each position and the power given to the holder is clearly specified. If this definition is accepted as the central characteristic of the concept, then it is possible to apply the concept of bureaucracy to religious organisations. In terms of this ideal type definition, organisations such as the Roman Catholic Church, the Church of England and the Mormons may be seen as examples of an advanced stage of bureaucratisation; and it is clear that there is a trend toward bureaucratisation in many other Western religious organisations. Indeed, as any movement increases in size, there are pressures towards the development of such an organisational structure which are brought about by the problems of the administration of property and the co-ordination of activity required to achieve the aims of the organisation.

All religious organisations are established, in the first place, with the aim of promoting certain clearly defined religious ends; for example, the worship of God, the salvation of souls, teaching God's message to the world and discovering God's will for the individual worshipper, or, more profoundly, to enable the member to experience a relationship with God or ultimate reality. As Thomas O'Dea (1963) pointed out, over time these motives become detached in the process of institutionalisation, and the members of an organisation may substitute other aims for the original ones. One of the problems that all religious organisations face is that of keeping alive the original goals of the movement, and not allowing these to be completely submerged in aims such as the survival of the organisation. It is clear that in order for an organisation to achieve its primary aim it must, of course, survive, but such survival is futile if the organisation has forgotten or deliberately abandoned these primary aims.

Many new movements within Christianity have come into existence mainly because the church of the time (or place) has apparently forgotten its primary aim. Many sects have as their primary aim a return to the belief and practices of an earlier period before the 'church' became corrupted. It is for this reason that I have suggested that the term sect should be reserved for such reform movements as usually start within the church but which frequently evolve into independent churches.

Centralisation

One of the major effects of both the growth of oligarchies and bureaucracies in religious movements is the concentralisation of power in a small group of leaders. Some movements, of course, start from a situation in which all power derives from the charismatic founder and remains in the hands of his legally appointed successor, or group of successors. In the latter case, the problem may then become one of decentralising power to the mass membership, but in the present context we are assuming that power is originally widely diffused; we shall seek to explain how it becomes concentrated and how such a process may be avoided. The cases we shall be considering, the Quakers, Spiritualists and Congregationalists, are movements that have consistently resisted attempts to concentrate power either in the hands of a bureaucracy or an oligarchy.

The third, broader trend that has been observed in both secular and religious organisations in recent years is that of professionalisation.

Professionalisation

The process of professionalisation has received considerable attention from sociologists in recent years. Although no agreed definition of a profession or model of the process has yet emerged, neverthelesss it is clear that over the past century an increasing number of occupations have sought the status of a profession. The reason for this is that the professions traditionally have a higher social status and, usually, greater monetary rewards than other occupations.

In the nineteenth century three occupations were generally accepted to be professions: medicine, the law and the church (though the role of the clergyman was even then distinguished from that of the doctor and the lawyer). Modern concepts of the 'ideal type' profession are usually based on traditional versions of the role of doctors and lawyers, but lack some of the distinguishing features of those professions.

Amongst the most important of the characteristics of such an 'ideal typical' profession are the following:

1   the existence of a professional organisation
2   that, in association with the state, can exercise control over the members of the profession and can control entry to the profession;
3   lengthy period of training required for entry;
4   members are 'self-employed', i.e. have a practitioner-client relationship with the public;
5   members are governed by a code of ethics;
6   members are motivated by the idea of service to the public.

Though the clergy have frequently been described as professionals they clearly do not comply with the first, second and fourth of these characteristics.

There is, however, a further definition of professional which is more widely used by laymen, though it seems to have been largely ignored by social-scientists, that is the definition which sees the professional as being the opposite of the amateur. Used in this way we may define the amateur as one who engages in a particular activity because of an intrinsic interest in and/or commitment to that activity, either full- or part-time, without consideration for any monetary reward. In contrast, the professional is one who earns his living through the practice of a particular occupation.

There are many examples of professionalisation that are based on this model. For instance, the game of cricket which was largely an amateur game at the highest level (county cricket) in the nineteenth century has now become a completely professional game at that level, though at local club level it still remains amateur.

The application of the concept of professionalisation to religious movements is largely concerned with this type of development. In the early stages a religious movement is largely run by amateurs, enthusiastic followers who give up their leisure time to organising and promoting the movement. The creation of a priesthood or full-time ministry marks the beginning of professionalisation and, as the movement increases in size and power within a society, the 'priesthood' may also become a profession in the sense of an occupation having a high status in society.

As a religious organisation becomes increasingly dominated by full-time professional workers, the role of the layman as an ordinary member of the organisation may decline, his power within the organisation being usurped by the professional. This is the situation with which we are concerned. Is it inevitable? How may it be prevented? For control by professionals inevitably leads to a suppression of the creativity of the lay members in a religious organisation.

Early Spiritualists were particularly aware of the dangers of 'Organisation'. An anonymous writer in the *Spiritual Magazine* in the 1860s admitted that organisation, 'Enables those engaged in the promotion of any cause to work more efficiently for certain ends.' He pointed to the strength and efficiency of religious movements such as Catholicism and Methodism, 'But do . . . not the members of those communions pay a fearful price for the benefits derived from their compact organisations in the loss of individuality and intellectual freedom?' He anticipated Robert Michels (1908) in pointing out the dangers of bureaucracy and oligarchy, and argued that a highly organised movement would be 'controlled by the lower stratum of minds – minds that live and work almost solely for the interests of organisations'. He continued to remark forcibly 'Should Spiritualists organise thoroughly there are thousands who would enlist in their ranks for the purpose of leading the organisation.'

On the whole Spiritualism has avoided the worst dangers of organisation (Nelson, 1969a) and has remained a movement through which religious and spiritual creativity may be expressed relatively freely.

The same is true of the Society of Friends (Quakers) but there have been increasing tendencies towards the development of bureaucracies and oligarchies even in Christian churches that have a tradition of democracy. In most cases the increasing centralisation of organisational structures has been a result of ecumenical and church unity movements. Ecumenism and the movement toward unifying churches has been one reaction to the declining support that some denominations have had to face. If there are three churches in a town and all are poorly attended, the simple economic answer seems to be close two and you will have a good congregation at the one surviving church. There is little evidence to support this idea (Nelson and Clews, 1971). Indeed many people seem to cease attending church at all when the church which they have frequented closes.

The closure of buildings and uniting of congregations are clear indicators of the decline of the denomination concerned, not only in the crude sense that they are losing members, but in the more profound sense that they have lost their religious creativity, their motivation to engage in mission and 'spread the word'. It is not surprising that such denominations continue to lose members in spite of rationalising their organisation.

A denomination which has suffered greatly at the hands of rationalising oligarchs is the Congregational movement. The freedom of the individual Congregational church was first curtailed by the establishment of a national Congregational church in England in 1962, to replace the looser Union that had existed as a fellowship of churches since 1831. In 1972 the Congregational church united with the Presbyterian to form the United Reformed church which produced a further centralisation of the organisation. But religious creativity was not dead in Congregationalism. At the formation of the Congregational church a small group of local churches had broken away to form the Evangelical Fellowship of Congregational Churches. When the United Reformed Church was formed a large number of local churches refused to participate and formed the Congregational Federation. Within the Fellowship and the Federation local congregations retain a large measure of autonomy and an environment in which spiritual freedom can flourish and creativity continue.

It is interesting to note that the United Reformed Church has continued to decline whereas the Federation and Fellowship have grown in membership.

9
Membership – recruitment and retention

Conversion

In the early stages of growth all religious movements rely on methods of conversion for the recruitment of new members. Niebuhr (1954) defined movements at this stage of development as sects, and went on to point out that in the strict sense the term could only be applied to the first generation of a religious organisation. Religious organisations in their second and subsequent generations come to rely on the recruitment of the children of existing members as the main source of new members.

Mature religious organisations may be classified in terms of their attitude towards conversion, the classificatory system ranging from those that actively proselytize to those that discourage recruitment by putting obstacles in the way of potential members.

At one extreme we have movements such as the Watch Tower Association (Jehovah's Witnesses) who devote a great deal of time and energy to proselytizing at the other occult orders which operate largely as secret societies and carefully select potential members.

The first type approximates to Wilson's type of Conversionist sect in which the motive for conversion is a concern for the salvation of the maximum number of people. Such movements tend to be not only Christian but also involved in a millennialist version of Christianity which holds the view that the 'end of the world' is at hand. Since they contend that only true believers will survive that event, and that only the 'saved' dead will be resurrected to life in the 'new world', they are driven by the urgency to 'save' as many of their fellow men as possible. Jehovah's Witnesses are highly and efficiently organised to carry out this task. The members are expected to devote a great deal of time to 'door-to-door' evangelism, talking to potential recruits and selling the literature of the organisation.

Another movement which devotes much time and energy to 'door-to-door' salesmanship is the Church of Latter Day Saints (The Mormons) (O'Dea, 1957). Young Mormons are expected to give up two years to full-time missionary activities and are frequently sent to foreign countries to carry out their tour of duty. They are extremely well trained in techniques of itinerant salesmanship and usually appear to have considerable success; indeed, this organisation, together with Jehovah's Witnesses, has been one of the most rapidly growing movements not only in Western countries but also on a world scale.

The process of conversion has been a subject of study for many years, in the early period mainly by psychologists and historians but more recently also by sociologists.

The definition of conversion has changed considerably over the past century. A major contribution to its study was made by William James (1936), who defined the process in the following words:

> To be converted, to be regenerated, to receive grace, to experience religion, to gain an assurance, are so many phrases which denote the process, gradual or sudden, by which a self hitherto divided and consciously wrong, inferior and unhappy, becomes unified and consciously right, superior and happy in consequence of its firmer hold upon religious realities (James, 1936).

James agrees with the earlier findings of Starbuck (1899) that 'Conversion is in its essence a normal adolescent phenomenon, incidental to the passage from the child's small universe to the wider intellectual and spiritual life of maturity.'

Starbuck also carried out one of the first empirical

investigations of the motives for conversion. His findings related to 'Protestants living in an American milieu' and he made no claim that they could be more generally applied. The concept of conversion in the thought of such nineteenth-century writers as Starbuck and James is inevitably located in the Christian culture of the society. The origins of conversion as a process of religious change in the Greek and Roman world during the last three centuries before Christ, and the first four of the Christian era, were examined by Nock (1933) in his study of a period which in many respects resembled the present in that it saw the rise and fall of many new religious movements.

The French psychologist Penido (1935) made an important distinction between two types of conversion, distinguishing it in terms of its origins: endogenous and exogenous. Exogenous conversion is one that results from events that occur outside the mind of the individual, whereas endogenous conversion takes place within the mind of the convert. An example of the second type was the case of Cardinal Newman, who claimed: 'My change did not arise from the shock of exterior influences but it came from the work of my own spirit and the happenings around me' (Carrier, 1965, p. 71).

Penido pointed out that 'a conversion appears to the psychologist as the disintegration on the religious level, of a mental synthesis, and its replacement by another.' Thus indicating that there were two stages in that process, a stage of disintegration and one of re-integration. In the case of exogenous conversion he argued that these occurred sequentially whereas in endogenous conversion they happened simultaneously.

Interest in conversion was revived amongst social scientists in the 1960s by the growth of new religious movements and since then research has largely been conducted within these limits. Some of the most influential work was that carried out by J. Lofland and R. Stark (1965). It was based on a study by Lofland (1978) of the introduction and early growth of a cult which he described as the Divine Pecepts but which was in fact 'the Moonies', now known as the Unification church. Lofland and Stark defined conversion as the process that takes place 'when a person gives up one perspective or ordered view of the world for another'. They argued that the process is complicated and that its analysis is best 'based on a "value-added conception"' (Smelser, 1963). 'That is, we shall offer a series of seven (more or less) successively accumulating factors, which in their total combination seem to account for conversion to the D.P.' (the cult they were studying). They went on to say that 'All seven factors seem necessary for conversion, and together they appear to be sufficient conditions.' The conditions they specified were that

for conversion a person must:
1 experience enduring, acutely felt tensions
2 within a religious problem-solving perspective
3 which lead him to define himself as a religious seeker
4 encountering the D.P. (Cult) at a turning point in his life
5 wherein an effective bond is formed (or pre-exists) with one or more converts;
6 where extra-cult attachments are absent or neutralised;
7 and, where, if he is to become a deployable agent, he is exposed to intensive interaction (Lofland and Stark, 1965).

While this model was developed from a study of a particular cult, the authors suggested that 'its terms are general enough, and its elements articulated in such a way as to provide a reasonable starting point for the study of conversion to other types of groups and perspectives', a conclusion with which few would disagree.

Lofland's interest in conversion has continued and in a more recent study (Lofland and Skonovd, 1981) he has joined with a colleague to attempt a classification of conversion in terms of what he defines as conversion motifs. A classification system which also provides a useful base for the further examination of conversion.

However, before we proceed to a critical examination of their scheme, there are some points that must be clarified. In the first place they adopt the definition of conversion used by Richard Travisano (1970) who describes it as 'a radical re-organisation of identity, meaning, Life', combining it with Max Heirich's (1977) view that conversion is 'the process of changing a sense of root reality ... a continuous shift in one's sense of grounding'.

Travisano (1970) was himself responsible for developing the idea of Berger that the term conversion should be replaced by 'alternation' because of the extent to which converts fluctuated between belief systems. Travisano rejected the notion of abandoning the concept of conversion, but propounded the view that the term alternation should be also introduced because of the substantial differences that existed between the two processes. The main distinction he made between the two processes is that conversion is a more radical and complete change than alternation. He argues that:

> Alternations are transitions to identities which are prescribed or at least permitted, within the person's established universe of discourse. Conversions are transitions to identities which are proscribed within the person's established universes of discourse, and which exist in universes of discourse that negate those formerly established ones. The ideal typical conversion can be thought of as the 'embracing of a negative identity. The person becomes something which was specifically prohibited' (Travisano, 1970).

He gives as an example of alternation the transition from being a Baptist to being an Episcopalian, and a Jew becoming a Christian as an example of a conversion. James T. Richardson (1980) pointed out that the distinction was important within the context of his study of a Jesus movement, since a recruit coming from a fundamentalist church could be considered a case of alternation, whereas one coming from a political protest movement or the drug culture might constitute an example of conversion. Thus new members of a particular religious movement may have experienced very different processes of recruitment.

Travisano suggests that the concept of alternation is more appropriate within the social context of the period in which he was writing because, 'we suspect converts because they are "true believers" and we do not trust people who have total commitments to a cause.' The young people who flocked to new movements in the 1960s were 'alternators', since not only did many of them move from one cult to another, but most of them ended up by returning to the 'straight' society from which they came. However, the concept of alternation has often been used in a loose sense to include slight changes in belief and identity or condition, for which I have suggested that the more appropriate term might be *alteration* (Nelson, 1984).

We shall return later to a consideration of Travisano's contribution to the discussion of the concept of identity and commitment, but now we turn to a consideration of the classification of conversion motifs.

Lofland and Skonovd sum up their scheme of six motifs and cross-classify these in terms of five major variations or motifs. In critically reviewing their typology we shall be following their discussion of these motifs.

1 *Intellectual*. A form of self conversion that results from private study of alternative systems of values and beliefs, through 'reading books, watching television, attending lectures and other impersonal or "disembodied" ways'. They quote the example of Roger Straus 'who while an undergraduate substantially converted himself to Scientology through extensive reading. His first contact with an actual Scientologist was for the predecided purpose of attaining full-membership.' Straus gave a full account of his conversion in a paper presented to the Pacific Association (Straus, 1979a). Straus's experience led to the promotion and development of the activist model of conversion (Straus, 1976; 1979b) which has also been developed by Lofland (1977) and Richardson (1979). As Lofland and Skonovd point out, the intellectual form of conversion is a relatively new phenomenon at least in the Western world, a fact which they attribute to the rapid growth of new and impersonal forms of communication. However, if this is broadened out to include all activist forms of conversion, then we may see it as relatively common in many Eastern societies. In the East it is widely accepted that the religiously inclined should devote themselves to a search for the truth during which they seek out and temporarily attach

themselves to religious teachers (gurus) until they find the guru whose teaching suits them best.

The concept of the seeker is one that is particularly appropriate for developing an understanding of the origins and growth of some contemporary religious movements. Not all religious leaders are prepared to wait in silence for the arrival of disciples, and consequently we have to consider the other types of conversion outlined by Lofland and Skonovd.

2 *Mystical*. Their second motif, which they describe as mystical, is in their own words 'historically speaking, the best known', but they have great difficulty in defining it, except to say that 'The prototypical instance within the Christian tradition is . . . the conversion of St Paul in a dramatic incident on the Damascus Road [which has] functioned as the ideal of how conversion should be in the Western world.' The most typical contemporary examples are those of the 'born again' Christians. This type differs from the intellectual in that the event is less connected with intellectual factors but highly charged with emotional content. Since, like the intellectual mode, it may occur in isolation, the authors argue that 'there is little or no social pressure on the convert'.

3 *Experimental*. Thirdly they propose an experimental motif. This involves a process in which the individual investigates and joins a movement. Conversion is the end product of a lengthy period in which the recruit becomes involved in the activities of the movement. They quote the work of Balch and Taylor (1977), on the followers of the process and Balch's conclusion that 'the first step in conversion . . . is learning to act like a convert' (1980) and also Beckford's (1975) study of Jehovah's Witnesses in which he points out that recruits are immediately involved 'in practical work alongside more mature witnesses'. This finding supports my own contention on the role of involvement in the development of 'commitment' within the Jehovah's Witness movement (Nelson and Walsgrove, 1980), to which we shall return in our discussion of the importance of 'commitment' mechanisms.

Lofland and Skonovd argue that 'experimental' conversions involve relatively low degrees of social pressure to participate since the recruit takes on a 'try-it-out' posture. This may be true of the initial decision to become involved, but once one has done so the pressure to accept the belief and practices and to become a true believer is intense, at least in movements such as Jehovah's Witnesses. In other movements such as the Spiritualists, the overt pressure is much less (Nelson, 1969a). My studies of the Spiritualist movement show that the majority of recruits make their first contact with Spiritualism in an 'experimental' context. The proportion of 'experimenters' who become converts is unknown. It would appear, however, that a large number of people occasionally attend meetings without becoming more fully involved or becoming members. The reason for this is that little social pressure is brought upon attenders to become more intensively involved.

While the 'experimental' motif is a valid type in accounting for the initial contact of potential recruits with a movement, the extent to which it can be considered a 'conversion motif' depends upon the approach to conversion characteristic of the religious movement concerned, a factor which is not considered by the authors.

4 *Affectional.* This fourth type of motif emphasises the importance of personal contacts in the conversion process. The identification of this motif is traced to the work of Lofland and Stark (1965) who pointed out the role of the 'positive effective bonds', and the more formal wording of Stark and Bainbridge (1980b) is quoted, where they argued that 'interpersonal bonds are the fundamental support for recruitment' in outlining a theory of the role of networks in recruitment to cults and sects. Not only do Lofland and Skonovd see social networks as an important way in which people make contact with movements, but they point out that the social relationships the convert experiences within the movement may also be seen as the rewards of membership. Their theory does not reject the factors of deprivation or ideological compatability, but adds to them the rewards of membership. These include not only the support and affection of fellow members and the possibility of achieving status within the group, but also, in the case of some movements such as the Moonies, the

Krishna movement and the Mormons, actual material rewards.

The findings of Bainbridge and Stark have been supported by the work of Snow, Zurcher and Ekland-Olson (1980) who found that 'the probability of being recruited into a particular movement is largely the function of two conditions: (1) links to one or more movement members through a pre-existing or emergent interpersonal tie; and (2) the absence of countervailing networks.'

5 *Revivalist*. This motif involves intense social pressure and great emotionalism and is often manifested in crowd situations. In recent years the work of Billy Graham (Pollock, 1979) has illustrated the revivalist mode of conversion.

6 *Coercive*. The final motif involves the use of force either physical or mental to achieve conversion. In recent years the term brainwashing has frequently been used for this type of conversion. The term became familiar in the 1950s following reports of the techniques used in Korea in attempts to change the attitudes and belief of American prisoners of war, and after similar accounts of the treatment of dissidents in eastern Europe. As William Sargant (1959) pointed out, similar techniques had been developed by religious movements at least since the time of Wesley. The essence of brainwashing involves two processes: (a) de-structuring – whereby the existing beliefs are broken down; and (b) re-structuring – whereby a new set of beliefs is inculcated. Somit (1968) outlined the seven characteristics of brainwashing as used by communists in Europe and China:

1 *total control* of the prisoner's life;
2 *uncertainty* about the future;
3 *isolation* from the world;
4 *torture* mental or physical;
5 *physical debilitation* and exhaustion;
6 *personal humiliation;*
7 *certainty of prisoner's guilt.*

With the rise of new religious movements in the 1960s, concern began to be expressed about the methods of recruitment used by some organisations, which led to the rise of anti-cult and deprogramming movements which are discussed in more detail in a later chapter.

As we have indicated in our discussion of church and sects, churches as long established and indeed often monopolistic religious organisations recruit most of their members from the children of existing members, except when they are conducting missions in non-Christian countries. They can consequently rely largely on methods of socialisation and education of children and the active support of the parents in recruitment. Sects and cults need to attract outsiders and must therefore use somewhat different methods of recruitment involving a variety of techniques of conversion.

Both sects and cults are to some extent at odds with the dominant cultural system. Since they operate within the broad Christian culture, sects share more of that common culture than cults, but the situation is complicated today by the fact that the dominant cultural pattern of the West is now only residually Christian. Modern Western culture is dominated mainly by scientific materialism, a pattern which has penetrated the thinking of all the major liberal Christian denominations. This means that any religious organisations that seek recruits are faced with the problem of completely re-orientating the 'world-view' of such potential recruits. This applies as much to conservative Christian churches as it does to non-Christian cults.

Both types of movement, therefore, tend to recruit those who are disaffected with the materialist values of the modern world. In this respect the West is no better than the communist world where religion has to struggle against a dominant dialectical materialism which, however, presents no greater threat to spiritual values than does the materialism of the West.

It is noticeable that the agents of many cults do not make a directly religious approach to potential converts. Whether it is 'Moonies' on the street corner, or Jehovah's Witnesses at the door, they will usually start by discussing the awful state of the world, with its increase in drug taking, crime, war and violence. Only if they find that the potential recruit agrees will they then proceed to hint that the only solution to these problems is to be found in the teachings of their movement.

The styles of proselytism vary considerably and different ones may be used by the same movement. A number of distinct styles may be distinguished: (1) interviewing passers-by in the street; (2) door-to-door canvassing; (3) holding public meetings; (4) demonstrating in the streets; (5) publication of books, magazines, etc.; (6) sale of literature; (7) approaching friends, work mates, neighbours etc. (networking); (8) flirty fishing (using sex as an incentive); (9) advertising; (10) employing the mass media (used much more in the USA where movements may buy time on radio and TV). Some movements use all these methods whereas others restrict their approach to a few. For instance, the Quakers rely largely on publication and personal contact.

Active and passive conversion

Roger Straus (1979b) drew a distinction between two types of theoretical explanation for conversion, that based on a passivist and that based on an active model.

The passivist model sees the individual as having little control over his own behaviour but as being driven into conversion by social or psychological factors that determine his behaviour.

On the other hand, the activist model conceives of conversion as a process through which the individual actively seeks and adopts a new interpretation of reality which is different from the one he previously held. The individual engages in interaction with others in the process of negotiating an understanding of reality. The process of conversion, understood in this way, must be distinguished from that of 'reality creation' in which individuals construct their own 'world-view'. The construction of reality is the process already referred to in our discussion of the work of religious innovators who creatively construct new religious ideas that may become objectified in the formation of cults. Conversion is the process whereby individuals come to understand and to accept as their own, religious realities that have already been objectified by religious founders. While being a process of subjective change which affects the minds of individuals, conversion is not an objectively creative process. Nevertheless, it may have considerable effects, not only upon the individual mind but also upon society, in so far as it produces changes in the attitudes, values and behaviour patterns of significant numbers of people within society. Before proceeding to an examination of the effects of conversion it is important to consider those studies that have affected our understanding of the process.

Straus's (1979b) account of his own conversion to Scientology while an undergraduate is a classic example of the activist model. As the result of wide reading, Straus converted himself to Scientology and did not make personal contact with a Scientologist until he decided to join the movement. He says

> although I was highly suspicious of any organised group, after several months I considered that the only way to check the whole thing out was to take the plunge. I walked into New York Org and asked the receptionist what I had to do to 'go clear' and become an auditer (*ibid.*).

My own experience of becoming a Spiritualist was similar. I had been brought up in a conventionally Christian church as a child, but in my early teens ceased to believe in the main doctrines of the church as the result of reading scientific literature, particularly biological texts that were based on evolutionary theory. I became a rationalist though I did not join any related society. As my reading widened, I became aware of the evidence of psychic research which led me to experiment with a small group of friends. There were no psychic societies or Spiritualist churches near my home and it was not until I moved to a larger city in my late twenties that I attended Spiritualist churches. It was even longer before I formally joined a Spiritualist organisation.

The whole process, in my case, was a personal achievement as a result of a long period of change. Consequently, I have never considered this an act of conversion, a procedure which I always associated with much more rapid and indeed sudden events.

A study of members of the Spiritualist movement (Nelson, 1969a) seems to indicate that while some members had undergone a slow process, others had experienced a 'sudden' conversion as the result of attending a meeting at which the medium had produced convincing evidence of the truth of Spiritualist teachings.

But while the activist model may fit the case of some individuals and some movements, the majority of new movements actively set out to recruit members.

Commitment and retention

The successful religious movement is one which not only recruits new members but also succeeds in retaining existing members. Some organisations that are very successful in prosyletizing lose members as rapidly as they recruit them, thus only just maintaining the overall size of the organisation; other groups that are less enthusiastic about conversion retain the loyalty and commitment of their members. The most rapidly growing movements manage to achieve both these aims.

While membership growth is frequently used as a measure of the success of an organisation, it must be remembered that it is an exceedingly crude measure and one that it perhaps only entirely valid when applied to conversionist movements. The success of a group must always be considered in terms of the aims of the group. This makes it difficult to assess the relative success of an organisation since it makes it impossible to use the same criteria for all the organisations studied.

However, it is clear that organisations as such cannot be said to have succeeded if they cease to exist, though during the period of their existence they may have been successful in providing the conditions in which the aims of their individual members could be achieved. For instance, a group of mystics might have the shared aim of achieving enlightenment, an aim which they might feel could be furthered by collective activity. If all the members of the group achieve enlightenment they may find the group redundant, in which case the success of its members as individuals may lead to the death of the group. Such situations must be rare partly because a group once formed comes to acquire collective aims that go beyond those of individual members, but which the individual members come to accept and seek to promote. For instance the survival of the group often becomes a goal that takes priority over the original aims for which the group was formed.

John M. Finney (1978) has argued that 'religious behaviour and beliefs are most accurately interpreted as being normative consequences of religious group membership.' A model which he uses as a base for developing a theory of religious commitment which rests on the conceptualisation of the dimension of religious commitment formulated by Glock and Stark (1965) and refined by them (Stark and Glock, 1968).

In their work Glock and Stark took the view that religiosity might be expressed in a number of different ways. In consequence they proposed the existence of five distinct dimensions of religious commitment. In their first formulation they defined these as: (1) belief; (2) practice; (3) experience; (4) knowledge; and (5) consequence. The consequential dimension was clearly of a different order from the others and in their reformulation they discarded it, but they also sub-divided the dimension of practice into two types, ritual and devotional.

The idea that these dimensions varied independently of each other led to suggestions that individuals could score high on one dimension but low on another, and to the view that classes might differ in the form in which their religiosity was displayed. For instance, it was suggested that working-class people might be high on belief but low on ritual practice whereas the middle class were high on ritual and low on belief. Differences between the United States and Britain were also explained in the same way.

Finney demonstrated the existence of a complex relationship between these dimensions and argued that ritual practice, which he identified with membership of a religious group, was the primary factor.

While this model may clearly be criticised on the grounds that some 'religious movements' do not require formal membership or participation in ritual, it may be applied to most of the types of movement we are considering in this study.

Given that membership is an important precondition for the development of other forms of religiosity, we may now turn to an examination of the ways in which religious groups maintain the loyalty of their members.

This means turning from a conception of commitment as an expression of being religious to a somewhat different conception. This views commitment as entailing a restriction on alternative modes of action as a consequence of involvement (Payne and Elifson, 1976); or of commitment as synonomous with loyalty to an organisation, or perhaps more accurately to see loyalty as the major expression of commitment.

Rosabeth M. Kanter defined commitment as

the process through which individual interests become attached to the carrying out of socially organised patterns of behaviour which are seen as fulfilling those interests, as expressing the nature and needs of the person ... one problem of collectivities is to meet organisational requisites in such a way that participants at the same time become positively involved with the system – loyal, loving, dedicated and obedient (Kanter, 1968).

In the course of conducting her classic study of commitment mechanism in communities (*ibid.*), she produced a model which is also applicable to religious and other types of movement.

Kanter says 'Commitment refers to the willingness of social actors to give their energy and loyalty to social systems.' She points out that there are three types of social system problems that involve the commitment of the actors within the system. These are continuance, cohesion and control.

The continuance commitment involves the commitment of actors to remaining members and is primarily to be seen in terms of their cognative orientations. As she says, 'If when profits and costs are considered, participants find that the costs of leaving the system would be greater than the costs of remaining' they will remain members.

Cohesion commitment involves the 'commitment of actors to group solidarity, to a set of social relationships', and 'forming positive cathartic orientations: effective ties that bond members to the community'.

Control commitment, 'involves – their forming positive evaluations ... orientations ... to uphold norms and obey the authority of the group'.

She argues that successful organisations develop mechanisms to ensure that members develop the three kinds of commitment indicated. In each case two type of mechanism (negative and positive) are involved. In the case of continuance commitment the mechanism are: (1) sacrifice; and (2) investment. Sacrifice involves the giving up of something as the price of membership; it 'operates on the basis of a simple principle – the more it "costs" a person to do something, the more "valuable" he will have to consider it, in order to justify the psychic "expense" and remain internally consistent.' Examples of sacrifice include giving up alcohol, tobacco or sex. On the other hand, investment is a process which 'provides the individual with a stake in the fate of the organisation, he commits his "profit" to the organisation, so that leaving it would be costly. It allows a person future gain from present involvement.' Investment may be financial or defined in terms of time or energy.

Cohesion commitment also involves two processes: (1) Renunciation; and (2) Communion. Renunciation involves giving up social relationships 'potentially disruptive to group cohesion'. In extreme cases a movement may require recruits to give up their families and more frequently to renounce certain types of association with the outside world. Jehovah's witnesses are forbidden to participate in political activities and many evangelical churches forbid attendance at cinemas, theatres, unbelievers. 'The process of *Communion* may be defined as becoming part of a whole and may be produced through such activities as communal sharing, working together, regular group mettings and ritual.'

Finally we come to control commitment mechanisms which Kanter divides into the two processes of (1) mortification; and (2) surrender.

Mortification reduces the self-esteem of the actor, through processes of confession, self-criticism and mutual criticism, and in so doing breaks down his identity in preparation for the imposition of a new identity derived from membership of the group. Surrender is the process through which the individual identifies himself with the group and accepts its authority.

Kanter was able to demonstrate that communes that used such commitment mechanisms were more likely to survive, and the model was adapted and applied to the study of religious movements by Nelson and Walsgrove (1980).

The importance of separating individuals from their previous environmental influences and incorporating them into the new movement has been recognised in the production of the concept of encapsulation. Greil and Rudy (1984) have recently described and discussed three types of encapsulation and examined the reasons for which different *identity transformation organisations* use specific types of encapsulation. Many new religious movements may be classified as identity transformation organisations, and the concept of encapsulation may consequently be used as a tool for explaining the methods used to retain members, though it is a blunt tool because it describes an inclusive process.

Conclusion

While the studies we have considered indicate that the success and indeed survival of religious organisations is dependent on their devising or adopting 'mechanisms of commitment', the very techniques that enable organisations to retain the loyalty of their members also involve the exercise of social control by the leadership over the members. In many cases, such control not only prevents the members from exercising their creativity, but also negates the spiritual aims of religion which are by definition the salvation of individuals through the development of their spiritual lives and the promotion of spiritual growth. Most organisations severely limit the ways in which people may develop their spirituality.

The individual searching for spiritual growth may find his effort inhibited rather than helped by becoming a member of a religious movement. The search for spirituality may therefore involve a struggle against the religious institutions that try to force the 'water of spiritual life' into restricted channels.

10
The rise of new religious movements

Social background

We have already examined some of the internal preconditions that are necessary for the rise of new religious movements; we now turn to an examination of external preconditions, that is to say those factors in the social and cultural environment that affect the chance of a new movement developing.

The first and major precondition appears to be the breakdown of the monopoly of control over the provision of religious services within the society in question, and its replacement by a situation in which religious entrepreneurship is tolerated. In this chapter we shall examine this process within the context of modern Western societies using the sociological concept of secularisation.

Secularisation

It has frequently been suggested that the growth of new religious movements, which as we have seen reached a peak in the 1960s, represented a reaction to the decline of institutional religion in Western societies. By institutional religion was meant conventional forms of Christianity which in America would be described as the 'mainline' church and in Britain would include the major denominations, the Anglicans, the Non-Conformists and the Catholics. As we have seen, this process which has been described as secularisation has been subject to considerable discussion and this has now been broadened out to include an examination of the relationship between secularisation and the rise of new religious movements; a development which might be seen either as part of a process of secularisation or as the consequence of that process.

Secularisation and sacralisation ⁻

One of the greatest sociologists of the twentieth century, Pitirim Sorokin, saw human history as an essentially recurrent process of development. This process passes through three major steps in which the cultural super-system of society moves from the ideational, to the idealistic and then to the sensate type of world outlook. The process is then repeated (Fig. 10.1), but the recurrence is never merely a repetition, but occurs at a different level, for history while cyclical can best be represented as a spiral or as a swinging pendulum (Fig. 10.2).

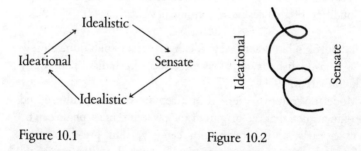

Figure 10.1   Figure 10.2

Each swing of the pendulum or of the points on the spiral of change represents a situation in which the cultural systems of a society are relatively well integrated around a particular view of the nature of reality. Sorokin described the sensate system as one in which 'The true, ultimate reality-value is sensory. Beyond it there is no other reality or any other non-sensory value' (1947).

The ideational system on the other hand, is based on the assumption that 'The true, ultimate reality-value is a supersensory and super-rational God (Brahma, Tao, "Divine Nothing" and other equivalents of God). Sensory and any other reality or value is either a mirage or represents inferior and shadowy pseudo-reality and pseudo-value'.

The idealistic type of system is described by Sorokin as based on the assumption that

> The true, ultimate reality value is the Manifold Infinity which contains all differentiations and which is infinite qualitatively and quantitatively. The finite human mind cannot grasp it, or define it, or describe it adequately in its infinite plenitude. This Manifold Infinity is ineffable and unutterable. Only by a very remote approximation can we discern three main aspects in it, the rational or logical, the sensory and the supernatural-supersensory. All three of these aspects harmoniously united in it are real; real also are its supernatural-supersensory, rational and sensory values. It has many names: God, Tao, Nirvana, the Divine Nothing of mystics, the Supra-Essence of Dionysus, Heidigger's Being, Jaspers' Transcendence, and Northrop's 'undifferentiated aesthetic continuency' (*ibid.*, 1947).

What Sorokin has described as idealistic corresponds quite closely to a non-dualistic system, as described in Indian philosophy (Chethimattan, 1971).

Modern Western society is in a sensate phase of culture and Sorokin argued that the origins of the present sensate phase can be seen as early as the fourteenth century, thus pre-dating the Reformation by some two centuries. Perhaps Protestantism could be seen as a sensate form of Christianity and thus as the religious expression of a developing sensate world-view. Certainly, modern science, capitalism and rationalism are all components of a sensate system as is modern sociology. The sensate world-view is ultimately based on sensory experience.

The process of secularisation which many sociologists have seen as characteristic of Western societies since at least the eighteenth century, is the process whereby sensate attitudes, beliefs and values replace those of a previously idealistic (or ideational) culture.

But here we shall digress for, as David Martin (1966) and Larry Shiner (1967) pointed out, the term secularisation has been used in many other ways. Shiner in particular made an attempt to classify the various definitions of the concept and we shall use his classification as the basis for our discussion. He distinguished six types of definition of secularisation.

I Decline of religion

'The previously accepted symbols, doctrines and institutions lose their prestige and influence. The culmination would be a religionless society.'

The most damaging criticism of Shiner's phrasing of this concept is that the second sentence of the definition does not follow as a logical necessity from the first. If, in a society, the previously accepted symbols, doctrines and institutions lose their prestige and influence, this does not necessarily imply that the society is becoming 'religionless' but may simply mean that it is changing its religion. A pagan society being converted to Christianity would pass through precisely this process; the old beliefs and practices die and are replaced by new. The anthropologist, Raymond Firth, has shown in detail how the old pagan belief and rituals of the Tikopia were replaced by Christian beliefs (Firth, 1967).

It is true that conservative members of the society in question may interpret the situation as one of religious decline, whereas those opposed to the tradition may interpret the change as progress.

Shiner interprets this definition in terms of the present situation within Western Christianity and refers to the usage of the concept in this way by Glock and Stark, who define secularisation as the replacement of 'mystical and supernatural elements of traditional Christianity, by a demythologised, ethical rather than theological religion' (Glock and Stark, 1965). In this sense the work of recent theologians such as Rudolf Bultman, Dietrich Bonhoffer and Paul Tillich and the popularisation of their ideas by John Robinson and

Paul Van Buren, must all be seen as part of a process of secularisation. Indeed, these theologians saw their work as being essentially concerned with presenting a 'religionless' Christianity as the appropriate faith for modern secular man.

The idea of a decline implies that at some period in the past men were more religious than they are today. Shiner repeats the arguments of Martin (1966) and Le Bras which show that it is extremely difficult to establish and ascertain that men were more religious in the past. It is true that at certain periods in the past men conformed more readily to the religious norms. This does not mean that they were any more basically religious than people are today. In the past men have attended church more frequently but this may have been for social or political rather than for religious reasons; they may have openly assented to the traditional beliefs expected of them, but this may have meant very little to them.

Whilst such arguments clearly have some force, they can scarcely outweigh the evidence that in some countries, England for example, there has been a steady decline in church attendance over the past sixty years, and that more people are now prepared to express their doubts about traditional belief than in the past. These facts seem to me to highlight quite significant changes in the situation of religious institutions in our society which can undoubtedly be described in terms of a decline. Since they seem to me to reflect not merely a turning from one supernaturalist interpretation to another, but a movement from supernaturalist interpretations as such towards a naturalist interpretation, then we may correctly apply the term secularisation to this process.

II Conformity with 'this world'

'The religious group or the religiously informed society turns its attention from the supernatural and becomes more and more interested in "this World".'

Shiner quotes Harold Pfautz and Will Herberg as the main exponents of this usage of the concept. Pfautz (1955; 1956) indeed used the term to describe the process by which sects as they develop towards becoming churches become increasingly a 'part of and like "the World"'. Will Herberg (1960) argued that religion in America had become secularised and that Protestants, Catholics and Jews were all expressing through their religion alternative and equally acceptable ways of being American. He extended Pfautz's typology concluding with the statement that 'The series can now be completed: *Cult – sect – denomination –socio-religious community – tri-faith systems.* Beyond this secularisation cannot go' (Herberg, 1962). Here again we may be looking, as Shiner implies, at religious change rather than secularisation.

It is possible that modern theologians are correct in arguing that they are not destroying, but only developing the tradition of their faith and that Christianity is essentially concerned with 'this World'. It is this sense that it has been suggested that Christianity has always exerted a secularising influence on man and society. Indeed, it has been suggested that Judaism, by emphasising the transcendence of God and man's role in this world, commenced the process (O'Dea, 1957). A transcendent monotheism replaces the pantheistic world-view. God is seen as standing above and outside the natural order, rather than being immanent in the material world. Supernaturalist beliefs other than those relating to the one God are devalued; the spirits, the demons and the gods that inhabited the world, animating and controlling it, disappear and God is increasingly seen as functioning through the operation of natural laws and impersonal forces. This development of religious thought was halted and partly reversed by medieval Catholicism, but with the Reformation it plays an important role in Protestant thought. By the eighteenth century rationalism and deism had developed and man had begun to question not only the pantheistic world-view, but the need for even a monotheistic God. The universe could be explained in terms of natural laws and forces and many men began to see no reason for belief even in a personal 'First Cause'.

Thus it is possible to argue that Christianity (at least in its Protestant form), by destroying a belief in a lower order of supernatural beings, led inevitably to a questioning of the existence of any such beings and consequently to the development of materialist philosophies. In this sense each development that has led to the denial of a supernaturalist interpretation can be seen as a stage in the process of secularisation.

This argument has applied in the past (before the late nineteenth century) only to intellectuals. As far as the masses are concerned, it is only in the present century that pantheistic and animistic belief have been seriously questioned; even today there are indications that those who have rejected Christianity have not necessarily rejected all supernaturalist interpretations. Indeed it is possible that people are turning from 'de-mythologised' Christianity towards new cults and what are sometimes referred to as popular superstitions. The evidence for this is difficult to assess but fortune-tellers, astrologers, healers and occultists of various types appear to flourish.

The turning of man's attention from other-worldly and spiritual concerns to a concern with this world is also said to be a feature of the influence of the ethic of Christianity. The Jewish, Christian and Islamic religions as ethical monotheisms tend to place more emphasis on man's *religious* duty to obey the will of God in this present life, and to see the will of God as being concerned more with the moral life of man than with his performance of ritual activities. This view of the will of God is particularly well developed in Protestant Christianity where man's attention is directed towards the service of God through work, through devotion to one's occupation as a calling and through the ideal of service to his fellow men. In this way Protestantism has from its inception cleared the path for a teaching which emphasises life in 'this world', and which at the extremes of Marxism and Humanism asserts that man is alone in the universe.

Whether a religion which becomes so denuded of a supernaturalist element can still be defined as such is a moot point. In so far as men turn from other-worldly to this-worldly interests, and in particular when this is related to a decreasing belief in a supernatural order, we may, I suggest, rightly use the term secularisation to describe this process.

If we consider the phrase 'conformity with the world' more

literally, we see that Shiner confuses the secularisation of religion with the secularisation of society. Religion may be very concerned with 'this world' without becoming 'this-worldly'. Thus the medieval church was very concerned with life in this world, but was concerned to make the world conform to Christian principles. In recent times the tendency is the opposite; now the concern for 'this world' is expressed in an attempt by the churches to conform to the secular and largely non-Christian principles of society.

III   'Disengagement of society from religion'

'Society separates itself from the religious understanding which has previously informed it in order to constitute itself an autonomous reality and consequently to limit religion to the sphere of private life.'

Shiner describes this as a process by which institutions such as the state, the family and education become autonomous and freed from the control of religious institutions. At the same time religious institutions also become clearly differentiated from society as a whole and from other social institutions. This process has been discussed in the work of Landis and more recently has formed the basis of D. E. Smith's study of *India as a Secular State* (Smith, 1963).

As Shiner points out, the concept of 'differentiation' developed by Parsons and Bellah is a more appropriate way of defining this process than the term secularisation.

IV   Transposition of religious beliefs and institutions

'Knowledge, patterns of behaviour, and institutional arrangements which were once understood as grounded in divine power are transformed into phenomena of purely human creation and responsibility.'

This appears to be concerned with the trend for religious ideas to give rise to secular ideas, for ideas and beliefs which were thought to be the possession of the church to be taken over, adapted and used by secular institutions. The attempts to attribute the rise of capitalism and modern science to the Puritan ethic are examples of this usage of secularisation.

V *'Desacralisation of the World'*

'The world is gradually deprived of its sacral character as man and nature become the object of rational-causal explanation and manipulation.'

This represents an aspect of Shiner's second definition and is difficult to separate from that definition. Shiner mentions Weber's concept of 'disenchantment' (Gerth and Mills, 1947), a process of increasing rationalisation, as one expression of this version of secularisation and also Eliade's views on the loss of the sense of the sacred (Eliade, 1959). A further example is to be seen in Henri Frankfort's world outlook of primitive man (Frankfort, 1949).

However it is formulated, there is little doubt, if we make comparative studies of pre-literate and modern industrial societies, that the world outlook of those two types of society differs greatly. In primitive and pre-literate societies man tends to interpret experience in mythopoeic terms, whereas when his outlook becomes 'disenchanted' he increasingly comes to interpret the world in rational terms.

VI *Movement from sacred to secular society*

Finally Shiner discusses a general concept of 'Movement from a "sacred" to a "secular" society'. Shiner's major example here is the theory of Howard Becker who saw sacred societies as mainly distinguished by resistance to change, whereas secular societies were open to change (Becker, 1957).

Becker's crucial variable which equates 'sacred' with resistance to change and 'secular' with openness to change has little relevance to the distinctions between societies based on supernaturalist and those based on naturalist belief systems.

Naturalist systems of an idelogical type, once established, may be as resistant to change as supernaturalist systems. Examples of this include a communist society based on Marxist belief.

Conversely, a supernaturalist system may be associated with openness to change where it perceives the existing social system as being contrary to the will of the gods, or where God is seen as actively working (with human co-operation) in the perfection of the world. Thus, early Christianity favoured change largely for the first of these reasons, and similar reasons have inspired the millennial cults (Cohn, 1970). Protestantism (particular of the Calvinist variety) has encouraged change largely for the second reason (Weber, 1930).

Secularisation as a general process of social change is more clearly seen in Sorokin's concepts of a development from ideational to sensate types of Society.

In general, Shiner may be criticised for ethnocentrism, the theories and empirical research he discusses are concerned with Christian societies and no attention is given to the secularisation process in Eastern societies. The work of Trevor Ling may indicate that some religions such as Buddhism and Hinduism may be putting up a more successful resistance to the growth of scientific scepticism than has Christianity (Ling, 1966). Shiner, in his discussion of the definition of religion, confused the issue (as indeed does David Martin) by suggesting that it is impossible to distinguish between the religious and the secular (Martin, 1966). The fact that religion is a term (like secularisation) which has been used and indeed misused in many ways, does not indicate that a clear definition cannot be arrived at, but only that religion is multi-dimensional.

Having considered the major alternative definitions of secularisation, we shall return to the consequences of viewing it as a process of development of a sensate super-system.

The sensate world-view discourages, though it cannot, of course, prevent, people having psychic or mystical experiences. In the first place it defines such experience as unreal, as illusory. It defines persons who have such experiences as abnormal and treats them as deviant or insane – which perhaps is saying the same thing. Sensate societies have engaged in a variety of techniques for discouraging contact with supersensory reality. Deviants who persist in such behaviour may be killed, as in the case of heretics in later medieval Europe and witches in the sixteenth and seventeenth centuries.

All forms of supersensory experience were condemned, and super-rational beliefs were irradicated until, by the eighteenth century, the 'religious elite' of the major churches were attempting to establish a 'natural religion', 'on basis of reason alone'. At this period we must remember a major justification for the persecution of Methodists was their 'enthusiasm'. The Methodists claimed a direct experience of God which expressed itself in 'irrational' behaviour. Other sects which indulged in supersensory experiences, such as the Quakers with their experience of the 'inner light', had managed to survive through the worst period of sensate bigotry but did not achieve respectability until late in the nineteenth century.

It is difficult to say at what point sensate culture reached its peak. Sensate attitudes have continued to spread amongst the masses well into the second half of the twentieth century, and in a desperate attempt to retain their members and to recover their position, the major Christian denominations have continued to offer an increasingly secularised form of Christianity which perhaps culminated in the 'death of God' school of theology in the 1960s.

However, the sensate system has constantly been threatened by the persistence of supersensory experience. From the middle of the nineteenth century, man began to attempt to establish the reality of psychic phenomena using the largely accepted methods of sensate science. It is true that the efforts of psychic researchers have either been ignored or condemned as fraudulent by conventional scientists, but their work has thrown doubt on the claims of positivism and on the treatment given to those who have supersensory experiences. Indeed, the whole definition of insanity has been questioned and its treatment condemned by writers such as Szasz (1971) and Laing (1960).

Sensate systems are inherently unstable because they attempt to deny the reality of an important form of human experience; since religion is the institutionalisation of that form of experience, a religious organisation that adopts sensate beliefs and values is doomed to failure. This is what has happened to the Christian churches. Protestant churches were more seriously affected, but in recent years the Catholic church has also moved in the same direction; already that church is being rent by internal dispute and at least in Britain, its growth has been arrested.

The only Christian churches which are growing in Western societies are those which have resisted the temptation to seek for popularity by adopting secular ideas. The growing Christian movements are those which challenge the sensate world-view and maintain a traditional Christian view. They include Evangelical churches which emphasise the experience by the individual of the presence of God and of Jesus, and the Pentecostal movement which adds to these the gifts of the Holy Spirit. One of the most interesting developments of the 1960s was the growth of a Pentecostal or Charismatic movement within the established denominations including the Catholic church.

The rise of such movements demonstrate that even in the sensate churches men feel the need for an experience of the supersensory world, and that not even the arid rigidity of the organisational structures can destroy the spontaneous expression of man's need for the divine, or his ability to experience the presence of the spirit world.

The sensate system at the height of its achievement was displayed in the philosophy of positivism, in the ethics of utilitarianism, in the materialism of nineteenth-century science, in the twin economic systems of capitalism and Marxism (both based on the assumption that material welfare was the ultimate value), in art, music and literature, and finally in the twin perspectives of sociology, one of which pictures man as the product of society and the other which sees him as the creator, but both of which exclude the intervention of super-human forces in the destiny of mankind.

The secularisation of religion in the sensate age left those with spontaneous experiences of the supersensory without any refuge in a cold and antagonistic world. Such men tended to rebel against Christianity as well as against the materialistic outlook of their time. They found inspiration in the knowledge of Eastern religions and the religious practices of primitive peoples which were becoming known in the West as a result of exploration which, by the mid-nineteenth century, was opening up the world to the Westerner.

The first major new religious movement, Spiritualism, was clearly influenced both by knowledge of Hinduism and by contact with American Indian Shamanism (Eliade, 1964). Theosophy was partly an offshoot of Spiritualism, but shows much more influence of Hindu thought. Amongst these early cults the only one during the nineteenth century to extend its teaching beyond a small circle of middle-class intellectuals was Spiritualism.

As the impetus of sensate culture has become exhausted, the initiative has passed to those movements which promote the idealistic culture. This is reflected in the proliferation of new cults in the second half of the twentieth century and the revival of old movements which had been submerged under the flood of materialism or driven underground by persecution. The popularity of the witchcraft and traditional occult movements has been as marked as the rise of new movements such as the Divine Light Mission, The Hare Krishna movement and Transcendental Meditation, which have Eastern origins, or the rise of pseudo-scientific cults such as Scientology or the Flying Saucer movement.

Secularisation has reached its limits as a movement promoting sensate values and beliefs, and the West is now moving into a period of sacralisation which is the process which promotes idealistic values and beliefs.

Human history consists of a conflict between these two processes. This conflict is endemic not only to the human condition, but also to the cosmic situation and this means that conflict can only be resolved when the apparent dualism of the cosmos is resolved in the non-dualistic character of ultimate reality.

On the human level, the end of struggle would be the end of

history and would coincide with the arrival of the whole race at what the Buddhist call 'enlightenment', or the Christian 'union with God'.

Religion is a human activity which operates at several levels, at the highest level it is the search of man for enlightenment, for at oneness with God, for the experience of cosmic consciousness. This is the aim of the mystics in all societies and at all periods of history. It represents the yearning of the differentiated for the undifferentiated condition.

At another level religion is man's instrument in the struggle between the cosmic opposites. It institutionalises the forces of the spirit of good, against the institutionalised forces of materialism and evil.

Religion may also be concerned with the relationship between incarnate and discarnate beings, between gods, spirits and ghosts on the one hand and human beings on the other.

Finally, religion may be the activity in which spiritual and moral principles are applied to the solution of material problems.

Religion is thus concerned with the whole range of human life. It is hardly surprising that it has been considered to be a basic human institution, a fundamental component of all human societies, by all the major sociological thinkers.

Unfortunately, sociologists have adopted a reductionist approach to the study of religion. They have seen it as 'untrue' though socially useful, while those of Marxist orientation have viewed it as both untrue and socially harmful.

It is clear that although most sociologists have seen religion as central to society, they have engaged in an attack upon religion which, directly or indirectly, is also an attack on the basic stability of society. In its assault upon the society which gave it birth, sociology has attacked religion which it has seen either as the major source of bourgeois society (Weber), or as the major source of stability and social control within society.

Sociology has failed totally to take religion seriously as a human activity having significance not only for its practitioners but for society as a whole in any other than a socially functional sense. In this study I have attempted to develop a sociological perspective which does take religion seriously, one which is not distorted by the narrow materialism of previous sociological perspectives, and to show how such a perspective can throw light on aspects of human life and the life of societies which have been but poorly illumined by the distorted views of the past. In other words, it is time that we discarded a sociology based on the outdated and unproductive outlook of sensate culture and developed a non-dualistic sociology appropriate to the new age of idealistic culture into which we are moving.

Bryan Wilson (1969; 1976) is one of the major advocates of the view that new religious movements are 'a feature of societies experiencing secularisation, and they may be seen as a response to a situation in which religious values have lost pre-eminence' (1969, p.207).

In his more recent works he has continued to press this point, arguing that such movements 'indicate the extent to which religion has become inconsequential for modern Society' (1976, p.96), and going on to say they 'add nothing to any prospective reintegration of society and contribute nothing towards the culture by which a society might live'. Wilson sees religion as a matter of purely personal choice. Individuals choose their religion from a wide variety on offer in the same way that they choose their car or their breakfast cereal, or washing-up liquid, and with as little effect on the wider society. Why the ability to exercise personal choice in any area of life should reduce the significance is not clear. The social structure has been considerably influenced in the past by consumer choice in economic products and by choice of political preference as expressed through the ballot box, is there any reason to assume that religious choices may be any less influential?

Wilson's thesis has been criticised by Greeley (1972) who argued that the secularisation model 'cannot cope with the new manifestation of the sacred', and who saw the rise of new religions as an indication of the continuing significance of religion for modern society. Bell (1977) also subjected Wilson's ideas to a critical examination, but a number of points need to be raised in the present context.

In the first place Wilson's secularisation model is open to a very basic criticism that has indeed been raised in various ways by previous authors. If secularisation is taken to mean a decline in the practice of religion we are faced with two problems. Firstly, how do we measure such a decline? and secondly, from what period do we date the beginning of this decline? Wilson assumes that a decline in religion can be measured by counting the number of people who attend church services. He produces a considerable amount of evidence to show that church attendance has declined during the twentieth century, as well as the number of church baptisms and marriages; yet the fact that there were twice as many members of 'main line churches' in Britain in 1970 as there had been in 1870 seems to have been ignored. There had, of course, been a considerable increase in the population of the country during that century but the actual proportion of the population who were church members had remained almost the same 17.5 per cent in 1870 and 18 per cent in 1970. Any decline in membership dated only from 1960 when 19.4 per cent of the population were church members.

The figures for 1970 do not include members of 'marginal' Christian organisations such as the Mormons and Spiritualists or of non-Christian religions. If these are included it would appear that at least 25 per cent of the population are recognised members of religious movements, a higher proportion than at any previous period since reliable records have been kept. In view of this I am tempted to ask, what secularisation? It is true that a smaller proportion of people attend worship regularly, but we must remember that in the Victorian period church attendance was considered to be a mark of respectability and that most people would attend in order to conform to the social norms. They may not have been inherently more religious than the mass of the present day population. On the other hand, at the present time church membership is not socially required and we may therefore assume that the majority of those who are church members maintain their attachment because they have a genuine religious

TABLE 10.1 *Church membership in Britain 1870–1970[+] (in thousands)*

Date	Church of England	Non-Conformist	Roman Catholic	Scottish Presbyterian	Total
1870	1206	1290	1213	822	4531
1880	1332	1465	1459	949	5205
1890	1614	1625	1691	1052	5982
1900	2089	1863	2016	1164	7132
1910	2418	2020*	2216	1232	7886
1920	2410	1963	2502	1281	8156
1930	2529*	2001	2781	1299	8610
1940	2255	1874	3023	1311	8463
1950	2077	1696	3499	1304	8576
1960	2398	1604	4346	1322*	9670*
1970	1804	1329	4829*	1179	9141

* Peak membership for each group.
[+]This Table is based on material in R. Currie *et al.*, 1977

TABLE 10.2 *Church membership in UK 1970–85**

Date	Anglican	Presby.	Meths.	Bapts.	Other Prots.	Roman Catholic	Total
1970	2258	1890	673	293	561	2524	8199
1980	2166	1574	536	237	609	2344	7466
1985	2058	1483	485	224	758	2265	7273

*Compiled from *Social Trends* London, HMSO, 1985. The base for the calculation of these statistics is different from that used for Table 10.1 and they cannot therefore be directly compared. It is clear that all denominations except 'Other Protestants' have declined in membership.

TABLE 10.3 *Other Christian churches (UK 1970–85)*
(in thousands)

Date	Mormons	Jehovah's Witnesses	Spiritualists	Other	Total
1970	70	62	45	–	177
1975	80	80	57	88	305
1985	102	92	53	101	348

Source: Compiled from *Social Trends* London, HMSO, 1985

TABLE 10.4 *Non-Christian religions (UK 1975–85) (in thousands)*

Date	Islam	Sikh	Hindu	Jewish	Other	Total
1975	400	115	100	111	85	811
1985	900	175	140	111	198	1524

Source: Compiled from *Social Trends* London, HMSO, 1985

commitment. In view of this we might claim that the population of Britain is more religious than it was in the Victorian period. If only one sixth of the population was a church member in the latter part of the nineteenth century, how is it that we consider that period to have been highly religious? Conversely, why do we consider contemporary Britain to be secularised when almost a quarter of the population are active members of religious organisations and one sixth of them are members of Christian churches?

The illusion of secularisation seems to have arisen out of a number of developments. In the first place there has been a marked decline in certain types of churches. In particular the non-Conformist churches, which taken together had more members than the Church of England in the early years of the twentieth century, have undergone a continuous decline since 1908. Secondly, this decline has been accompanied by a break in the relationship between religion and politics that has reduced the influence of the churches on public policy in Britain. Thirdly, too much emphasis was placed by some scholars on the statistics of church attendance which was declining, and too little attention was given to social factors that had affected the subjective meaning which church attendance and membership had for the majority of the population.

In Victorian and Edwardian Britain, religion was considered to be a social norm and an indicator of respectability. The upper and middle class were meticulous church attenders: Mudie-Smith's (1903) study of London showed that 50 per cent of the residents of the outer-city districts attended church on the day of the survey, whereas only 33 per cent of the inhabitants of the inner-city districts were in church. Those members of the working class who aspired to upward social mobility, to social respectability, or who had deferential attitudes to their employers also attended church. It seems clear that social rather than religious motives may have determined the high level of church attendances at that time. The fact that church attendance was higher than church membership seems to support the idea that attendance was affected by social expectations, though this must also to some extent have applied to membership since that tended to confer additional status. But membership also carried with it additional commitments that many people might not want to undertake. For instance most non-Conformist churches required members to participate in many church activities and make regular financial contributions, and those who did not conform to these demands and also maintain the high moral standards required might be expelled from the church, an ignominy which would affect their status in the local community.

By the 1960s church attendance was no longer socially required. It no longer conferred status and was no longer necessary either as a means of retaining or of gaining social position. Church membership, in ceasing to be a means of social advancement, is now clearly to be seen as an expression of genuine religiosity. It is much more likely that the churchgoer in modern Britain will be intrinsically rather than extrinsically religious. If this is the case, we may claim that Britain is a more religious rather than a less religious country, since the churches have largely got rid of their marginal or extrinsic supporters while increasing the number of their intrinsic adherents.

We must consider briefly the reasons that led to the decline of non-Conformity in England and Wales, and examine why a decline in one sector of Christianity should be seen as a decline in religion as such, in spite of the fact that losses in the Non-Conformist denominations were more than compensated for by growth in the Anglican and Roman Catholic sectors, a factor which must be related to the change that occurred in the relationship between religion and politics.

In the nineteenth century there were two main religious groupings in England. On the one hand there was the Church of England which, as the established church, claimed but could no longer enforce, a religious monopoly. The Church of England was an organisation that closely approximated to Troeltsch's model of a church. It was highly centralised, supported the established social order, and was described by a contemporary as 'the Tory [Conservative] Party at prayers'. The Conservative Party of that period promoted the interests of the landed aristocracy. On the other hand stood the Non-Conformists, a loose grouping of denominations, the main elements of which were the Congregationalists, the Baptists and the Methodists. The Methodists were divided into a number of small denominations, while the Congregationalists and Baptists consisted of largely independent local congregations organised into federations or unions at the national level. The Non-Conformists were strongest in the urban areas where they constituted a middle-class denomination. As the political interests of the upper class and landowners was represented by the Tory Party, the interests of the middle class and the towns was represented by the Liberal Party – a party which was concerned with promoting change and reform that was to a great extent stimulated by what became described as the 'Non-Conformists' conscience. Throughout the nineteenth century, therefore, the churches were involved in the political struggle for power, but by the early years of the twentieth century a new contender for power was entering the arena. The working class who for so long had seen the trade unions as its source of influence, decided that it was necessary to enter the field of parliamentary politics and the Labour Party was formed.

Many leaders of the trade union and Labour movements were Non-Conformists, but the majority of the working class were not attached to any denomination; as Wickham (1957) observed 'the churches have not lost the urban working class, they have never had them.' In consequence, the Labour Party has never had a close attachment to a Christian denomination, and has remained a secular organisation.

In 1906 the Liberal Party gained a landslide victory in the general election when they won 387 seats in the House of Commons and obtained 49 per cent of the votes in the country. By a '*strange coincidence*' the membership of the Non-Conformist churches reached its highest level in the years between 1905 and 1908.

By 1910 the membership of the Non-Conformist churches and support for the Liberal Party were beginning to show clear signs of decline, a decline which was almost continuous for both movements at least up to 1970. Since that date support for the Liberal Party has improved but support for the Non-Conformist church has continued to decline. These recent differences in the success of the two movementns are probably related to the fact that the new Liberal Party is not appealing to the same sector of the electorate which supported the Party in the early years of the century.

The common feature of the Liberal Party and the Non-Conformist church in the early part of the twentieth century lay in the fact that they recruited their membership from the same social class, the middle and lower sections of the middle class. A class composed of small industrialists and business men, of shop-keepers and professionals.

Napoleon had made a contemptuous reference to Britain as a nation of shop-keeepers and the class to which he referred continued to have considerable influence throughout the nineteenth century where it embodied many of the Victorian values so admired by the present government. The core of these values can best be expressed in the concept of self-help, a virtue extolled by Samuel Smiles (1859) in a book of that title which was a best-seller for several years in Victorian Britain. This class put a high value upon independence, on being their own master, on not being dependent on others, values that were expressed not only in their work and economic relationships but also in their religious lives. The direction of influence is not easy to trace. Was it independent businessmen who became independent in religion and formed or joined Non-Conformist or dissenting churches? Or was it the influence of a theology of independence and the experience of being brought up within 'Independent' churches that led men to seek independence in their economic lives? There seems to have been an inevitable connection between the two. Puritan forms of Protestantism which emphasise the direct relationship of the individual with God seem to be related not only logically but also empirically to the rise in capitalism and socialism in the economic field, to democracy as a political form and to churches in which the power is shared democratically between all members of the organisation. A change in any one of these areas is thus likely to provoke changes in the others. Historically, it is not clear which changes triggered the decline that has occurred in Non-Conformity, Liberalism, and the class of independent small businessmen in the first half of the twentieth century. It was this decline in what had been a very influential sector of British society that created the illusion of a general decline in religion.

But decline in Non-Conformity was to a great extent offset by an increase in the membership of the Anglican Church and of Roman Catholicism. We may see this as related to the way in which, in the economic sphere, small businesses were being replaced by large industries, and small shops by department stores and chain stores. The independent worker was being replaced by the employee, the small shop-keeper by the manager of a large supermarket. The social relationships were thus changing; the professional being replaced by the bureaucrat is a process taking place within the 'professions' that paralleled that taking place in the business world. In the medical field, the 'private practitioner' became an employee of the National Health Service. Most lawyers and accountants ceased to be self-employed and worked for government departments, local authorities and large corporations.

Such people found their political views better expressed either by the Conservative Party, in so far as they identified with the interests of their employers, or with the Labour Party if they perceived themselves to have other interests in their role as employees. The party of the independent person no longer had a wide base of support.

In the same way this new middle class, in so far as it was religious, saw no particular virtue in small independent churches. Since it accepted the large centralised and authoritarian organisation in its economic life, it also tended to join the large centralised authoritarian churches.

Many saw all large organisations as being more efficient and sought to extend this concept into their religious organisation. Therefore those who had been brought up within independent Non-Conformist churches often sought to transform these organisations by a process of amalgamation with other similar organisations in order to increase efficiency. In 1930 a wide variety of Methodist denominations were invited to form the Methodist church. Later independent Congregational churches were invited to form a national Congregationalist church which went on to unite with the Presbyterian church to form the United Reformed Church. Many such developments occurred throughout the Western world; they were legitimated by the development of a theology of ecumenism, which suggested that ultimately God's will was that there should be one church.

In each case, not only was the size of the organisation increased but power was centralised and an authoritarian structure established. That is to say the individual members lost much of their independence and power to control the organisation.

It has been necessary to outline these developments, since the new religious movements are to some extent a reaction against these developments in the traditional religious organisations.

The reactions have not all been so extreme as to be defined as cults, for many of them have occurred within the Christian tradition. These have taken two forms: (1) the formation of new independent sects, that have sought to retain or revive the traditions lost through the union of organisations; and (2) movements within existing churches.

A major example of the formation of a new sect to preserve a tradition is the Congregational Federation. When the Congregational Church of England and Wales decided to unite with the Presbyterians in 1972, approximately a third of the local congregations of that church refused to become members of the new United Reformed Church. Most of these continuing Congregational churches got together to form a loosely organised federation which restored to the local congregation the independence which it had enjoyed before the formation of the Congregational Church of England and Wales.

The best known example of the second type of reaction has been the development of the charismatic movement within a number of denominations, including the Catholic Church. Charismatics do not wish to withdraw from the church but seek to form groups consisting of people who wish to supplement traditional forms of worship in their denomination with practices which they believe bring them into direct contact with the 'Holy Spirit'.

Both these types of movement may be seen as expressions of religious creativity since in both cases the attempt is being made to establish direct contacts between the human individual and God. This is the case in the instance of the Congregational church, since the core of the concept of Congregationalism is that the church is a group of people who feel that they are called by God to meet together locally for worship. The group which in its church meeting refers all decisions to God, who is thought to guide the members in the making of such decisions relating to the organisation and conduct of the church. The charismatics also wait in their meetings for God to speak directly to them, usually through the process of glossolalia, or speaking in tongues.

The Congregational church is clearly not a new religious movement in the same sense as many considered here, because it had its origins in the late sixteenth century. The Congregational Federation, however, may be considered in that way, since it was necessary that such a movement be formed in the 1970s to ensure that spirituality was not suppressed by the growth of bureaucratic structures.

Another example of a Christian denomination which has retained its core of creative spirituality by consistently refusing to develop a bureaucratic structure is the Society of Friends, the Quakers. Charismatic movements have periodically arisen within the Christian church throughout its history, some have been institutionalised as an order within the church, and an example of this might be the Franciscan movement, but others such as the early Methodist movement and the Pentecostal movement were only able to survive by withdrawing from the church (in both cases the Church of England) in Britain, and forming their own organisations.

Britain and the USA

The claims made in the 1960s that Britain had become secularised which were rooted in the statistics of attendance, led to certain problems when comparisons were made with the United States of America. At that period both the attendance and membership of churches in the USA were increasing; the proportion of Americans attending church services regularly was over 50 per cent and consequently at least as high as it had ever been in Britain. This led to a discussion of the reasons why the Americans were becoming more 'religious' at the time at which it was thought the British were deserting the churches. Berger (1961) and Herberg (1960), amongst others, suggested that the churches in America had survived by becoming secularised and promoting a religion of 'the American way of life' rather than by adhering to a more spiritual form of Christianity. The evidence seems to indicate that they were probably correct in their assessment of the theological direction that many American churches were taking toward a more 'liberal' form of theology. But the same trends were apparent in Britain. However, the liberalisation of many churches seems to have had the opposite effect from that intended, for from the 1960s it became clear that support for liberal churches was declining in America as well as Britain. Indeed, a decline in membership of the Christian church in both countries is apparent in the 1960s. But the rapid decline in liberal churches was, to some extent, offset by a growth in conservative churches, that is to say in fundamentalist, evangelical and Pentecostal churches and in extreme Christian cults as well as by the rise of new religious movements and, in Britain, the growth of non-Christian religions often introduced by immigrants.

The controversy over the alleged differences between Britain and America in the 1960s was clearly based on a misunderstanding of the situation derived from a failure to compare membership statistics rather than figures of attendance. In both societies religion has retained its significance in the lives of many individuals though it has ceased to be so attractive as a collective activity. In other words, the trend has been towards the privatisation of religion, about which there has been considerable discussion in America.

11
The functions of
new religious
movements

In a very useful review of the literature, Robbins and Anthony (1978) discussed the role and functions of new religious movements in modern Western societies, and pointed out that the theories offered may be classified into four types: (1) those that claim that such movements have unintended and unanticipated integrative consequences for society; (2) those that claim that new religious movements have disintegrative consequences; (3) those that propose that these movements contribute to socio-cultural transformation; and (4) those who see them as marginal and socially irrelevant in Western societies.

We shall follow Robbins and Anthony in their critique of each of their types though we shall arrive at rather different conclusions, since they are themselves committed to the integrative hypothesis. As they point out (Robbins, Anthony and Curtis, 1975), they had 'sought to formalise the notion of latent integrative consequences of contemporary new religion and specify the symbolic processes which mediate these consequences' and they quote from that paper. Their hypothesis 'states that youth culture religious movements have the consequences of reconciling and adopting alienated young persons to dominant institutions, and in so doing... perform latent pattern maintenance and tension management functions for the social system.' A typical attempt of structural functionalists is to suggest that all signs of conflict are 'really' integrative for societies, and which reminds one of earlier attempts to deal with the problems of crime and deviancy by proclaiming that such behaviour is ultimately having integrative effects. Of course, new religious movements are expressions of deviance, and in some circumstances their activities may be labelled as criminal. In this context we have only to refer to the activities of anti-cult movements and repressive measures taken by the state against some new religions. It is clear from this that some people perceive new religions as being disintegrative and consequently a danger to both church and state.

But to return to the argument for the integrative function of such movements we must consider Robbins, Anthony and Curtis's study in more detail. They identified four processes or ways in which these movements facilitate institutions and contribute to social stability and maintenance of the 'status quo'. Let us describe the four processes. First, *adjustive socialisation* 'which refers to the tendency of many of the new movements to socialise converts in norms, skills and attitudes which are conducive to successful coping and adaptation to conventional institutional milieux.' They quote Robbins's (1969) study of the Meher Baba cult, in which he argues that the cult provided a way for those in the drug culture to become rehabilitated. In a later article Robbins and Anthony (1972) argue that Baba deprives the drop-out life style of legitimacy, endows work with expressive meaning and facilitates his followers' reassimilation into conventional work roles. The second proces, *combination*, is more complex and entails the capacity of many of the new movements to evolve symbol systems and expressive styles which are 'able to combine or synthesize counter cultural values with traditional or mainstream orient-ations, thereby making it easier for former "alienated" participants in deviant expressive milieux to act in accordance with conventional expectation' (Robbins *et al.*, 1975, p.51). They point to Gordon's (1974) study of the Jesus Movement and Tipton's (1982) study of Erhard Seminars Training and his other studies of Zen converts and Jesus converts (Tipton, 1982) as evidence for the effectiveness of this process.

Their third integrative process, *compensation*, 'refers to the renewal of commitment to conventional routines which derives from having the expressive needs that these routines cannot be gratified elsewhere (i.e. in religious groups)' (Robbins *et al.*, 1975, p.52). They quote Harvey Cox (1974) as suggesting that such cults may provide members

> with a compensatory community of feelings and affections which, ironically, may enable them to turn the wheels of the big impersonal bureaucracies even more efficiently. In this way what began as a revolt against automated culture could end up by making it more efficient.

Finally, they identify the process of *redirection* 'through which movements "channel" or "redirect" protest and alienated expressivity in areas which do not involve overt conflict with authorities or seriously threaten the status quo.' In this context they quote Howard's (1974) study of the Krishna Consciousness movement as providing a harmless outlet – but no threat to the establishment since its members can be defined as mad. It is of course possible to interpret the labelling of cult members as mad as a deliberate strategy of social control, through which the real threat they are perceived to present to society is diffused.

Robbins and Anthony imply that many studies support their integrative hypothesis, but in fact they quote very few. The claim dates back at least to Johnson's (1961) study of sects in which he pointed out that they could frequently be seen as 'socialising in dominant values'. The major evidence that at least some of the new religious movements of the 1960s and early 1970s had the function of returning their members to the dominant culture, is to be found in the fact that the majority of 'drop-outs' of that generation did 'drop back' into straight society. Whether this was the result of the socialisation they received within new religious movements is doubtful for that thesis has never been tested. It is doubtful because although some movements discouraged drug taking and encouraged the virtue of work, they also invariably inculcated other values that were at variance with the dominant culture. For example, most cults encourage collective values that were clearly opposed to the individualism of Western societies. Thus, while such movements as the Moonies and Krishna

Consciousness encouraged their members to work, this was always work for the benefit of the organisation, not the individual. Such movements tend to discourage the materialistic value of 'straight' society and encourage spiritual values that are frequently considered deviant in the outside world.

If there are difficulties for the integrative hypothesis, we must turn to a serious consideration of the view that new religious movements have disintegrative consequences for society.

Durkheimian and structural-functional theory locate religion as the central integrative institution in society, but this theory is based upon the assumption that a specific *religion* has a monopoly of control over the beliefs and values upon which the system is based. Religion in this sense is integrated within the type of society Becker (1957) described as 'sacred'. However, in most societies the processes of modernisation are producing secular societies throughout not only the Western world but the Third World. The communist world has been rather more successful in maintaining its 'sacred' quality, for the state and Party retain a nominal monopoly on the definition of value and beliefs, but even in those societies *religion* (in its spiritual form) has not only survived but shows some indications of growth.

Religion within a secular society no longer provides the source of social integration, and the rise of new religions may be taken to indicate either that anomie has replaced the normative consensus and that a disintegrative process has commenced, or on the other hand, that the rise of such movements is a causal factor in the disintegration of the system. There is insufficient evidence to indicate the priority of causation but, at least at a certain stage of development, there appears to be a relationship between the rise of new religious movements and the disintegration of pre-existing systems.

A frequently quoted work that argues that the rise of new religions was disintegrative in a specific case was Gibbon's study (1776–88) of *The Decline and Fall of the Roman Empire*, in which he claimed that the rise of Christianity undermined the traditional values of Roman civilisation. On the other hand, it can be argued that the rise of new religion in ancient Rome was a reaction to the collapse of the earlier religion.

Tiryakian (1972) following Talcott Parsons's structural-functionalist analysis of social systems, has argued that an increase in such non-institutionalised religious activity indicates a breakdown of the normative sub-system which he believes to be the first stage of the disintegration of the system as a whole.

Ethical aspects of new religious movements

An important approach to the understanding of new religious movements is to be found in the work of Steven Tipton (1982). Tipton argued that the youth of the 1960s joined new religious movements in order to 'make moral sense of their lives'.

He pointed out that the youth of the early 1960s rejected the traditional ethics of American society and tried drugs, sex, communes, sit-ins and be-ins, but finding them unrewarding turned to religion, in one or other of the three main forms. The first of these he described as 'born again' charismatic Christianity, which he examined in detail in his case study of the Living World Fellowship. Secondly, he examined the way of enlightment in his study of the 'Pacific Zen Centre'. Finally his study of EST (Erhard Systems Training) provides an insight into the work of the human potential movement which aims at self realisation.

Tipton's examination of the nature of American moral culture provides a useful framework for the study of new movements. This is based on a classification of styles of ethical evaluation (see Table 11.1) derived from the work of R. B. Potter (1965):

According to Tipton, American moral culture takes three main forms.

1 *Biblical religion.* This is strongly rooted in the Anglo-Saxon Protestant tradition. It starts from the belief that God who is the creator of the universe and the father of the human race reveals his will in the Scriptures. God's commandments so given, are the basis for moral goodness. Revelation not reason is the base of moral evaluation, clearly fitting the authoritative style. The individual has moral duties which do not derive from society but from the

TABLE 11.1 *Styles of ethical evaluation*

Style/dimension	Oriented to	Mode of knowledge	Discourse	Right making characteristics	Virtue
Authoritative	Authority	Faith conscience	What does God Command?	Commanded by God	Obedience
Regular	Rules	Reason	What is relevant rule or principle?	Conforms to rule	Rationality
Consequential	Consequences	Cost benefit Analysis	What do I want?	Produces good consequences	Efficiency
Expressive	Self and situation	Intuition feelings	What's happening?	Expresses self: responds to situation	Sensitivity

absolute demands of God.

2   *Utilitarian individualism.* Another important element in American culture and one which derives from the Enlightenment of the eighteenth century. In this conception the individual spends his life seeking to satisfy his own wants and interests. The goodness of an action is defined by its consequences. Does it satisfy the want of the individual? While this style might seem to differ considerably from that of Biblical religion, the two are often linked in practice, for the rhetoric and symbols of Biblical religion have frequently been used to give religious legitimation to utilitarian values.

3   *Counterculture.* Tipton describes the counterculture which he sees as rooted in the expressive dimension. The individual is seen as a personality that experiences, knows and 'is'. The morality is that of love, 'Don't hurt anybody', an ethic that derives directly from the conception of the universe as a unity. If all things are one than the 'individual' is harming himself if he harms 'others'. As he points out, there is a utilitarian aspect to such an ethic since actions may be judged by their consequences, but the type of consequences sought are very different from those sought by utilitarian individualists. The search is for consequences that benefit all, since in benefiting all one benefits the individual self.

The ethics are both situational and expressive as shown in the common sayings of the period, such as 'Do your own thing', 'Be what you are' and 'Let it all hang out' on the expressive side, and 'Go with the flow' and 'Different strokes for different folks' on the situational. Knowledge is intuitive and involves an 'affectively centred self awareness' an 'empathetic feeling for others' and a 'relaxed nonanalytical attention to the present situation'.

Tipton saw the central virtue of the counterculture to be sensitivity of feeling. He summed up this part of his discussion by pointing out the alternative attitudes to society offered by the counterculture:

1   ecstatic experience v. technical reason;
2   holism v. analytic discrimination;
3   acceptance v. problem solving activism;

4   intuitive certainty v. pluralistic relativism.

While his characterisation of the counterculture constitutes a useful 'ideal type' model for the classification of new movements he seems to be using it as a more concrete descriptive type and thus to overstretch the model. Clearly, there are movements that approximate to his 'ideal' type, in particular those that have their roots in Eastern religions, but not all new religions fall into this category. The counterculture is by no means a unitary movement, but if it is taken to include all movements that vary widely from the 'establishment', then it can be seen to include a great diversity of types.

Finally, Tipton offers an interesting explanation for the rise of the counterculture and one which seem unrelated to his classifications of ethics, for he sees it as the result of economic and technological changes in society. He argues that as the proportion of the labour force engaged in production declines, and the proportion in service industries expands, so work becomes 'a game' between persons instead of 'a game' by persons against nature. This is an interesting idea but one which needs developing. It is not entirely clear why such changes in the economic system should have the effect of turning youth against the system and setting them off in search of alternatives.

The second explanation that Tipton offers is that technological advances in production have produced possibilities of great increases in personal consumption and an increase in leisure time. Both these developments in the economic and technological systems probably played some part in producing the reaction of youth against traditional culture in the 1960s, but other factors also need to be taken into consideration. In particular, we must note that the counterculture was largely a product of middle-class youth, and there are few indications of working-class young people being involved.

The increase of deviant social movements is not so much an indication of the internal workings of a society but rather of its internal strength. Only a strong and self-confident society, which of course means a self-confident ruling class, can tolerate the existence of deviant or non-conforming groups within society.

Society in which new religions movements are tolerated are those in which the internal differences, based on material or non-material factors, are subordinate to a general consensus of values which is often not clearly articulate, but exists at the emotional rather than the intellectual level.

If we take mainland Britain as an example, we can draw out some of the factors involved. (I excluded N. Ireland from this analysis since this is a province in which an underlying consensus has not existed, at least for some three hundred years.)

In mainland Britain principal differences exist which may be classified in the following way:

1 *Economic.* Conflict exists and at times becomes acute between workers and employers, resulting in strikes. This rarely escalates to violence except when the state intervenes, because in Britain workers and employers generally agree that differences should be settled through negotiations, and industrial action usually occurs only when one side refuses to negotiate. The most violent strike of recent times, the Miners' Strike of 1985, resulted largely from the intervention of the government who restricted the freedom of the state-owned National Coal Board to negotiate with the unions. The Printers' Strike of 1986 arose out of the refusal of a private enterprise employer to negotiate. Trade unions in Britain are not aimed at political revolution or at effecting large-scale changes in the social system, but solely with maintaining or improving the position of their members within the system.

2 *Political.* While some extreme political parties of both right and left exist and are tolerated, political differences are focused in three major parties. None of these pursues revolutionary aims but seeks simply to modify the system.

3 *Nationalism.* At least three areas, Scotland, Wales and Cornwall, have political parties that aim at some form of self-government, but these work through the democratic parliamentary system, though there have been occasional

acts of terrorism by fanatical nationalists.

4 *Religions.* The numerous Christian sects, non-Christian religions and new religious movements generally tolerate each others' activities and are tolerated by the religiously detached.

5 *Ethnic minorities.* In this case there is more evidence of conflict based on racism and prejudice, which sometimes leads to riots.

The underlying consensus that covers all differences, except perhaps those based on race, appears to be a broad tolerance of the rights of others to differ from one's own values. Beyond that there is little consensus, but the emphasis placed on that value and those of honesty and 'fair play' provides the basis for a relatively well integrated society.

The existence of deviant movements could only create disintegration if any one such movement attempted to impose its own intolerant views on the majority. The British are wary of extremist movements that hold intolerant views, and measures are sometimes taken to prevent such movements taking oppressive action against others.

The situation is similar in many other Western democracies in particular in those with a long tradition of democratic institutions, where there is little fear that the existence of new movements will cause a disintegration of the system.

All systems do change over time and we now turn to the theories that claim that new religions act as agents of socio-cultural transformation.

The new religious movements seem to be more the product of disintegrative processes in society as a whole than the source of disintegration, but since they arise out of, or as a reaction to disintegration they may well be seen as having the potential to transform society. The new movements of the 1960s, which became collectively known as the 'counter-culture' (Roszak, 1968), tended to be seen as the basis for a new type of socio-cultural system, a view that was most forcibly expressed by Charles Reich (1970), who saw the diffusion of countercultural values as producing a slow non-violent revolution in America. The values of the counterculture were seen as the opposite of those of the materialist individualism of 'straight' society, and were embodied typically in the hippy communes.

By the mid-1970s the counterculture had largely disappeared, and the hope for a transformed society seemed to have faded, at least in the short term. However, by the 1980s the counterculture had been replaced by the New Age movement which encompasses a wide variety of social movements and cults, some of which have survived from the 1960s but many of which have developed on the foundation laid by the counterculture. Society has not yet been transformed, but the transformative influences are still at work. The fountain of creativity is still flowing in a number of directions, all of which converge on a group of values that may be seen as the basis for a new type of social system.

New Age movements are basically of two types, personal and social. Personal movements are concerned with the trans-formation of the values of individuals. Such movements vary from secular encounter groups to meditation groups which expand the awareness of the individual and in so doing change his social values. These groups approach the solution of human problems directly but deal only indirectly with social problems.

On the other hand are groups that are concerned to deal directly with social, collective and global problems. The most important of these are the Green movements which are concerned with a variety of problems that arise out of the human exploitation of the Earth; they range from political parties to groups such as Greenpeace, the Friends of the Earth and a variety of conservationist groups with more specific but limited aims.

The Green movement is the most direct of the consequences of the work of Reich (1970) and the counterculture, it rejects the same set of values in the dominant culture. A set of values that, although often thought of as characteristic of capitalism, is also central to the communist system at least as displayed by the Soviet Union and more recently by China. A system which emphasises materialism and a growth economy.

The Green movement is clearly the movement of the future but the transformation will take some time to achieve. However, the foundation for any such transformation will have been laid by the new religious movements; the social and economic transformation that will become inevitable within the next century can only be achieved if the values and beliefs of a significant proportion of the population have been changed.

Weber was undoubtedly correct in his view that the religious Reformation was a necessary precondition for the rise of a capitalist system, and an equally drastic change in attitudes must take place before an expanding acquisitive society can be replaced by a stable, sharing community.

Finally, we must consider briefly Wilson's view that new religious movements are irrelevant.

Wilson (1976) sees modern Western societies as secularised because of the decline of 'institutionalised religion', a view which we have already questioned because of the lack of evidence for any real decline in support for institutional religion. He interprets the rise of new religions as only another manifestation of secularisation, because he seems to have a restricted definition of religion. He fails to see that the most important achievement of 'secularisation' was to break the monopoly of institutionalised religion and set free the individual to be religious in his own way, that religion is concerned with creativity and spirituality and can simply flourish more fruitfully in what he defines as a secular society.

As we have already seen, a secular society is by no means inimical to religion, indeed the plural nature of such societies implies that a great variety of systems of beliefs and values will freely compete for members.

The fact that a religion does not have a monopoly within a society does not mean that it has no influence, that it is socially irrelevant. No doubt most of the citizens of Rome thought that Christianity was socially irrelevent in the first century AD, but within 200 years it had displaced the institutional religion and become the state church. It is possible that somewhere amongst the 'irrelevant' cults of the present, the future world religion waits for its time to come.

Indeed, the survival of the human species may depend upon the ability of humans to create a religion that can act as the ideological base for a world society, a religion that can unite humanity and integrate a planetary civilisation. If we have lost the desire and will to return to the fountain of religious creatively, then we may not only destroy our species but the Earth with it.

The new religious movements of the past, the present and presumably the future display creativity in an immense variety of forms. We cannot expect that all new religions will have the same functions. Some may be integrative, others disintegrative while the most hopeful sign is that some are transformative. These transformative movements must to some extent also be disintegrative as they attack the existing system, but they are also positive in that they seek to replace it with an alternative way of life. The functions of movements of this type change over time from disintegrative, through transformative to integrative, Christianity is a classic example of this form of movement.

Movements not only change their functions over time but their functions may vary from one society to another. Again, this may be seen in the case of Christianity, which may be integrative in certain Western societies but seen as socially and politically dangerous in some Communist societies.

The function of a particular religious movement may thus vary through space and time, being related to the structure of the social system within which it exists.

Some of the movements studied by Robbins and his associates clearly had the integrative functions they described, but other movements equally clearly oppose the existing system and may be seen to have disintegrative functions. The latter included not only extremist political movements of both left and right, but also religious movements such as the 'Moonies' and Jehovah's Witnesses who both severely criticise the social system and attempt to remove their members from that system as far as is possible.

To sum up, it is questionable whether it is either possible or appropriate to treat *all* cults or new religions as being either integrative, disintegrative or tranformatory. The category of new religious movements is not a unitary category, but has been constituted by lumping together a large number of movements having a wide variety of characteristics. As we have seen in our discussion of the concept of a cultic *milieu*, there are difficulties including *all* cults in a single category (*milieu*), and that a number of different cultic *milieux* may be distinguished. On the basis of such findings it is possible to postulate that

1   some movements may have either (a) integrative, (b) disintegrative, or (c) transformative consequences at a particular point in history;
2   some movements may be socially irrelevant;
3   some movements may be disintegrative in certain ways, transformatory in other ways, and also have some integrating consequences;
4   movements may proceed through a series of developmental stages from integrative to disintegrative, or from disintegrative to integrative;
5   movements that are highly significant at one period may become irrelevant, and socially irrelevant movements may become highly relevant either as a result of change within the movement itself or of changes in the wider society;
6   movements that are highly relevant in one specific society may be irrelevant in another contemporary society.

Considerable research needs to be undertaken to test these hypotheses, and here we shall only attempt a brief assessment of their use based on the relevant literature.

A problem that must be faced in all such studies is that of the self-fulfilling prophecy. Research that is based on the assumption that a movement has a particular function (set of consequences) is likely to find evidence to support that model.

Structural functionalists define religion as having an integrative function in society. They tend to be concerned about the process of secularisation and the way in which the 'decline of institutional religion' leads to the disintegration of society. In consequence they interpret new movements as either attempts to provide functional alternatives to institutional religion or as 'socialising in dominant values'. The first of these types of functionalised reaction can be seen in the controversy that has continued in America for some years over the subject of civil religion.

12
The social problem of new religions

Recently religion, and not only new religious movements, has become a controversial subject in America, not just amongst sociologists but more widely. The religious right and the Moral Majority have been described as anti-American and as endangering fundamental freedoms in the writings of Conway and Sigelman (1983) and McGuire (1982) as well as in the popular media.

Thomas Robbins (1983) has suggested that 'religious movements ... [are] increasingly being viewed as social problems', and in a following article (Robbins, 1985) he supports the suggestion of Horrowitz (1982) that religion needs to be studied as a social problem. In other parts of the Western world it is largely new religious movements that have been seen to present problems (Beckford, 1985), though religion is more generally considered to present a problem in the communist world. But first we shall turn to a consideration of the controversy surrounding new religious movements, some of which may be seen as a conservative backlash by the religious traditionalists, but much of which is an attack by what would be seen as liberals in America on the alleged authoritarian practices of some new movements.

In Britain the religious right has attracted much less attention than in the USA largely because it has gained less popular support and also because the political connection is more tenuous. A paradoxical situation, for in Britain where there are ancient institutional connections between church and state, the actual political significance of religion has declined continuously during the present century. Conversely, in America where the Constitution forbids such as arrangement between church and state, the political significance of religion has increased in recent years during which two 'born again' Christians have been elected to the presidency.

The religious right can be seen as a danger in America largely because of its potential influence on the political system, through which it might obtain the power to suppress other religious movements. In Britain there is little danger of politics being 'resacralised', so that movements of the religious right are seen as no more dangerous than any other pressure group.

There is, however, a sense in which all religion in Britain may be seen as deviant by the majority of the population. As we have seen, about 25 per cent of the population are members of religious organisations. Seventy-five per cent of the population are either totally divorced from institutional religion or only slightly involved. This produces a general attitude of tolerant indifference towards religion, in which the religious are viewed as being slightly deviant, 'different from most of us', but not looked upon as so different that they create a problem. There are some exceptions though, and religious extremists are the subjects of some derision. In general this is good humoured, and they are more likely to be ignored than to be persecuted, a situation that has changed considerably since the early years of this century. Then the Salvation Army was the subject not only of derision but persecution in some towns. In a certain small town in Norfolk at that time the opponents of the Salvation Army formed a rival brass band which they called the Skeleton Army. This followed the Salvation Army band around town playing music hall songs loudly to drown out the music of the hymns being played by the Salvation Army.

In recent years the Hare Krishna people singing in the city streets have received a far more courteous reception, though most people have simply 'passed them by'. Incidentally, the Salvation Army bands have disappeared from most cities today, possibly because indifference is more difficult to face than antagonism.

The general indifference of the British public to religion provides a somewhat stony ground upon which to sow one's seed.

New religious movements do not grow as rapidly in Britain as, for example, in America, but they do not have to contend with violent antagonism and can 'bloom unseen' in quiet corners of the social system. It is perhaps this latter characteristic that led Wilson to see them as irrelevant. Such movements may grow more slowly in Britain, but they become firmly rooted over time and exert considerable influence on society as a whole. Congregationalism never attracted widespread support while the Quakers and Spiritualists reached even fewer numbers, but each of these movements had an important influence on British society.

We must turn to an examination of more recent reactions to new religious movements.

Origins of anti-cultism

The rapid growth of new religious movements in the USA in the 1950s soon caused suspicion and reaction, mainly by members of conventional churches. This seems to have manifested itself in action and organisation in America in 1971 when a couple living in California discovered that their daughter had left home and given up her career as a nurse to join a group of the Children of God, an extreme Christian communitarian sect. They eventually traced her living at a COG commune in Texas, and made unsuccessful attempts to extricate her. In the course of their efforts they held a press conference in Dallas which led to their being sued for libel of the sect. The publicity they received led to their being contacted by a number of parents who had experienced similar problems in dealing with the Children of God. This in turn led to the formation of an organisation called Free the Children of God (FREECOG) at a meeting held in San Diego in 1972.

It gradually became apparent that the parents of young people involved in other cults were having similar problems in making contact with their children and a wider movement called the Citizens Freedom Foundation (CFF) was formed at Denver in 1974. This was only the first of a number of such movements that arose in the early 1970s, which include Citizens Engaged in

Freeing Minds, Return to Personal Choice, Love our Children and Citizens Engaged in Reunited Families.

At first these groups tended to work in isolation but they soon realised that co-operation at the national level would greatly facilitate their work, and in 1977 an organisation called the International Foundation for Individual Freedom (IFIF) was established.

The concern expressed through the formation of these societies arose out of the claim that cults used 'brainwashing' methods to recruit members and violence to prevent members from leaving the movement.

While the anti-cultist movement had its origins in reaction to the activities of the Children of God, attention soon focused on the Moonies, though many other cults also received the attention of the anti-cultists. The Moonies have received more attention from scholars as well as lay writers than any other new movement. The reason for such a wide interest in the Moonies would appear to be that they have been open to attack from a wide number of directions. Indeed, all the criticisms that could be made of a cult have been directed at the Unification Church.

In the first place, from the point of view of parents and families of members or potential recruits, they have been criticised for the methods of recruitment, for the treatment of members, for their attempts to prevent members from withdrawing, and to bring ex-members back into the fold. All religious movements may attempt to achieve these ends, so that the criticism by other organisations may be directed mainly at the methods used, and may be motivated by the perception of the relative successes of the Unification Church in achieving these aims.

This perception of the Unification Church was somewhat illusory for, while the movement appeared to be growing rapidly in the 1970s, Beckford (1985, p.151) reported that 'roughly 75% of recruits disengaged from the movement in Britain within a year of joining', and Barker (1984) went further in her estimate that no more than 12 per cent of those who took part in the Unification Church's 21-day workshop became full members, and 9 per cent became home church members. Such statistics tend to suggest that the danger represented by the Moonies was greatly exaggerated and that the 'public concern' over their activities had been amplified by the mass media, probably as a result of the concern of other pressure groups.

Many workers who have dealt with the question of cult movements and the reaction to cults have tended to see anti-cultists as being opposed to *all cults*. This is only true if the term cult is used in a theological rather than a sociological sense, to mean all religious movements with which the writer disagrees. Christians are inclined to use the terms sect and cult in this way, which creates a situation in which 'my church' is your 'cult', and vice versa. The membership of many cults may be strongly opposed to other cults, and the idea that all cults have sufficient in common to present a united front against anti-cultism is also clearly mistaken. Most cults make claim to some exclusive revelation or esoteric knowledge and consequently tend to either ignore or reject the claims of others. In other words, cults like sects and churches tend to be intolerant. However, not all new religious movements are intolerant, and 'cults' such as Spiritualism are generally tolerant towards other religious movements, though it is possible to detect a recent growth of intolerance within British Spiritualism which has taken the form of verbal attacks by national Spiritualists on Christian Spiritualists as well as on traditional Christian churches.

Few religious movements are prepared to treat all other movements as having equal claims on truth or access to inspiration. Historically Taoism is an example of such a movement, while in the modern world we may note organisations such as the World Congress of Faiths. Amongst the most important of such pressure groups are the mainline Christian churches who see the Unification Church as heretical, while evangelical Christians see it in even more extreme terms – as an agent of the devil (Satan).

State reaction is largely concerned with the extent to which the Unification Church may infringe the liberty of the subject or break other laws on the one hand, and on the other with the potential danger that is presented by its political aims. Many people on the political left are scared by Moon's overt anti-communism, and these are joined by liberals who seen the Unification Church as having similarities with fascist movements, as an authoritarian organisation. Other critics have commented on the way in which Moon exploits his followers as low paid sales people, and on the fact that he owns armament factories in Korea.

As already noted, the media has been highly critical of the Moonies and in 1981 the Unification Church sued the *Daily Mail* for libel. The case was dismissed by the court and the Unification Church's appeal against that verdict finally failed in 1983, a result that led to a decline in the activities of the organisation in Britain.

Beckford's (1985) discussion of 'the societal responses to the New Religious Movements' directs our attention to some of the dangers of the state regulation of religion. It is true that new religions may indeed threaten contemporary values and the institutional structures of society, but how else can change occur? It is inevitable that change which threatens the power and status of the existing establishment of both state and church will be resisted, and consequently that these elites will act to repress, suppress or discredit all new ideas that threaten their control of society.

The methods used to discredit the opposition may be crude as in Nazi Germany or Stalinist Russia, or more subtle as in most modern Western societies, but there is no doubt that the establishment will seek to control access to the fountain of youth in order to prevent society being flooded by creative thought and spiritual inspiration. But we must always be aware of the fact the new religious movements may also be attempts to limit access to the fountain, and represent an effort by potential counter-elites to gain control of the minds of the majority.

The real problem presented by new religious movements may be not that they threaten the existing power structure, but that they may provide new means whereby people may be subjected to control. The saving grace here would seem to be that there are many new religions and that freedom is best maintained by a situation in which no ideology has a monopoly, but in which the fountain remains open to all.

13
World-wide creativity

World developments

Secularisation has not been restricted to the West. If the term is used in the way that Becker defined it, it has been a common feature of the processes of social change everywhere. Existing religious and ideological monopolies have been challenged and at least temporarily replaced by periods of toleration, though in some cases the old ideology has been rapidly replaced by a new monopolistic system. For example, the Russian Revolution broke the monopoly of the Orthodox church which had been supported by the Tsarist regime, but rapidly replaced it with a monopolistic communist ideology enforced by the Party and the state. The brief interval of toleration in Germany that followed the First World War ended with the imposition of Nazi ideology in 1933, though this was replaced, at least in West Germany, by a secular regime after the Second World War. In Japan defeat in the Second World War led to the end of a state-supported ideology and to an outburst of religious creativity that may even have exceeded the outburst in North America.

Throughout the Third World contact with Western culture, which included the activity of Christian missionaries, Marxist propagandists and teachers of scientific philosophies, has led in many cases to the questioning and decline of traditional religions, and the rise of numerous new religions.

Wherever traditional religions fail to adapt to social change, or where a culture is threatened by the effects of culture contact new religions arise. In most cases new religions are synthetic, they combine elements of the traditional religion with those introduced from other cultures.

Central Africa

De Craimer, Vansina and Fox (1976) have argued that religious movements are an essential part of the common culture of Central Africa and that

> contrary to the allegations of some writers, these movements were not purely or even primarily reactions to the stresses of the colonial experience or modernisation. They were an integral part of the precolonial Central African tradition and they were primarily religious in nature (*ibid.*).

They argue that 'a movement is initiated by a visionary leader who reinterprets the relationships between the main religious symbols and rituals prevalent in the community.' The leader may take 'several years before he or she announces to the local community that [their visions] are true'. They go on to point out that 'when the community accepts the message, it observes the newly proposed rituals that are expected to bring fortune to the village and do away with affliction and witchcraft.... Once the first congregation is formed – it develops an internal organisation' a feature commonly observed in cults elsewhere, in which a hierarchy of specialists develops. If it is successful, the 'movement spreads as neighbouring settlements become convinced that the new movement seems to offer better protection against misfortune.'

Some movements spread widely and may last for many years; the authors claim that

> [it is] not unusual for one to last twenty to thirty years [but] some lose their vitality fairly quickly after their installation and remain dormant until they are replaced by another movement,

in others the local visions and innovations keep the movement very much alive and in the centre of social life for many years. Eventually all movements end by being replaced by others (*ibid*).

The authors list the goals and values of the movements they studied some of which seem to be very traditional – such as 'successful hunt' or 'abundant harvests', while others give some indication of Western influence, such as 'become like a European' or 'Africanisation of Christianity' but they claim that all these goals and values represent 'facts of a single cultural creation usually expressed in a single word, inadequately translated as "force" or "the good life".'

It is clear from their descriptions that in Central Africa such movements represent a culturally approved outlet for creativity, and that in many cases this is religious creativity since it is rooted in 'visionary' experiences.

Numerous other studies have shown the wide distribution of spirit mediumship in African societies; Beattie and Middleton (1969) edited a collection of such studies. In most African societies mediums hold a specific place in the social system which locates them as part of the existing religious establishment. Individual mediums may attract a specific clientele, but within traditional society only rarely do they establish a distinctive movement. The arrival of Christianity has modified this situation in many societies.

Amongst the best known and most widely studied of the new religious movements of the Third World is a type commonly known as a cargo cult.

Millennial movements

Cargo cults are one form of millennial movement which has been characteristic of colonial and ex-colonial Third World countries, particularly during the past half century. Millennialism, however, has been a persistent though usually subterranean element of

Christianity since, at least, St John's publication of the *Book of Revelations*.

Millennialism as strictly defined is restricted to societies that have been influenced by Judaeo-Christian-Islamic faiths, and can only be found where there is a particular attitude towards history, one in which time itself is seen as a linear process leading towards a final conclusion. The Christian perception of history is archetypical of this approach and is one in which God is seen as having created the world and the human race. Over time humanity has drifted further from God as the result of the activities of Satan, the personification of evil. Present society is consequently seen as being totally corrupt, but faith is maintained in a final resolution in which God will return to Earth, his faithful followers will be rewarded and the evil will be punished. Within this general conception there are many variations, but one seems to predominate in Western movements and has influenced many Third World movements. It is based on an interpretation of Biblical prophecies, particularly those found in the Book of Daniel and the Book of Revelations.

It starts from the concept of the Messiah, the Judaic idea that God will send a leader who will save his people from oppression. The early followers of Jesus claimed that he was the promised Messiah but, when this claim was rejected by the majority of the Jews, they transformed and universalised the concept by extending the promise of salvation to all the followers of Jesus no matter what their racial origin, and to cover not simply the liberation of the Jews but all peoples. The promise, however, was projected into an unspecified future, though many have subsequently claimed that a careful reading of the Biblical text reveals the exact date, and many movements have arisen throughout the history of Christianity that have been based on the claim by a leader to have discovered the date of the Second Coming of Jesus Christ.

Norman Cohn (1962) provided an excellent review of millennialist movements in the period between the tenth and sixteenth centuries in Western Europe. He compared these to modern political totalitarian movements and saw people as driven by the anxieties of life in the urbanised area of Europe to turn to a fantasy, 'a coherent social myth which was capable of taking entire possession of those who believed in it'. He went on to point out that

So it came about that multitudes of people acted out with fierce energy a shared fantasy which though delusional yet brought them such intense emotional relief that they could live only through it and were perfectly willing to die for it [and that] is not irrelevant to the growth of totalitarian movements, with their Messianic leader, their millennial mirages and the demon's scapegoats in the present century (*ibid.*).

Norman Cohn as a psychologist applied psychoanalytic concepts to his study of these social movements, which he saw as the result of the 'delusion of despair' and a 'collective paranoid fantasy born out of irrational fears and fantastic expectations' (Talmon, 1962), a situation in which the individual comes to see himself as a good person, persecuted by demonic forces, yet certain of final victory.

Cohn's analysis give rise to much discussion and critical comments. Worsely (1957) for instance, pointed out quite correctly that the social conditions which gave rise to such movements were understandable and not irrational. People who are involved in these movements are not necessarily behaving in a paranoid way since the oppression from which they are suffering is real, not illusory.

The kind of situation which gave rise to millennarian movements in pre-industrial Europe now tends to produce political movements in Western societies. Worsley and other Marxists have interpreted millennarian movements as pre-political movements of protest. They argue that they are the precursors of political activity, and that protest takes a religious form in societies in which political action is either not institutionalised or not available to certain groups or classes within society. In such societies the only institution that gives access to power is religion, and in consequence protest takes a religious form. While the explanation is adequate for pre-industrial societies not only of the past but also of contemporary Third World countries, it hardly explains the survival of millennialist movements in the West in the present century. A classic example of a contemporary millennialist movement which is still growing even in industrial societies is Jehovah's Witnesses. The membership tends to be recruited from the working class in Britain, but this is a class which has been extensively politicised and the natural reaction of members of that class to feelings of oppression is to act through trade unions and left-wing political parties.

It may well be that millennialist movements in Western democracies attract sectors of the population who have become disillusioned by the political system. Such persons may join extremist political factions such as the Trotskyist and fascist parties, become involved in terrorist movements or in millennialist or other types of new religious movement, and therefore religious movement may be seen as socially significant political forces within modern societies.

We now turn to a consideration of various types of millennialist movements in non-Western societies.

Cargo cults

The term cargo cult seems to have originated as a descriptive name for a type of religious movement that appeared most characteristically in the South Pacific islands. There are records of movements occuring in the nineteenth century (Worsley, 1957) but attention was drawn to this type of movement by The Vailala Madness. This cult seems to have been founded in 1919 by one, Evana, who is said to have fallen into a trance while hunting. He prophesied that the ancestors would return in a large steamship laden with white-mans goods and including rifles to drive the white man out.

In spite of the failure of such prophecies, cults of this type reappeared throughout the South Pacific. Probably one of the most typical was the John Frum movement (Guiart 1956) which arose on the island of Tanna in 1940. Tanna was first contacted by a white man in 1774 when it was visited by Captain Cook. The island seems to have been visited by other white men during the following century, but it was only in 1869 that a Christian mission was established there by a group of British Presbyterians. It took thirty years of steady work before Christianity became firmly established. In 1900 the arrival of some 'young energetic and harsh' missionaries, who set out to complete the Christianisation of Tanna as quickly as possible, gave rise to conflict between the Christians and heathens, and between the missionaries and white traders on the island, which involved the representatives of the two conflicting colonial powers, the French and the British. The island was eventually included in the condominium of the New Hebrides and jointly administered by Britain and France.

By 1920 the island was effectively Christianised and the population was estimated to consist of 4000 Christians and 1000 heathens. In 1932 a new mission of the Seventh Day Adventists was established and in the following year a Catholic mission. These provided some opposition to the Presbyterians from whom they gained members, for in 1939 there were reported to be 3381 Presbyterians, 656 Adventists, 72 Catholics and 1659 heathens.

In 1940 a man called John Frum started preaching about a future golden age which would follow the abandonment of Christianity and the return to traditional ways. It was claimed that he was the reincarnation of Karapenmun, a former heathen god. The authorities captured a man thought to be John Frum and imprisoned him. But it appears that the real John Frum – if such a person ever existed – must have escaped. He rapidly gained a mass following and the churches were emptied.

Cargo cults such as the John Frum movement appear to be direct reactions to culture contact with white men. The native culture in which religion is inexplicably involved in everyday life is shattered in two ways. Firstly by the deliberate attempt to replace the native religious tradition with Christianity, a process that involves the suppression of many of the spontaneous contacts that the native people have with the spirit world and the latter's replacement by a more restricted access to God mediated through white priests or ministers. The ancient gods are condemned as devils and reverence for the ancestors, which has been the mainstay of the social structure, is reduced as contact with them is forbidden or ridiculed. Western morality is imposed on the people and traditional customs forbidden. Tom Harrison (1938) described the ways in which the civilisation of the Pacific islands had been destroyed by the arrival of the white men and particularly the missionaries. Raymond Firth (1967) and Margaret Mead (1961) in follow-up studies to their original research were also able to trace the effects of culture contact on particular South Pacific societies.

The second major influence was that of the traders who introduced Western goods into the islands. It is easy to imagine the reaction of a native who has lived in a 'Stone-Age' culture to the first sight of a steamship and an aeroplane, or to smaller domestic objects such as canned food, paraffin lamps and radio sets. Such objects are totally beyond his understanding and his technology. He cannot conceive of how they might be made by men and attributes their product to the gods and the ancestors. Furthermore, he sees that the white men who use these goods do not make them and, in fact, seem to do no productive work, yet ships and aeroplanes arrive bringing 'cargo' of such goods for the use of the white men. The natives came to understand the situation as involving two elements. The goods are sent by the ancestors, but because the natives have deserted the traditional ways of the ancestors, it is easy for the white men to appropriate the goods for their own use.

The leaders of cargo cults offer a solution to this problem by suggesting that a return to the cultural traditions of the past will please the ancestors who will then ensure that the goods are received by the natives. This is, however, often linked with the need to adopt certain significant elements of the white man's culture which are seen as directly related to the arrival of the 'cargo'.

In most of these cults we therefore see that a rejection of Christianity and many of the trappings of a Western way of life is a precondition for the arrival of 'cargo'. While imitation radio sets may be constructed to enable them to communicate with the ancestors or, as in the present case, with John Frum. In the case of the John Frum cult the followers went further and constructed a dummy landing strip in preparation for the arrival of the aircraft bringing the 'cargo'.

This type of explanation has been seen as a variation of the relative deprivation theory, in that the natives perceive themselves as deprived when they compare themselves with the white men. Their turning to a religious solution arises naturally from their traditional culture, modified by the apocalyptic vision of the Christian religious traditions. Such a reaction is not the only possible form; in other cultures different types of social movements arise out of culture contact.

Robert Linton was one of the first anthropologists to attempt a theoretical study of the effects of culture contact. He coined the term 'nativistic' movements to cover all movements that arise from the contact between different cultures. He classified movements in four types based on the opposition between revivalist and perpetuative aspects which form one dimension, and the rational and magical aspects which constitute the other.

	Magical		
	(1) Revivalist-magical	*Perpetuative-magical*	
Revivalist			Perpetuative
	(2) Revivalist-rational	*Perpetuative-rational*	
	Rational		

FIGURE 13.1 *Nativistic movements*

1	Revivalist-magical	Return to the past based on irrational-magical ideas and methods.
2	Revivalist-rational	Return to the past based on rational ideas and methods.
3	Perpetuative-magical	Irrational clinging to the present state.
4	Perpetuative-rational	Rational desire to perpetuate present conditions.

As Lanternari (1974) pointed out, a major defect of Linton's model was that he over-emphasised the 'backward-looking aspects [and] overlooked their regenerative transformative components'.

However, the term 'nativistic' has continued to be used generally in a broad and ill-defined way to refer to a wide range of movements in the Third World. Movements that are 'deliberate, conscious, organised efforts by members of a society to construct a more satisfying culture' have been defined by Wallace (1966) as 'rvitalisation movements'.

Crisis cults

The term crisis cult was proposed by Weston Le Barre who argued

> I have adopted the simple term 'Crisis Cult' both for its brevity and its indecisiveness, intending only to imply the insight of Malinowski that there is no cult without a crisis. That is to say, there must be an unresolved problem or crisis, chronic or acute, and unresolved by ordinary secular means, before there is a cult response (Le Barre, 1972).

While he uses the concept generally, Le Barre applies it in particular to the rise of religious movements among the North American Indians, where the Ghost Dance cults offer useful case studies of the processes involved.

From the first, the American Indians have resisted any intrusion of the white men, but their superior military technology enabled them to dispossess the Indians of much of their land and by the second half of the nineteenth century many Indian tribes had become dispirited. A stream of prophets had arisen in many tribes offering solutions to the crisis that faced the Indians. As early as 1806 the Shawnee prophet Tenskwatawa had sought to turn his people away from the ways of the white man and his ideas spread to other tribes.

In 1852 Patheske of the Winnebago tribe had a vision of a new dance that he was to teach the people which would ensure success in their conflict with the Sioux people.

While these events were of significance, the source of the ideas that were embodied in the Ghost Dance seems to have arisen amongst tribes in the North West of America where a movement known as the Prophet Dance flourishes.

The first Great Ghost Dance movement arose in 1870 and was initiated by a Paccite Indian from Nevada named Tavibo. He had a vision which led him to predict a great earthquake that would swallow up the whites leaving the earth once more to the Indians. He also introduced a new ritual dance. His dance spread widely to other tribes, but other dance cults were springing up independently. In 1881 an Apache named Nakaldoklin also devised a dance.

In 1890 Wovoka, who claimed to be the Son of Tavibo, started the second Great Ghost Dance movement. As early as 1941 Barber attempted to explain the rise of the Ghost Dance movements in terms of a form of deprivation theory. He also pointed out that the failure of the Ghost Dance as an attempt to resist the influence and power of the 'white man' led many American Indians to turn to the Peyote cult which, as a retreatist form of religion, leads to 'passive acceptance and resignation in the face of continuing deprivation' (Barber, 1941). The Payote cult has been the subject of numerous studies including those of Le Barre (1938) and Slotkin (1955–6).

The deprivation theory which we have discussed in previous chapters was also used to explain these movements by Yonina Talmon (1962) and David Aberle (1962). While remembering the weaknesses of that theory, it is clear that deprivation of any kind may break the bonds that all societies place upon their members..

Deprivation of the human need for spiritual experience that results from the enforced conformity of established religion leads people to reject that religion and seek more direct ways of relating to the spiritual nature of the universe. Deprivation of the human need for spontaneous expression and creative action leads to rebellion against the controls of a repressive society.

Spontaneous and creative action at all levels is facilitated by the breakdown of the existing social and cultural system, whether this had been caused by largely internal processes as in the case of the Western world, or by the intervention of external forces as in the case of the Third World. While the new movements in the Third World differ superficially from those in the West, they arise from essentially the same factors.

14
Return to the source

Conclusion

We started out with a problem, or perhaps more accurately a series of problems that arose out of attempts to understand what is happening to religion in the second half of the twentieth century. Our explanation took us via myth and legend into social-scientific studies of religion, in the course of which we followed a number of paths which converge on to the pivotal concept of religious creativity.

Human beings are naturally creative but, as we contend, creativity can by no means be explained by biological factors, though they may play some part. We have argued that the main source of creativity is the psychic forces that constitute the base of the cosmic process itself. Further, we have argued that the form in which creativity is expressed is determined by socio-historical factors, which means that only through a sociological analysis can we understand the manifestations of human creativity.

While creativity is a universal aspect of human life, the extent to which individual creativity affects others is determined by the attitude towards creativity within the society in question. The attitude toward creativity varies between the extremes of encouragement and repression.

The type of society described as 'sacred' by Becker attempts to repress any creativity that may endanger the stability of the system. This means that creativity is limited to minor variations on the central themes of the dominant culture. In this situation religious creativity is restricted to such activities as might be included in the process of preaching a sermon or writing a new hymn, where the form of expression may be innovative but the content is conformatory. On the other hand, Becker's 'secular' society is one in which creativity is at least tolerated and may even be encouraged. While modern Western societies may be placed towards the secular end of Becker's continuum, they are by no means pure secular societies for powerful elites are able to exercise control over freedom of expression.

As indicated in chapter 3, 'Parapsychology and the sociology of religion', there are two themes running through this book, one is that of the repression of human creativity as represented specifically in the effort to re-present and communicate experiences of the ultimate.

The experience of the ultimate is beyond the reach of sociology or indeed any form of scientific study since it is a non-rational experience which can only be destroyed by rational analysis. This is a message of the legend of the fountain of youth; but not the only message, for the study also sums up the process whereby people attempt to control and exploit the 'experience' for material benefit.

At this level it becomes possible to treat the problem sociologically. How do humans attempt to control such experiences? By the creation of organisations that enable a minority of the 'elite' to restrict the supply of 'spiritual goods' to the majority of the population. Churches are created and orders of priesthood instituted with the power to act as mediators between the individual and the *all* (God). Indeed, gods are invented since it is easier to pretend to act as an intermediary between an individual god and an individual human than it would be to control the relationship between the individualised self and the true Self that exists at the core of each being. However, the attempt to control access to knowledge is not restricted to 'religion'. Even social science has developed its priesthood who systematically guard knowledge by the use of techniques of mystification, as has been explained by Andreski (1974) and others.

Religion as a social organisation may easily become merely an instrument for the exercise of power, a means of social control and a way in which people may be manipulated in the interests of elites. It was this that both Marx the atheist and Kingsley the Christian meant when they described religion as 'the opiate of the masses'.

Spirituality is an essential component of the human situation, but when it becomes organised, controlled and directed it may become perverted until the individual's access to the source for satisfying his spirit needs is blocked. But so strong is the creative urge that in spite of the efforts to repress it through the processes of institutionalisation, socialisation, bureaucratisation and the growth of oligarchy, creativity spontaneously bursts forth giving rise to new religions, new philosophies, new ideas and new arts.

Rise of new religions

We have discussed the necessary and sufficient conditions for the rise of religious movements. In summarising our conclusions, we believe that the situation may be best understood as a value-added process (Smelser, 1962) which may be most logically expressed in the following ways:

a   The decline of influence of traditional institutional religion
b   creates a situation in which many people seek answers to fundamental question of meaning (beliefs) and morality (values) which are needed as a basis for mental, moral and spiritual security in a rapidly changing social environment.
c   Some may find this in a return to a more dogmatic, fundamentalist form of traditional faith (the growth of 'conservative' and evangelical sects (churches)). For sects are able to flourish only when religious monopolies have been destroyed.
d   Others seek it in the adoption of religious faiths derived from other cultures, e.g. Buddhism, Hinduism, Islam in Britain,
e   or in a revival of older indigenous faiths, e.g. paganism,

witchcraft, occult movements,

f   but some find it necessary to formulate their own systems of values and beliefs.

g   From these private faiths new religions (cults) may arise.

h   Some creative individuals who have developed their own religions seek to communicate these to others.

i   Private faiths may become new religious movements – if the innovators have charisma and are able to attract followers.

j   In order to be successful new movements must adopt techniques for the recruitment and retention of members.

k   For continued success religious movements must remain flexible and continually adapt to the changing social environment.

l   Failure to respond to changing needs of individuals and society leads to the decline and death of movements.

m   Successful movements may attract a large following which enables them to become monopolistic religions.

n   A monopolistic religion is one that has exclusive rights to the provision of religious or ideological knowledge and beliefs and has the power to enforce that monopoly.

o   Such power is often provided by the state within a specific geo-political unit.

p   Monopolistic religions commonly engage in the repression of rival faiths.

q   State enforced ideological monopolies tend to create discontent,

r   which leads to revolt and revolution.

s   That opens up the situation, at least temporarily, to creative thought and the rise of new religious and ideological movements.

This cycle tends to be repeated over varying periods of time and subject to the intervention of external forces such as conquest or peaceful penetration of a culture by alien cultural influences.

Sorokin's cyclical theory of cultural change provides us with a basis for an explanation of the cycle of development not only within the civilisations he examined, but also within institutions, though specific institutions alter in rhythm with changes in other institutions and with the general trends in society as a whole.

Sorokin did not imply any directionality in change that went beyond the swing of the pendulum from sensate to idealistic cultures. However, an examination of history indicates that the swings of the pendulum are not exact repetitions and that history may be better represented as a spiral rather than a simple repetitive cycle, provided that we do not consider the movement within the spiral to illustrate progress or regression, but simply as indicating that no repetition is a complete re-enactment of a previous stage in the process.

In our examination of concepts of human nature we were then led on to consider the metaphysical basis for certain of these which, having their origin in Eastern religions, have emerged in many new religious movements. The metaphysical cosmology which we explored briefly treats the universe as an existential whole in the process of becoming; human history plays an important part in that process. All events are essential to the completion of the whole, as are the parts of a jigsaw puzzle which must be put in place if the picture is to be complete.

Sorokin's theory in combination with this holistic metaphysic provides us with a basis for understanding the contribution of new religious movements to the completion of the 'picture', which is immensely complex and exists in four not three dimensions. Viewed in this way, we must try to understand new religions as parts that emerge within the evolutionary process of the *whole*. Their existence is essential to the life of the whole, as the mystic Angelus Silesius once remarked (Gollancz, 1950), within a Christian context,

'Come I to naught, then God's own death must be: He would give up the ghost for lack of me'.

Within a sociological context all that exists, individuals, groups or ideas, play a part in the whole; their manifestation at a particular time is indicative of the condition of the whole society and indeed of the human species. Particularly at the present time the species must increasingly be the unit of study of the sociologist. The world-wide new forms of religiosity are thus clearly indicative of the current socio-cultural conditions and of the future development of humanity.

This relates to the ideas of creativity through the view that individuals are channels through which the creative processes of the universe work at the human level. Social change is the outcome of creativity in the field of ideas. Ideas originate in the universal mind which flows eternally like the fountain of youth, and human creativity is nourished by drinking of that fountain. Like all things, our argument returns to its source.

In Britain, America and Europe the outburst of religious creativity that was an obvious part of the culture of the 1960s and early 1970s had subsided by the early 1980s. Little attention has yet been given to this decline of religious activity. As we have seen, Tipton suggested that the new religious movements of the 1970s which he studied were a reaction against the wilder excesses of the drug and psychedelic movements of the 1960s. While there may have been a development in the direction he indicated, most commentators have not clearly distinguished between the movements of the 1960s and those of the following decade.

By the end of the 1970s the media were beginning to ask 'Where have all the hippies gone?' A question which requires more serious attention.

One of the most interesting features of the new movements of the 1960s and 1970s was their social composition. It is clear that these movements recruited their members almost exclusively from the middle-class youth, amongst whom students predominated. These young people appeared to be rebelling against the life style of their parents' generation, a style marked by affluence and materialism. They were certainly not stimulated by economic deprivation, but perhaps by ethical and spiritual deprivation. However, the 'drop-outs' always had a safety net, not only in the fact that they came from relatively well-off families, but also because the wider social environment of that time was one of full employment. If they wanted to drop back in there was always a job waiting for them, and in fact as they grew older the majority did precisely that; they accepted conventional employment and became conforming members of society. A sociological study of the careers of the 1960s' drop-outs would be a most useful piece of work, but so far little attempt has been made to undertake such research.

By the end of the 1970s the economic environment was changing, the age of affluence was over, and unemployment was beginning to prove a serious problem. The attitude of middle-class youth changed dramatically, and students sought to train seriously for career opportunities. They appeared to take little interest in spiritual matters, a trend which seems to confirm Maslow's model of a hierarchy of needs, in which spiritual needs only became dominant when basic biological, economic and social requirements are satisfied.

It is paradoxical that spirituality seems to increase in periods of affluence, as a reaction to excessive materialism rather than as a result of economic deprivation.

In the West, political extremism appears to be a more usual reaction to economic deprivation, though this is represented not only in the growth of groupings to the political right such as the National Front, and the Marxists and Anarchist movements of the extreme left, but also in the growth of parties such as the Greens, the pacifists, the anti-nuclear lobby and feminism.

The main lesson that may be learned from a study of new religious movements is one of hope. The human spirit can never be finally crushed by oppression, but will continue to seek expression in spite of all attempts to suppress it.

Bibliography

Aberle, David (1962), 'A Note on Reading Deprivation Theory as applied to Millenarian and other Movements', in Sylvia C. Thrupp, *Millenila. Dreams in Action*, The Hague, Mouton, pp.209–14.

A. E. (1918), *The Candle of Vision*, London, Macmillan.

A. E. (1932), *Song and its Fountains*, London, Macmillan.

Aidala, A. A. (1985), 'Social Change, Gender Roles and New Religious Movements', *Sociological Analysis*, 46, pp. 287–314.

Andreski, S. (1974), *Social Science as Sorcery*, Harmondsworth, Penguin.

Anthony, Dick and Robbins, Thomas (1974), 'The Meher Baba Movement. Its effects on Post Adolescent Youthful Alienation', in Irving Zaretsky and Mark Leone (eds), *Religious Movements in Contemporary America*, Princeton, Princeton University Press, pp.479–511.

Anthony, Dick, and Robbins, Thomas (1975), *Youth Culture, Spiritual Ferment and the Confusion of Moral Meanings*, paper presented to Society for the Scientific Study of Religion, Milwaukee.

Anthony, Dick, and Robbins, Thomas (1978a), 'The Effect of the Detente on the Rise of the New Religions. The Unification of Reverend Sun Myeing Moon', in Jacob Needleman and George Baker (eds), *Understanding the New Religions*, New York, Seabury.

Anthony, Dick, and Robbins, Thomas (1978b), 'A Typology of Non-Traditional Religious Movements in Contemporary America', *Journal of Social Issues*.

Anthony, Dick, and Robbins, Thomas (1982), 'Spiritual Innovation and the Crises of American Civil Religion', *Daedalus III* (1) Winter, pp.215–34.

Austin, Roy (1977), 'Empirical Adequacy of Loflands' Conversion Model', *Review of Religious Research*, vol 19, no. 3, pp.282–7.

Backster, Cleve (1968), 'Evidence of a primary perception in plant life', *International Journal of Parapsychology,* Institute of Parapsychology, vol 23, pp.81–9.

Bainbridge, William S. and Stark, Rodney (1979), 'Cult Formation, Three Compatible Models', *Sociological Analysis*, vol 40, no. 4 pp.283–95.

Bainbridge, William S. and Stark, Rodney (1980a), 'Scientology: To be Perfectly Clear', *Sociological Analysis*, vol 41, no. 2, pp.128–30.

Bainbridge, William S. and Stark, Rodney (1980b), 'Client and Audience Cults in America', *Sociological Analysis*, vol 41, no. 2 pp.137–43.

Baird, A. (ed.) (1944), *One Hundred Cases for Survival After Death*, London, S.P.C.K.

Baker, D. (1977), *The Opening of the Third Eye*, Wellingborough, Aquarian Press.

Balch, Robert W. and Taylor, David (1976), 'Salvation in a UFO', *Psychology Today*, vol 10, pp. 56–68.

Balch, Robert W. and Taylor, David (1977), 'Seekers and Sources. The Role of the Cultic Milieu in Joining a UFO Cult', *American Behavioural Scientist*, vol 20, no. 6, pp.839–60.

Balch, Robert W. and Taylor, David (1980), 'Looking Behind the Sciences in Religious Cult. Implications for the Study of Conversion', *Sociological Analysis*, vol 41, no. 2, pp.137–43.

Balleine, G. R. (1956), *Past Finding Out*, London, S.P.C.K.

Barber, B. (1941), 'Acculturation and Messianic Movements', *American Sociological Review* VI, pp.663–9.

Barfield, O. (n.d.), *Saving the Appearances*, New York, Harcourt, Brace & World.

Barker, E. (ed.) (1982), *New Religious Movements – a Perspective for Understanding Society*, New York, Edwin Meller Press.

Barker, E. (1983a), *Of Gods and Men, New Religious Movements in the West*, Macon, Georgia, Mercer University Press.

Barker, E. (1983b), 'New Religious Movements in Britain – The Context and the Membership', *Social Compass*, vol 30, no. 1, pp.33–48.

Barker, E. (1984), *The Making of a Moonie*, Oxford, Blackwell.

Barnes, D. F. (1978), 'Charisma and Religious Leadership: An Historical Analysis', *Journal of the Scientific Study of Religion*, vol 17, pp.1–18.

Beattie, J. and Middleton, S. (1969), *Spirit Mediumship and Society in Africa*, London, Routledge & Kegan Paul.

Becker, Howard (1932), *Systematic Sociology*, New York, Wiley.

Becker, Howard (1957), 'Current Sacred Secular Theory', in Howard Becker and Alain Boskoff (eds), *Modern Sociological Theory, Continuity and Change*, New York, Dryden Press.

Beckford, James (1973), 'Religious Organisations', *Current Sociology*, pp.20–2.

Beckford, James (1975), *The Trumpet Shall Sound*, Oxford, Blackwell.

Beckford, James (1977), 'The Explanation of Religious Movements', *International Social Science Journal*, vol 29, no. 2, pp.235–49.

Beckford, James (1978), 'Through the Looking Glass and out the other side. Withdrawal from Reverend Moon's Unification Church', *Archives de Sciences Sociales des Religions*, vol 45, no. 1, pp.95–116.

Beckford, James (1981), 'Cults Controversy and Control: A Comparative Analysis of the Problems Posed by New Religious Movements in the Federal Republic of Germany and France', *Sociological Analysis*, vol 43, no. 3, pp.249–64.

Beckford, James (1983a), 'The Public Response to New Religious Movements in Britain', *Social Compass*, vol 30, no. 1, pp.49–62.

Beckford, James (1983b), 'Young People and New Religious Movements', *Social Compass*, vol 30, no. 1, pp.5–12.

Beckford, James (1985), *Cult Controversies*, London, Tavistock.

Bell, Daniel (1960), *The End of Ideology*, Glencoe, Ils Free Press.

Bell, Daniel (1976), *The Cultural Contradiction of Capitalism*, New

York, Basic Books.

Bell, Daniel (1977), 'The Return of the Sacred. The Argument on the Future of Religion', *British Journal of Sociology*, vol 28, no. 4, pp.419–49.

Bellah, Robert (1970), 'Christianity and Symbolic Realism', *Journal for the Scientific Study of Religion*, vol 9, no. 2, pp.89–99.

Bellah, Robert (1974), 'New Religious Consciousness', *New Republic*, vol 171, no. 31, pp.33–41.

Bellah, Robert (1975), *The Broken Covenant*, New York, Seabury.

Bellah, Robert (1976), 'The New Religious Consciousness and the Crisis of Modernity', in C. Glock and R. Bellah (eds), *The New Religious Consciousness*, Berkeley, California, pp.333–52.

Beloff, J. (ed.) (1974), *New Directions in Parapsychology*, London, Elek.

Belshaw, Cyril (1965), 'The Significance of Modern Cults in Melanesian Development' in W. A. Lessa and Evon Z. Vogt, *Reader in Comparative Religion*, second edition, pp.517–22.

Benge, Ronald (1976), 'Identity Confusion and the Third World', *Communication*, vol 2, no. 2, September, pp.205–20.

Bennett, J. (1963), *Gurdjieff: A Very Great Enigma*, Ripon Coombe Springs Press.

Bensman, Joseph and Givant, Michael (1975), 'Charisma and Modernity', *Social Research*, vol 42, pp.570–614.

Berdyaev, N. (1952), *The Beginning and the End*, London, Bles.

Berger, P. (1961), *The Science of Solemn Assemblies*, New York, Doubleday.

Berger, P. (1969), *The Social Reality of Religion*, London, Faber.

Bergson, H. (1911), *Creative Evolution*, London, Macmillan.

Bernstein, M. (1956), *The Search for Bridey Murphy*, London, Hutchinson.

Bibby, R. W. and Brinkerhoff, M. (1974a), 'Sources of Religious Involvement', *Review of Religious Research*, vol 15, no. 2, pp.71–9.

Bibby, R. W. and Brinkerhoff, M. (1974b), 'When Proselytising Fails', *Sociological Analysis*, vol 25, pp.189–200.

Bird, Frederick (1979), 'The Pursuit of Innocence, New Religious Movements and Moral Accountability', *Sociological Analysis*, vol 40, no. 4, pp.335–46.

Bird, F. and Reimer, B. (1982), 'Participation Rate in New Religious and Para Religious Movements', *Journal for the Scientific Study of Religion*, vol 21 (1), pp.1–14.

Blatchford, R. (1926), *More things in Heaven and Earth*, London, Methuen.

Bocock, R. (1974), *Ritual in Industrial Society*, London, Allen & Unwin.

Bottomore, T. B. (ed.) (1963), *Karl Marx: Early Workings*, Harmondsworth, Penguin.

Branford, Victor V. (1923), *Science and Sanctity*, London, Le Play House.

Branford, Victor V. (1924), *Living Religions*, London, Le Play House.

Britten, E. H. (1870), *Modern American Spiritualism*, New York, privately published.

Britten, E. H. (1873), *Nineteenth Century Miracles*, Manchester, privately published.

Brockington, A. Allen (1934), *Mysticism and Poetry*, London, Chapman & Hall.

Bromley, David and Hodges, Susan (eds) (1978), *Moonies in America: Cult, Church and Crusade*, Beverley Hills, Sage.

Bromley, David and Shupe, Anson D. (1979), 'The Trevnoc Cult', *Sociological Analysis*, vol 40, no. 4, pp.361–6.

Bromley, David, Shupe, Anson D. and Ventimiglia, J. C. (1979), 'Atrocity Tales, the Unification Church and the Social Construction of Evil', *Journal of Communication*, vol 29, no. 3, Sumner, pp.42–53.

Bromley, David and Shupe, Anson D. (1981), 'Repression of Religious "Cults"', Research in Social Movements', *Conflicts and Change 4*, pp.25–45.

Bucke, R. M. (1972), *Cosmic Consciousness*, London, Olympia.

Bullett, G. (1950), *The English Mystics*, London, Michael Joseph.

Burke, Kathryn L. and Brinkerhoff, Merlin B. (1981), 'Capturing Charisma: Notes on an Elusive Concept', *Journal for the Scientific Study of Religion*, vol 20 (3) pp.274–84.

Burridge, K. (1969), *New Heaven and New Earth*, Oxford, Blackwell.

Camic, C. (1980), 'Charisma', *Sociological Inquiry*, vol 50, pp.5–23.

Campbell, Bruce (1978), 'A Typology of Cults', *Sociological Analysis*, vol 39, no. 3, pp.228–40.

Campbell, Colin (1969), 'Humanism in Britain' in D. Martin (ed.), *A Sociologist Yearbook of Religion in Britain*, London, S.C.M.

Campell, Colin (1972), 'The Cult, The Cultic milieu and Secularisation', in D. Martin (ed.), *Sociological Yearbook of Religion in Britain*, London, S.C.M.

Campbell, Colin (1977), 'Clarifying the Cult', *British Journal of Sociology*, vol 28, no. 3, pp.375–88.

Campbell, Colin (1978), 'The Secret Religion of the Educated Classes', *Sociological Analyses*, vol 39, no. 2, pp.146–56.

Carlyle, T. (1870–72), *Collected Works*, Centenary Edition, London, Chapman & Hall.

Carrier, H. (1965), *The Sociology of Religious Belonging*, London, Darton, Longman & Todd.

Carrington, H. (1946), *Thought Transference*, New York, Creative Age Press.

Carroll, Michael (1985), 'The Virgin Mary and La Salette and Lourdes, "Whom did the Children See"', *Journal for the Scientific Study of Religion*, vol 24 (1), pp.56–74.

Cashmore, Ernest (1977), 'The Rastaman Cometh', *New Society*, August 25, pp.382–4.

Cassirer, Ernest (1925), *Philosophie der Symbolischen, Forman II. Das mythesche Denken*, Berlin, Bruno Cassirer.

Catton, W. R. (1957), 'What kind of People does a Religious Cult attract?', *American Sociological Review*, vol 22, pp.561–6.

Champlin, C. (1978), 'Neo-Oriental Religious Sects in America', *The Social Science Forum*, vol 2 (1), pp.22–35.

Chethimattan, J. B. (1971), *Consciousness and Reality*, London, Geoffrey Chapman.

Clark, James M. (1957), *Meister Eckhart: an Introduction to the study of his works*, London, Nelson.

Cohn, Norman (1962), *The Pursuit of the Millenium*, London, Mercury.

Cohn, Norman (1970), *Europe's Inner Demons*, London, Heinemann.

Colpe, Carston (1977), 'Syncretism and Secularisation: Complementary and Anti-thetical Trends in New Religious Movements', *History of Religions*, vol 17, no. 2, pp.158–76.

Comte, A. (1875), *Positive Philosophy* (translated by H. Martineau), London, Geoffrey Chapman.

Conway, F. and Siegelman, J. (1983), *'Holy Terror: The Fundamentalist War on American Freedom in Religion, Politics and Our Private Lives'*, New York, Seabury.

Conze, E. (1956), *Buddhist Meditation*, London, Allen & Unwin.

Cooper, Paulette (1971), *The Scandal of Scientology*, New York, Tower.

Cox, Harvey, review of Irving Zaretsky and M. Leone (eds), (1974), *Religious Movements in America*, in *Times Sunday Book Review*, New York, December 22, pp.12–13.

Cozin, Mark (1973), 'A Millenarian movement in Korea and Great Britain', in D. Martin, (ed.), *Sociological Yearbook of Religion in Britain*, London, S.C.M.

Crookall, R. (1961), *The Supreme Adventure*, London, Clarke.

Currie, R., Gilbert, A. and Horsley, J. (1977), *Churches and Churchgoers*, Oxford, Clarendon Press.

D'Aygalliers, A. Wautier (1925), *Ruysbroeck the Admirable*, London, Dent.

Daner, Francine J. (1976), *The American Children of Krisna: A Study of the Krisna movement*, New York, Holt, Rinehart and Winston.

Davis, A. J. (1959), *The Great Harmonia*, USA, Austin Publishing Co.

De Coppens, P. R. (1976), *Ideal Man in Classical Sociology*, London, Pennsylvania State University Press.

De Craimer, W., Vansina, S. and Fox, R. (1976), 'Religious Movements in Central Africa', *Comparative Studies in Society and History*, vol 18, pp.458–75.

Dohrman, H.T. (1958), *The California Cult*, Boston, Beacon.

Dsouza, D. (1985), 'Moon Planet – The Politics and Theology of the Unification Church', *Policy Review*, 32 Spring, pp.28–34.

Dufrenne, M. (1953), *Le Phenomenologie de L'experience esthetque*, Paris, Presses Universitaires de France.

Durkheim, E. (1938), *The Rules of Sociological Method*, Chicago, University of Chicago Press.

Durkheim, E. (1954), *The Elementary Forms of the Religious Life*, London, Allen and Unwin.

Earhart, H. Bryan (1980), 'Towards a Theory of the Formation of the Japanese New Religions', *History of Religions*, vol 20, pp.175–97.

Eccles, Sir John (1970), *Facing Reality*, London, Longman.

Eccles, Sir John and Popper, K. (1977), *The Self and its Brain*, London, Springer.

Eddington, A. S. (1928), *The Nature of the Physical World*, Cambridge, Cambridge University Press.

Einstein, A. (1920), *Relativity: The Special and General Theory*, London, Methuen.

Eister, Allan W. (1972), 'An Outline of the Structural Theory of Cults', *Journal for the Scientific Study of Religions*, vol 11, no. 3, pp.319–34.

Eister, Allan W. (1974), 'Culture Crises and New Religious Movements. A Paradigmatic Statement of a Theory of Cults', in I. Zaretsky and M. Leone (eds), *Religious Movements in Contemporary America*, Princeton, Princeton University Press, pp.612–27.

Eliade, Mircea (1958), *Patterns in Comparative Religion*, London, Sheed & Ward.

Eliade, Mircea (1959), *The Sacred and the Profane*, New York, Harcourt, Brace & World.

Eliade, Mircea (1964), *Shamanism*, London, Routledge & Kegan Paul.

Ellis-Davidson, H. R. (1964), *The Gods and Myths of Northern Europe*, Harmondsworth, Penguin.

Elwood, R. S. (1979), *Alternative Altars, Unconventional and Eastern Spirituality in America*, Chicago, University of Chicago Press.

Enroth, Ronald (1977), *Youth Brainwashing and Extremist Cults*, Grand Rapids, Michigan, Zundervan.

Eucken, R. (1912), *Main Currents of Modern Thought*, London, Fisher Unwin.

Evans-Wentz, W. Y. (1911), *The Fairy Faith in Celtic Countries*, Oxford, Oxford University Press.

Fenn, Richard (1972), 'Towards a New Sociology of Religion', *Journal for the Scientific Study of Religion*, vol 11, no. 1, pp.16–32.

Ferguson, M. (1981), *The Aquarian Conspiracy*, London, Routledge & Kegan Paul.

Festinger, L. and Riecken, M. (1956), *When Prophecy Fails*, Minneapolis, University of Minnesota Press.

Finney, John M. (1978), 'A Theory of Religious Commitment', *Sociological Analysis*, vol 39 (1), pp.19–33.

Firth, Raymond (1967), *Tokopia Ritual and Belief*, London, Allen and Unwin.

Flammarion, C. (1907), *Mysterious Psychic Forces*, London, Unwin.

Flammonde, Paris (1975), *The Mystic Healers*, New York, Stein and Day.

Foss, Daniel and Larkin, R. W. (1978), 'Worshipping the Absurd. The Negation of Cause among the Followers of Guru Maharaji Ji', *Sociological Analysis*, vol 39, no. 2, pp.157–64.

Foss, Daniel, (1979), 'The Roar of the Lemming. Postmovement Groups and the Life Construction Crises', *Sociological Inquiry*, vol 49, nos. 2–3, pp.264–85.

Frankfort, H. and Frankfort, H. A. (1949), *Before Philosophy*, Harmondsworth, Penguin.

Freud, S. (1928), *The Future of an Illusion*, London, International Psychoanalytical Library.

Galanter, Marc; Robbins, Richard; Rabkin, Judith and Deutsch, Alexander (1979), 'The "Moonies": A Psychological Study of Conversion and Membership in a Contemporary Religious Sect', *American Journal of Psychiatry*, vol 136, no. 2, February pp.165–70.

Galanter, M. (1983), 'Unification Church (Moonie) Dropout – Psychological Readjustment After Leaving a Charismatic Religious Group', *American Journal of Psychiatry*, vol 140, no. 8, pp.984–9.

Garrett, E. (1939), *My Life*, London, Psychic Book Club.

Garrett, E. (1948), *Adventures in the Supernatural*, New York, Age Press.

Garrett, W. R. (1974), 'Troublesome Transcendence: The Supernatural in the Scientific Study of Religion', *Sociological Analysis*, vol 35 (3), pp.167–80.

Garrett, W. R. (1975), 'Maligned Mysticism: The Maledicted Career of Troeltsch's Third Type', *Sociological Analysis,* vol 36, pp.205–23.

Gauld, A. (1968), *The Founders of Physical Research*, London, Routledge & Kegan Paul.

Gerth, M. M. and Wright Mills, C. (eds) (1947), *From Max Weber*, London, Routledge & Kegan Paul.

Ghiselin, B. (ed.) (1952), *The Creative Process*, New York, Mentor Books.

Gibbon, E. (1776–88), *The Decline and Fall of the Roman Empire*, London, Dent.

Gilbert, P. S. (1971), 'Joanna Southcott: The Case of a Conservative Millenarian Movement', *New Sociology*, vol 1, no. 1, pp.27–56.

Glock, Charles and Stark, Rodney (1965), *Religion and Society in Tension*, Chicago, Rand McNally.

Glock, Charles and Bellah, Robert (1976), *The New Religions Consciousness*, Berkeley, California, University of California Press.

Goldsmith, Edward (1978), 'The Religion of a Stable Society', *Man-Environmental System*, vol 8, no. 1, pp.13–24.

Gollancz, V. (1950), *A Year of Grace*, London, Gollancz.

Gordon, David (1974), 'The Jesus People: An Identity Synthesis Interpretation', *Urban Life and Culture*, vol 3, no. 2, pp.159–79.

Gottschalk, S. (1978), *The Emergency of Christian Science in American Religious Life*, Berkeley, University of California Press.

Grant, S. and Kelsey, D. (1969), *Many Lifetimes*, London, Gollancz.

Greeley, Andrew M. (1972), *Unsecular Man*, New York, Schoeken Books.

Greeley, Andrew M. (1973), 'Implications for the Sociology of Religion of Occult Behaviour in the Youth Culture', in Edward Tiryakian (ed.), *On the Margin of the Visible*, New York, Wiley, pp.295–302.

Greeley, Andrew M. (1974), *Ecstasy – A Way of Knowing*, Englewood Cliffs, New Jersey, Prentice-Hall.

Greeley, Andrew M. (1975), *Sociology of the Paranormal, A Reconnaisance*, Beverley Hill, Sage.

Greil, Arthur (1977), 'Previous Dispositions and Conversion to Perspectives of Social and Religious Movements', *Sociological Analysis*, vol 38, no. 3, pp.115–25.

Greil, A. and Rudy, D. (1984), 'Encapsulation and Identity Transformation Organisations', *Social Inquiry*, vol 54(3) Summer, pp.260–78.

Gris, M. and Dick, W. (1980), *The New Soviet Psychic Discoveries*, London, Sphere Books.

Groethuysen, B. (1968), *The Bourgeois*, London, Barrie and Rockliff.

Guiart, Jean (1956), 'Culture Contact and the John Frum Movement on Tanna, New Hebrides', *Southwestern Journal of Anthropology*, vol 12, no. 1, pp.105–16.

Guirdham, A. (1970), *The Cathars and Reincarnation*, London, Neville Spearman.

Guirdham, A. (1971), *The Lake and the Castle*, London, Neville Spearman.

Gurdjieff, G. (1950), *Beelzebubs' Tales to his Grandson*, London, Routledge & Kegan Paul.

Habermass, Jurgan (1973), *Legitimation Crisis*, New York, Beacon.

Haekel, E. (1910), *The Evolution of Man*, (translated by S. McCabe), London, Watts for Rationalist Press.

Hagen, E. E. (1966), *On the Theory of Social Change*, London, Tavistock.

Hampshire, A. P. and Beckford, J. A. (1983), 'Religious Sects and the Concept of Deviance – The Mormons and the Moonies', *British Journal of Sociology*, vol 34, no. 2, pp.208–29.

Hardy, Sir Alister (1966), *The Divine Flame*, London, Collins.

Hardy, Sir Alister (1979), *The Spiritual Nature of Man*, Oxford, Clarendon Press.

Hargrove, Barbara (1978), 'Problems in Studies of New Religions, Definitions and Classifications', in J. Needleman and G. Baker (eds), *Understanding the New Religions*, New York, Seabury.

Harper, C. (1982), 'Cultural Communities', *Journal for the Scientific*

Study of Religion, vol 21 (1), pp.26–38.

Harrison, Michael (1974), 'Preparation for Life in the Spirit: The Process of Initial Commitment to a Religious movement', *Urban Life and Culture 2*, pp.387–414.

Harrison, Paul (1959), *Authority and Power in the Free Church Tradition*, Princeton, Princeton University Press.

Harrison, Thomas (1938), *Savage Civilisation*, London, Gollancz.

Hashimoto, Hideo and McPherson, W. (1976), 'Rise and Decline of Sokagakkai in Japan and the U.S.', *Review of Religious Research*, vol 17, no. 2, pp.83–92.

Hay, D. and Morisey, A. (1977), *Reports of Ecstatic Paranormal or Religious Experience in Great Britain and the United States*, Oxford, Religious Experience Research Unit.

Haynes, R. (1973), *The Hidden Springs*, London, Hutchinson.

Heasman, K. (1962), *Evangelicals in Action*, London, Bles.

Heirich, M. (1977), 'Change of Heart. A Test of some widely held theories about Religious Conversion', *American Journal of Sociology*, vol 83, no. 3, pp.653–80.

Herberg, W. (1960), *Protestant, Catholic, Jew*, New York, Anchor.

Herberg, W. (1962), 'Religion in a Secular Society', *Review of Religious Research*, vol 4, Fall, pp.33–45.

Hill, C. (1958), *Puritanism and Revolution*, London, Secker & Warburg.

Hill, Michael and Thong, Simon (1977), 'Guns for the God Squad', *New Society*, vol 41, no. 778, September, pp.433–5.

Hitchcock, J. and Jones, R. (eds), (1976), *Spirit Possession in the Nepal Himalayas*, Warminster, Aris and Phillips.

Hitty, Dale *et al.*, (1984), ' Dimensions of Religious Involvement', *Journal for the Scientific Study of Religion*, vol 23, pp.252–66.

Hodges, D. L. (1974), 'Breaking a Scientific Taboo', *Journal for the Scientific Study of Religion*, vol 13, pp.393–408.

Holm, N. (1982), 'Mysticism and Intense Experience', *Journal for the Scientific Study of Religion*, vol 21, pp.268–76.

Hood, Ralph (1973), 'Forms of Religious Commitment and Intense Religious Experience', *Review of Religious Research*, vol 15, no. 1, pp.29–36.

Hopkinson, T. and Hopkinson D. (1974), *Much Silence*, London,

Gollancz.

Horrowitz, I. L. (1979), 'The Politics of New Cults. Non-Prophetic Observations on Science, Sin and Scholarship', *Soundings*, vol 62, no. 2, pp.209–19.

Horrowitz, I. L. (1982), 'A Reply to Critics and Crusaders', *Sociological Analysis*, vol 414 (3), pp.221–5.

Howard, John R. (1974), *The Cutting Edge. Social Movements and Social change in America*, New York, Lippincott.

Hoyt, J. K. (1907), *The Cyclopedia of Practical Quotations*, London, Funk and Wagnalls.

Hume, David (1956), *The Natural History of Religion*, London, Library of Religious Thought.

Humphrey, Betty (1944), 'Paranormal occurrences among pre-literate people', *Journal of Parapsychology*, vol 8, pp.214–29.

Huxley, T. (1967), *The Essence of T. H. Huxley*, (ed. C. Bibby), London, Macmillan.

Isichei, E. A. (1967), 'From Sect to Denomination among English Quakers', *British Journal of Sociology*, vol 15, no. 3, pp.207–22.

Iverson, J. (1977), *More Lives than One*, London, Pan Books.

Jackson, John and Joblin, Ray (1968), 'Towards an Analysis of Contemporary Cults', in David Martin (ed.), *Yearbook of Sociology of Religion in Britain*, London, S.C.M., pp.94–105.

Jacobs, J. (1974), 'The Economy of Love in Religious Commitment', *Journal for the Scientific Study of Religion*, vol 23, pp.155–71.

James, W. (1902), *Varieties of Religious Experience*, New York, Modern Library.

Jeffries, Richard (1883), *The Story of my Heart*, London, Longmans.

Johnson, Benton (1961), 'Do Holiness Sects Socialise in Dominant Values?', *Social Forces*, vol 39, pp.319–36.

Johnson, Benton (1971), 'Church and Sect Revisited', *Journal for the Scientific Study of Religion*, Summer, pp.124–37.

Johnson, Benton (1977), 'A Sociological theory of Religious Truth', *Sociological Analysis*, vol 28, no. 4, pp.268–88.

Johnson, Doyle Paul (1979), 'Dilemma of Charismatic Leadership. The Case of the People's Temple', *Sociological Analysis*, vol 40, no. 4, pp.319–23.

Johnson, Gregory (1976), 'The Hare Krishna in San Francisco', in C. Glock and R. Bellah, *The New Religious Consciousness*, Berkeley, University of California Press, pp.31–5.

Johnson, Raynor (1953), *The Imprisoned Splendour*, New York, Harper & Row.

Judah, J. Stilton, (1974) *Hare Krishna and the Counterculture*, New York, Wiley.

Julian of Norwich (1901), *Revelation of Divine Love* (ed. G. Warrack), London, Methuen.

Jung, C. (1916), *The Psychology of the Unconscious*, London K. Paul.

Kanter, Rosabeth (1968), 'Commitment and Social Organisation', *American Sociological Review*, vol 33, no. 4, pp.499–517.

Kanter, Rosabeth (1972), *Commitment and Community*, Cambridge, Massachussetts, Harvard University Press.

Kelly, Dean M. (1972), *Why Conservative Churches are Growing*, New York, Harper and Row.

Kelly, Dean M. (1978), 'Dialogue on the Theory of Religious Truth', *Sociological Analysis*, vol 39, pp.351–7.

Kitzinger, Sheila (1969), 'Protest and Mysticism. The Rastafari Cult in Jamaica', *Journal for the Scientific Study of Religion*, vol 8, no. 2, pp.240–62.

Klapp, Orrin, (1969), *Collective Search for Identity*, New York, Holt, Reinehard and Winston.

Knight, W. F. Jackson (1970), *Elysion*, London, Rider.

Koestler, A. (1974), *The Roots of Coincidence*, London, Hutchinson.

Kuhn, T. (1970), *The Structure of Scientific Revolutions*, Chicago, University of Chicago Press.

Lane, C. (1982), 'The New Religious Life in the Soviet Union', *International Journal of Sociology and Social Policy*, vol 2, no. 1, pp.44–57.

Laing, R. D. (1960), *The Divided Self*, London, Tavistock.

Lanternari, V. (1963), *The Religions of the Oppressed*, London, Knopf.

Lanternari, V. (1974), 'National and Socio-religious Movements', *Comparative Studies in History and Society*, vol 16, pp.483–503.

Le Barre, W. (1938), *The Payote Cult*, Yale University Press, (revised edition, 1960).

Le Barre, W. (1972), *The Ghost Dance*, London, Allen and Unwin.

Leech, Kenneth (1973), *Youthquake: The Growth of a Counter Culture*. London, Sheldon Press.

Leuba, –. (1896), 'Studies in the Psychology of Religious Phenomena', *American Journal of Psychology*, vol 7.

Levi, Ken (1982), *Violence and religious commitment: implications of Jim Jone's Peoples Temple Movement*, London, Pennsylvania State University Press.

Lewis, I. M. (1971), *Ecstatic Religion*, Harmondsworth, Penguin.

Lin YuTang (1949), 'The Book of Tao', in Lin YuTang, *The Wisdom of China*, London, Michael Joseph.

Ling, T. (1966), *Buddha – Marx and God*, London, Macmillan.

Lipset, S. M. *et al.* (1956), *Union Democracy*, Glencoe, Free Press.

Locke, John (1706), *An Essay Concerning Human Understanding*, London, Dent.

Lodge, Sir Oliver (1915), *Raymond*, London, Methuen.

Lofland, John and Stark, Rodney (1965), 'Becoming a World Saver', *American Sociological Review*, vol 30, pp.862–74.

Lofland, John and Skonovd, Norman (1981), 'Conversion Motivs', *Journal for the Scientific Study of Religion*, vol 20, December, pp.373–85.

Lofland, John (1977), 'Becoming a World Saver Revisited', *American Behavioural Scientist*, vol 20, no. 6, pp.800–19.

Lofland, John (1978), *Doomsday Cult*, New York, Irvington, (revised edition).

Lofland, John and Richardson, James T. (1984), 'Religious Movement Organisations: Elemental Forms and Dynamics', *Research in Social Movements, Conflict and Change,* vol 7, pp.29–53.

Long, J. (1976), 'Shamans, Trance, Hallucinogens and Physical Events', in A. Bharatti, *The Realm of Extra-Human Agents and Events*, The Hague, Mouton, pp.301–13.

Long, T. and Hadden, J. (1983), 'Religious Conversion and the Concept of Socialisation', *Journal of the Scientific Study of Religion*, vol 21, no. 1, pp.1–14.

Luckman, Thomas, *The Invisible Religion*, New York, Macmillan.

Lytton, Lord (1888), *Zanoni*, London, Routledge & Kegan Paul.

McDougal, W. (1915), *Body and Mind*, London, Methuen.

McDougal, W. (1934), *Religion and the Science of Life*, Durham, North Carolina, Duke University Press.

McGavran, Donald (1970), *Understanding Church Growth*, Grand Rapids, Michigan, Eerdmans.

McGuire, M. (1975), 'Toward a Sociological Interpretation of the Catholic Pentecostal Movement', *Review of Religious Research*, vol 16, no. 2, pp.94–104.

McGuire, O. (1982), *The New Subversive, Anti-Americanism of the Religious Right*, New York, Continuum.

McIntosh, C. (1980), *The Rosy Cross Unveiled*, Wellingborough, The Aquarian Press.

Marais, E. (1937), *The Soul of the White Ant*, London, Methuen.

Martin, David (1962a), 'The Denomination', *British Journal of Sociology*, vol 12, no. 1, pp.1–14.

Martin, David (1962b), *Pacifism*, London, Routledge & Kegan Paul.

Martin, David (1966), 'Utopian Aspects of the Concept of Secularisation', *International Year Book for the Sociology of Religion 2*, Westdeutsch Verlag, Kohn and Oploden.

Martin, David (1969), *The Religious and the Secular*, London, Routledge & Kegan Paul.

Martin, David (1978), *A General Theory of Secularisation*, Oxford, Blackwell.

Martin, Marty (1970), 'The Occult Establishment', *Social Research*, vol 37, Summer, pp.212–30.

Marx, John and Burkhardt, Holxner (1975), 'Ideological Primary Groups in Contemporary Cultural Movements', *Sociological Forces*, vol 8, no. 4, pp.312–29.

Marx, K. and Engels, F. (1955), *On Religion*, Moscow, Foreign Language Publishing House.

Maslow, A. (1964), *Religions, Value and Peak Experiences*, New York, Columbia University Press.

Maslow, A. (1973), *The Further Reaches of Human Nature*, Harmondsworth, Penguin.

Mayrl, William (1976), 'Marx's Theory of Social Movements and the Church Sect Typology', *Sociological Analysis*, vol 37, no. 1, pp.19–31.

Mead, G. H. (1934), *Mind, Self and Society*, Chicago, University of Chicago Press.

Mead, Margaret (1961), *New Lives for Old*, New York, Mentor.

Melton, J. Gordon (1982), *The Cult Experience, Responding to the new religious pluralism*, New York, Pilgrim Press.

Merton, T. (1938), 'Science, Religion and Technology in 17th Century England', *Osiris IV*, pp.360–632.

Messer, Jeanne (1976), 'Guru Maharaj-Ji and the Divine Light Mission', in C. Glock and R. Bellah, (eds), *The New Religious Consciousness*, Berkeley, University of California Press, pp.52–72.

Michels, Robert (1908), *Political Parties*, New York, Dover.

Moberg, D. O. (1961), 'Potential Uses of Church Sect Typology in Comparative Religious Research', *International Journal of Comparative Sociology*, vol 2, pp.47–58.

Mol, Hans (1976), *Identity and the Sacred*, Oxford, Blackwell.

Molinari, P. (1959), *Julian of Norwich*, London, Catholic Book Club.

Moss, P. and Keeton, J. (1979), *Encounters with the Past*, London, Sidgwick and Jackson.

Mudie-Smith, R. (1904), *The Religious Life of London*, London, Hodder and Stoughton.

Murray, M. (1921), *Witch Cult in Western Europe*, Oxford, Oxford University Press.

Myers, F. W. H. (1903), *Human Personality and its Survival of Bodily Death*, London, Longman Green.

Needleman, Jacob (1970), *The New Religions*, New York, Doubleday.

Needleman, Jacob (1975), *A Sense of the Cosmos. The Encounter of Modern Science and Ancient Truth*, New York, Doubleday.

Nelson, Geoffrey K. (1968a), 'The Concept of Cult', *Sociological Review*, vol 16, no. 3, November, pp.351–62.

Nelson, Geoffrey, K. (1968b), 'The Analysis of a Cult', *Social Compass*, vol 15, no. 6, pp.469–81.

Nelson, Geoffrey K. (1969a), *Spiritualism and Society*, London, Routledge & Kegan Paul; New York, Shoken.

Nelson, Geoffrey, K. (1969b), 'The Spiritualist Movement and

Need for a redefinition of Cults', *Journal for the Scientific Study of Religion*, vol 8, pp.152–60.

Nelson, Geoffrey K. and Clews, Rosemary (1971), *Mobility and Religious Commitment*, Birmingham, Institute for the Study of Worship and Religious Architecture.

Nelson, Geoffrey K. (1972), 'The Membership of a Cult', *Review of Religious Research*, vol 13, no. 3, pp.170–7.

Nelson, Geoffrey K. and Campbell, J. A. (1977), 'Centralisation in English Congregationalism', Birmingham Polytechnic, Working Paper.

Nelson, Geoffrey K. (1978), 'The adaptation of British Spiritualism to Social Change'. Paper given at World Congress of Sociology, Uppsalla.

Nelson, Geoffrey K. and Walsgrove, D. (1980), 'Fundamentalism and Church Growth', Paper presented to Sociology of Religious Group, British Sociological Association, Birmingham.

Nelson, Geoffrey K. (1982), 'Re-animating the Sociology of Religion', Birmingham Polytechnic, Working Paper.

Nelson, Geoffrey K. (1984), 'Cults and New Religions', *Sociology and Social Research*, vol 68, no. 3, pp.300–25.

Niebuhr, H. R. (1954), *The Social Sources of Denominationalism*, Hamden, Connecticut, Shoestring Press.

Nisbet, R. (1980), *History of the Idea of Progress*, London, Heinemann.

Nock, A. (1933), *Conversion*, Oxford, Oxford University Press.

Nordquist, Ted (1978), *Ananda Cooperative Village*, Uppsala, Borgstroms.

O'Brien, Leslie N. (1973), 'Some Defining Characteristics of the Hare Krishna Movement', *Australian and New Zealand Journal of Sociology,*

O'Dea, T. (1957), *The Mormons*, Chicago, Chicago University Press.

O'Dea, T. (1963), 'Sociological Dilemmas. Five Paradoxes of Institutionalisation', in E. Tiryakian (ed.), *Sociological Theory, Values and Sociocultural Change*, New York, Free Press of Glencoe, pp.871–90.

Ofshe, Richard (1980), 'The Social Development of the Synanon Cult', *Sociological Analysis*, vol 41, no. 2, pp.109–27.

O'Hara, M. (1980), *New Hope through Hypnotherapy*, Tunbridge Wells, Abacus Press.

O'Toole, Roger (1976), 'Non-religious uses of the Sect Concept', *Journal for the Scientific Study of Religion*, vol 15, pp.145–56.

Otto, Rudolf (1959), *The Idea of the Holy*, Harmondworth, Penguin, (first edition, 1917).

Paine, T. (1794), *The Age of Reason*, Paris, Barrois.

Park, R. and Burgess, E. (1921), *Introduction to the Science of Sociology*, Chicago.

Parsons, T. and Shils, E. (1937), *The Structure of Social Action*, New York, McGraw-Hill.

Parsons, T. and Shils, E. (1965), *Toward a General Theory of Action*, New York, Harper.

Patanjali, (1978), *The Authentic Yoga*, (translated by P. Y. Deshpande), London, Rideer.

Paton, L. B. (1921), *Spiritism and the Cult of the Dead in Antiquity* London, Hodder and Stoughton.

Pavlos, Andrew (1982), *The Cult Experiences*, Westpoint, Connecticutt, Greenwood Press.

Payne, Barbara P. and Elifson, Kirk (1976), '"Commitment" a comment on the uses of the concept', *Review of Religious Research*, vol 17, pp.209–15.

Penido, M. T. L. (1935), *La Conscience Religieuses,* Paris, Pierre Téque.

Pfautz, Harold (1955), 'The Sociology of Secularisation: Religious Groups', *American Journal of Sociology*, vol 261, pp.121–8.

Pfautz, Harold (1956), 'Christian Science. A Case Study of the Social Psyhological Aspects of Secularisation', *Social Forces*, vol 34, pp.246–51.

Piddington, T. R. (1962), 'Malinowski's Theory of Needs', in R. Firth (ed.), *Man and Culture*, London, Routledge & Kegan Paul.

Pilarzyk, Thomas (1978), 'Conversion and Alternation Processes in the Youth Culture', *Pacific Sociological Review*, vol 21, no. 4, pp.379–405.

Podmore, F. (1963), *Mediums of the 19th Century*, New York,

University Books.

Pollock, J. (1979), *Billy Graham, Evangelist to the World*, San Francisco, Harper and Row.

Potter, R. B. (1965), 'The Structure of Certain Christian Responses to the Nuclear Dilemma, 1959–63', Doctoral Thesis, Harvard Divinity School.

Prabhapada A. C. and Bhaktivedanta Swami (1979), *The Path of Perfection*, Los Angeles, Bhaktivedanta Book Trust.

Puharich, A. (1973), *Beyond Telepathy*, London, Pan Books.

Quarantelli, E. and Wenger, D. (1973), 'Characteristics and Conditions for the Emergency of an Ouija Board Cult', *Urban Life and Culture*, vol 1, no. 4, pp.379–400.

Rambo, Lewis (1982), 'Charisma and Conversions', *Pastoral Psychology*, vol 31, no. 2, pp.96–108.

Randall, J. (1977), *Parapsychology and the Nature of Life*, London, Abacus.

Randi (1976), *The Magic of Uri Geller*, Ballantine Books, London.

Rao, Ramakrishna (1966), *Experimental Parapsychology*, Springfield, USA, C. Thomas.

Reich, C. A. (1970), *The Greening of America*, New York, Random.

Rhine, J. B. (1936), *Extra-Sensory Perception*, London, Faber.

Rhine, J. B. (1948), *The Reach of the Mind*, London, Faber.

Rhine, J. B. (ed.) (1971), *Progress in Parapsychology*, Durkheim, North Carolina, Parapsychology Press.

Rhine, L. E. (1972), *Mind Over Matter*, London, Collier-Macmillan.

Richardson, James T. (1977), *Conversion Careers: In and Out of the New Religions*, Beverley Hills, Sage Publications.

Richardson, James T. (1978), 'An Oppositional and General Conceptualisation of Cult', *Annual Review of the Social Sciences of Religion*, vol 2, pp.29–52.

Richardson, James T., Stewart, Mary and Simmonds, Robert (1978), *Organised Miracles: A Study of a Contemporary Communal Fundamentalist Organisation*, New Brunswick, New Jersey, Transaction Books.

Richardson, James T. (1979), 'From Cult to Sect. Creative Eclecticism in New Religious Movements', *Pacific Sociological*

Review, vol 22, no. 2, pp.139–66.

Richardson, James T. (1980), 'Conversion Careers', *Transaction*, March/April, pp.47–50.

Ritzer, G. (1975), 'Sociology: A Multi-Paradigm Science', *American Sociologist*, 10, pp.156–67.

Robbins, Thomas (1969), 'Eastern Mysticism and the Resocialisation of Drug users. The Meher Baba Cult', *Journal for the Scientific Study of Religion*, vol 8, no. 2, pp.308–17.

Robbins, Thomas (1983), 'The Beach is Washing Away: Controversial Religion and the Sociology of Religion', *Sociological Analysis*, vol 33, no. 3, pp.207–12.

Robbins, Thomas (1985), 'Nuts, Sluts and Converts', *Sociological Analysis*, vol 46, no. 2, pp.171–8.

Robbins, Thomas and Anthony, Dick (1972), 'Getting Straight with Meher Baba: A Study of Mysticism Drug Rehabiliation and Postadolescent Role Conflicts', *Journal for the Scientific Study of Religion*, vol 11, no. 2, pp.122–40.

Robbins, Thomas and Anthony, Dick (1978), 'New Religious Movements, Integration Disintegration, Transformation', *Annual Review of the Social Sciences of Religion*, vol 2, pp.1–27.

Robbins, Thomas, Anthony, Dick and Curtis, Thomas (1973), 'The Limits of Symbolic Realism, Problems of Emphathetic Participant Observation in a Sectarian Context', *Journal for the Scientific Study of Religions*, vol 12, no. 3, pp.259—73.

Robbins, Thomas, Anthony, Dick and Curtis, Thomas (1975), 'Youth Culture Religious Movements, Evaluating the Integration Hypothesis', *Sociological Quarterly*, vol 16, no. 1, pp.48–64.

Robbins, Thomas, Anthony, Dick, Curtis, Thomas and Doncas, M. (1976), 'The Last Civil Religion – The Unification Church', *Sociological Analysis*, vol 37, no. 2, pp.11–25.

Robbins, Thomas, Anthony, Dick and Richardson, J. (1978), 'Theory and Research on Today's New Religions', *Sociological Analysis*, vol 39, pp.95–122.

Robertson, Roland (1970), *The Sociological Interpretation of Religion*, Oxford, Blackwell.

Robertson, Roland (1977), 'Individualism, Societalism. Worldiness Universalism. Thematising Theoretical Sociological of

Religion', *Sociological Analysis*, vol 38, no. 4, pp.281–308.

Robertson, Roland (1979), 'Religious Movements and Modern Society: Towards a Progressive Problem Shift', *Sociological Analysis*, vol 40, no. 4, p.299–314.

Robertson, R. and Chirco, S. (1985), 'Humanity Globalisation, and Worldwide Religious Resurgence', *Sociological Analysis*, vol 46, no. 6, pp.219–42.

Robinson, J. (1963), *Honest to God*, London, S.C.M.

Roszak, Theodore (1968), *The Making of a Counter Culture*, New York, Anchor.

Rowe, David L. (1978), 'A New Perspective on the Burned-over District', *Church History*, vol 47, no. 4, pp.408–20.

Rudhyar, Dave (1977), *Culture Crisis and Creativity*, Wheaton, Illinois, Theosophical Publishing House.

Sandon, Leo (1979), 'Responding to New Cult Politics', *Soundings*, vol 62, no. 3. pp.323–8.

Sargant, William (1959), *Battle for the Mind*, London, Pan.

Schnapper, Edith (1965), *The Inward Odyssey*, London, Allen and Unwin.

Schneiderman, Leo (1969), 'Ramakrishna: Personality and Social Factors in the growth of a religious movement', *Journal for the Scientific Study of Religion*, vol 8, no. 1, pp.60–7.

Schopenhauer A. (1891), *Selected Essays* (ed. Belfort Box), London, G. Bell.

Schul, B. (1978), *The Psychic Power of Animals*, London, Coronet.

Seve, Lucien (1978), *Man in Marxist Theory*, Atlantic Highlands, Humanities Press.

Shankara (1964), *The Crest Jewel of Wisdom*, (translated by C. Johnston), London.

Shepherd, William C. (1971), 'Religion and the Counter Culture. A New Religiosity', *Sociological Inquiry*, vol 42, no. 1, pp.3–9.

Shepherd, William C. (1979), 'Conversion and Adhesion', *Sociological Inquiry*, vol 49, nos. 2-3, pp.251–63.

Shils, E. (1975), *Centre and Periphery*, Chicago, Chicago University Press.

Shiner, L. (1967), 'The Concept of Secularisation', *Journal for the*

Scientific Study of Religion, vol 6, no. 2, pp.207–20.

Shweder, R. A. and Le Vine R. A. (eds) (1984), *Culture Theory*, Cambridge, Cambridge University Press.

Shupe, Anson and Bromley, David (1978), 'Witches, Moonies and Evil', *Society*, vol 15, no. 4, pp.75–6.

Shupe, Anson and Bromley, David (1979), 'The Moonies and the Anti-Cultists. Movement and Counter Movements in Conflict', *Sociological Analysis*, vol 40, no. 4, pp.425–34.

Shupe, Anson, D. L. and Bromley, David G. (1980), 'Reverse Missionizing: Sun Myung Moon's Unificationist Movement in the United States', *Free Inquiry in Creative Sociology*, vol 8, no. 2, November, pp.197–203.

Shupe, Anson (1984), *The Anti-Cult Movement in America – a bibliography and historical survey*, New York, Garland.

Slotkin, J. S. (1955-6), 'The Payote Way', *Tomorrow*, vol 4, pp.64–70.

Slotter, R. (1977), 'Exoteric and Esoteric Modes of Apprehension', *Sociological Analysis*, vol 38, no. 32, pp.185–208.

Smelser, N. J. (1962), *Theory of Collective Behaviour*, London, Routledge & Kegan Paul.

Smith, Donald E. (1963), *India as a Secular State*, London, Oxford University Press.

Snow, D. A., Zurcher, L. A. and Ekland-Olson, S. (1980), 'Social Networks as Social Movements. A Microstructural Approach to Differential Recruitment', *American Sociological Review*, vol 45, October, pp.787–801.

Snow, D. A. and Machalek, R. (1984), 'The Sociology of Conversion', *Annual Review of Sociology*, vol 10, pp.167–90.

Somit, A. (1968), 'Brainwashing', in Vol 2 of D. Sills (ed.), *International Encyclopaedia of the Social Sciences*, New York, Macmillan, pp.135–43.

Sorokin, Pitirim (1947), *Society Culture and Personality*, New York, Harper and Row.

Sorokin, Pitirim (1966), 'The Western Religion and Morality of Today', *International Year Book for the Sociology of Religion*, vol 2, pp.9–63.

Staal, F. (1975), *Exploring Mysticism*, Harmondsworth, Penguin.

Stainton, Moses W. (1949), *Spirit Teachings*, London, Spiritualist Press.

Starbuck, E. D. (1899), *The Psychology of Religion*, London, Walter Scott.

Stark, Rodney and Glock, Charles Y. (1968), *American Piety: The Nature of Religious Commitment*, Berkeley, University of California Press.

Stark, Rodney and Bainbridge, William (1978), 'Of Church, Sect and Cults', *Journal for the Scientific Study of Religion*, vol 18, no. 2, pp.117–33.

Stark, Rodney and Bainbridge, William (1979), 'Cults of America: A Reconnaissance in Space and Time', *Sociological Analysis*, vol 40, no. 4, pp.347–59.

Stark, Rodney and Bainbridge, William (1980a), 'Towards a Theory of Religious Commitment', *Journal for the Scientific Study of Religion*, vol 19, pp.114–28.

Stark, Rodney and Bainbridge, William (1980b), 'Networks of Faith: Interpersonal Bonds and Recruitment to Cults and Sects', *American Journal of Sociology*, vol 85, no. 6, pp.1376–95.

Stark, Rodney and Bainbridge, William (1981), 'Secularisation, revival and Cult Formation', *Annual Review of the Social Sciences of Religion*, vol 4, The Hague, Mouton.

Stark, Rodney and Skonovd, D. (1981), 'Conversion Motifs', *Journal for the Scientific Study of Religion*, vol 20, no. 4, pp.373–85.

Stein, Michael, (1977), 'Cult and Sport. The Case of Big Red', *Mid-American Review of Sociology*, vol 2, no. 2, pp.29–42.

Steiner, R. (1969), *Knowledge of Higher Worlds*, London, Rudholf Steiner Press.

Stevenson, I. (1974), *Twenty Cases Suggestive of Reincarnation*, Charlottesville, University Press of Virginia.

Stevenson, I. (1975-1977-1980), *Cases of the Reincarnation Type*, 3 vols, Charlottesville, University Press of Virginia.

Stoner, C. and Parke, J. A. (1977), *All God's Children. The Cult Experience – Salvation or Slavery*, Rador, Pennsylvania, Chiltons.

Straus, Roger (1976), 'Changing Oneself: Seekers and the Creative Transformation of Life Experience', in J. Lofland, *Doing Social Life*, New York, Wiley, pp.252–72.

Straus, Roger (1979a), 'Inside Scientology'. Paper presented to Pacific Sociological Association.

Straus, Roger (1979b), 'Religious Conversion as a Personal and Collective accomplishment', *Sociological Analysis*, vol 40, no. 2, pp.159–65.

Streiker, Lowell D. (1984), *Mind-bending brainwashing, cults, and deprogramming in the 80's*, Garden City, New York, Doubleday.

Swatos, William (1976), 'Weber and Troeltsch? Methodology. Syndrome and the Development of Church Sect Theory', *Journal for the Scientific Study of Religion*, vol 15, no. 2, pp.129–44.

Swatos, William (1981a), 'Church-Sect and Cult. Bringing Mysticism Back In', *Sociological Analysis*, vol 15, no. 2, pp.17–26.

Swatos, William (1981b), 'The Disenchantment of Charisma', *Sociological Analysis*, vol 42, no. 2, pp.119–36.

Swatos, William (1984), 'Iceland and Secularisation Theory', *Journal for the Scientific Study of Religion*, March, pp.32–43.

Szasz, T. (1971), *The Manufacture of Madness*, London, Routledge & Kegan Paul.

Talmon, Yonina (1962), 'The Pursuit of the Millenium', *Archives Europeenes de Sociologie III*, pp.125–48.

Tawney, R. H. (1921), *The Acquisitive Society*, London, G. Bell.

Tawney, R. H. (1926), *Religion and the Rise of Capitalism*, London, John Murray.

Thiessin, G. (1978), *The First Followers of Jesus*, London, S.C.M.

Thomas, K. (1971), *Religion and the Decline of Magic*, London, Weidenfeld and Nicolson.

Tipton, Steven (1979), 'New Religious Movements and the Problems of a Modern Ethic', *Sociological Inquiry*, vol 49, nos. 2-3, pp.286–312.

Tipton, Steven (1982), *Getting Saved from the Seventies*, Berkeley, University of California Press.

Tiryakian, Edgar (1967), 'A model of Social Change and its Lead Indicators', in S. Klausner, (ed.), *The Study of Total Societies*, Garden City, New York, Anchor, pp.69–97.

Tiryakian, Edgar (1972), 'Toward the Sociology of Esoteric Culture', *American Journal of Sociology*, vol 78, pp.491–512.

Tiryakian, Edgar (1974), *On the Margin of the Visible*, New York, Wiley.

Tobey, Alan (1976), 'The Summer Solstice of the Healthy-Happy-Holy Organisation', in C. Glock and R. Bellah (eds), *The New Religious Consciousness*, Berkeley, University of California Press, pp.5–30.

Towler, Robert (1984), *The Need for Certainty, a sociological study of conventional religion*, London, Routledge & Kegan Paul.

Travisano, R. (1970), 'Alternation and Conversion on Qualitatively Different Transformations', in G. P. Stone and M. Garvern, (eds), *Social Psychology Through Symbolic Interaction*, Waltham, Massachussetts, Gunn-Gloisdell, pp.594–606.

Troeltsch, E. (1931), *The Social Teaching of the Christian Churches*, (translated by O. Wyon), New York, Harper Torchbrook.

Truzzi, Marcello (1972), 'The Occult Movement and the Revival as Popular Culture', *Sociological Quarterly*, vol 13, pp.16–36.

Turner, F. M. (1974), *Between Science and Religion*, New Haven and London, Yale University Press.

Tweedale, C. L. (1947), *News from the Next World*, London, Psychic Book Club.

Tylor, E. B. (1958), *Primitive Culture*, New York, Harper Torch Books.

Uphoff, W. and Uphoff, M. A. (1975), *New Psychic Frontiers*, Gerrards Cross, C. Smyth.

Wach, Joachim (1944), *Sociology of Religion*, Chicago, Chicago University Press.

Wach, Joachim (1958), *The Comparative Study of Religion*, New York, Columbia University Press.

Waley, A. (1958), *The Way and its Power*, New York, Grove Press.

Wallace, Anthony (1959), 'Revitalisation Movements', *American Anthropologists*, vol 58, pp.264–81.

Wallace, Anthony (1966), *Religion: An Anthropoligical View*, New York, Random House.

Wallis, Roy (1974), 'Ideology, Authority and Development of Cults', *Social Research*, vol 41, no. 2, pp.299–327.

Wallis, Roy (1975), 'The Cult and its Transformation', in R. Wallis (ed.), *Sectarianism*, New York, Holstead, pp.35–49.

Wallis, Roy (1977), *The Road to Total Freedom*, New York, Columbia University Press.

Wallis, Roy (1981), *The Elementary Forms of the New Religious Life*, London, Routledge & Kegan Paul.

Wallis, R. and Bruce, S. (1982), 'Network and Clockwork', *Sociology 16*, no. 1, February, pp.102–7.

Wallis, R. and Bruce, S. (1984), 'The Stark – Bainbridge Theory of Religion: A Critical Analysis and Counter Proposals', *Sociological Analysis*, vol 45, no. 1, Spring, pp.11–27.

Wambach, M. (1979), *Reliving Past Lives*, London, Hutchinson.

Weber, Max (1930), *The Protestant Ethic and the Spirit of Capitalism*, New York, Scribners.

Weber, Max (1965), *The Sociology of Religion*, London, Methuen.

Westley, Francis R. (1978), '"The Cult of Man" Durkheim's Predictions and New Religious Movements', *Sociological Analysis*, vol 39, no. 2, pp.139–65.

Westley, Francis R. (1983), *The Complex Forms of the New Religious Life*, Chico, California, Scholars Press.

White, S. W. (1970), *The Sokagakki and Mass Society*, Stanford, Standord University Press.

Wickham, E. R. (1957), *The Church and People in an Industrial City*, London, Lutterworth Press.

Wickland, C. A. (n.d.), *Thirty years Among the Dead*, London, Spiritual Press.

Wiener, Martin J. (1981), *English Culture and the Decline of the Industrial Spirit 1850–1980*, Cambridge, Cambridge University Press.

Wilhelm, R. (translator) (1972), *The Secret of the Golden Flower*, London, Routledge & Kegan Paul.

Wilson, Bryan (1966), *Religion in a Secular Society*, London, Watts.

Wilson, Bryan (1970), *Religious Sects*, London, Weidenfeld and Nicholson.

Wilson, Bryan (1976), *Contemporary Transformations of Religion*, London, Oxford University Press.

Wilson, B. (1978) (ed.), *The Social Impact of New Religious Movements*, New York, Rose of Sharon Press.

Wilson, B. (1980), *Religion in Sociological Perspective*, Oxford, Oxford University Press.

Wilson, Colin (1978), *Mysteries*, London, Hodder and Stoughton.

Wood, E. (1961), *Yoga*, Harmondsworth, Penguin.

Worsley, P. (1957), *The Trumpet Shall Sound*, London, Methuen.

Wuthnow, Robert (1976a), 'The New Religions in Social Context', in C. Glock and R. Bellah, (eds), *The New Religious Consciousness*, Berkeley, University of California Press, pp.267–93.

Wuthnow, Robert (1976b), *The Consciousness Reformation*, Berkeley, University of California Press.

Wuthnow, Robert (1978a), *The Post Christian Perephery*, Berkeley, University of California Press.

Wuthnow, Robert (1978b), 'Religious Movements in the Transformation of World Order' in J. Needleman and G. Baker (eds), *Understanding the New Religion*, New York, Seabury Press.

Wuthnow, Robert (1978c), *Experimentation in American Religion*, Berkeley, University of California Press.

Yates, F. (1972), *The Rosicrucian Enlightenment*, London, Routledge & Kegan Paul.

Yinger, J. Milton (1957), *Religion, Society and the Individual*, New York, Macmillan.

Zald, Mayer and Ash, Roberta (1966), 'Social Movement Organisation', *Social Forces*, vol 44, pp.327–41.

Zaretsky, Irving and Leone, Mark (eds) (1974), *Religious Movements in Contemporary America*, Princeton, Princeton University Press.

Index of names

Subject index

244